THE AutoCAD Database Book

Accessing and Managing CAD Drawing Information

Third Edition

Frederic H. Jones
Lloyd Martin

Ventana Press
Chapel Hill, North Carolina

The AutoCAD Database Book—Accessing and Managing CAD Drawing Information Third Edition. **Copyright © 1989 by Frederick H. Jones and Lloyd Martin.**

Library of Congress Catalog No.: 88-051342

ISBN: 0-940087-28-6

Book design by David M. Kidd, Oakland, CA.

Concept and cover design by Suzanne Anderson-Carey, Berkeley, CA.

Cover illustration by Marc W. Ericksen, San Francisco, CA.

Typesetting by Johnna Webb, **Pixel** Plus Desktop Publishing, Chapel Hill, NC.

Third Edition, First Printing

Printed in the United States of America

Ventana Press, Inc.
P.O. Box 2468
Chapel Hill, NC 27515
919/942-0220

About the Authors

Frederic H. Jones is C.E.O. of éclat Intelligent Systems, Inc., producers of ei:MicroSpec™ and ei:VersaSpec™, two integrated CAD expert design systems. He is the author of four books on architecture, design and CAD.

Lloyd Martin is the president of Creative Technologies, Inc., a firm involved in the development of systems applications software based on AutoCAD. He is currently involved in developing an expert design system, based on AutoLISP, for facilities design.

Both of the Authors can be reached at:
éclat Intelligent Systems, Inc.
14470 Doolittle Dr.
San Leandro, CA 94577
(415) 483-2030

Acknowledgments

The authors and publisher wish to express appreciation to Greg Malkin and Robert Siletzky, who provided many valuable suggestions during the production of this book.

We also express our gratitude to the following individuals who assisted in the writing and production of this book:

Shanna Compton	Lynn Echnoz
John Sergneri	Lindy Martin
Judith K. Jones	Rob Holmes
J. B. Compton	Karen Wysocki

Limits of Liability and Disclaimer of Warranty

The authors and publisher of this book have used their best efforts in preparation of the book and the programs contained in it. These efforts include the development, research, and testing of the theories and programs to determine their effectiveness. The authors and publisher make no warranty of any kind, expressed or implied, with regard to these programs or the documentation contained in this book.

The authors and publisher shall not be liable for incidental or consequential damages in connection with, or arising out of, the furnishing, performance, or use of the programs, associated instructions and/or claims of productivity gains.

Trademark Acknowledgments

Contents

Chapter One: Getting Started

Chapter Two: Data Basics

Chapter Five: AutoLISP Programming

Chapter Six: Drawing Database and AutoLISP

Chapter Seven: Understanding the Drawing Database

Chapter Eight: Modifying the Drawing Database

Chapter Nine: Understanding and Using DXF Files

chapter 1 GETTING STARTED

CAD's IMPORTANT OTHER HALF

If you've been using AutoCAD® for any length of time, you've probably experienced great leaps in productivity over traditional "board & pencil" techniques — that's why you (or your company) bought all that equipment and software in the first place!

Drawings can quickly be revised and updated, repetitive graphic images can be accessed from symbol libraries, elements from one drawing can be easily transferred to another. In short, drafting with CAD allows you more time for creative tasks.

But what about CAD's important other half — the database? One of the great things about CAD is that while you make your drawings, your computer can be quietly creating databases full of information which save you even more time.

For example, a civil engineer can automatically link map data to road intersections. A mechanical engineer can track the VAV boxes for the HVAC system. An architect drawing a fifteen-story building can simultaneously keep track of how much conduit is needed.

For nearly every design project, there's an associated need to access and manipulate the information contained in your drawings. A properly managed database can result in enormous time-savings and free creative juices.

Linking various views of data together forms the foundation of object-oriented data design. Being able to call up your design from the viewpoint of the architect, cost estimator, structural engineer, HVAC engineer, etc., all from the same electronic "drawing," is the real power and future of automated design. With the inclusion of AutoLISP, an object-oriented language, AutoCAD lays the groundwork for true object-oriented CAD.

With the help of *The AutoCAD Database Book*, any user in any discipline can learn important techniques for saving hours of project time every week.

WHAT'S INSIDE

The AutoCAD Database Book addresses both the principles and practice of database use, design and programming for the CAD environment. You'll learn how to create and revise attributes, create data extraction files, and use blocks and symbols in database management. You'll learn basic techniques of data conversion and transfer between CAD systems. And you'll be exposed to many useful database utilities in AutoLISP®, BASIC and dBASE®.

Because AutoCAD is actually a database, nearly any AutoCAD-related subject could be considered appropriate for *The AutoCAD Database Book*. The next eight chapters focus on extracting visible and invisible information from a drawing, putting this information into a readable format, then translating it to a different environment (such as a word processor, spreadsheet or database manager) to generate bills of materials, reports, charts, material take-offs and other useful information. Parametric programming and other topics indirectly related to CAD database management fall outside the scope of this book.

After reading the book, you should be able to create your own non-graphic database link for a bill of materials and similar applications. You also will become more familiar with methods of manipulating **DXF** files to modify drawings and check data.

The programs and procedures can be typed in and used as presented, or form the foundation of more complex custom implementations that you create. To save typing time, an optional diskette is available that contains the programs and routines featured throughout the book.

INCREASED TIME-SAVINGS

The three primary elements of contract document development for engineers and architects consume varying percentages of the project's resources. In fact, in many design offices, the nongraphic database is more central than CAD itself!

In the typical project, 30 percent of the designer's resources are spent on drawings, 50 percent on the selection and specification of products and materials, and 20 percent on managing logistics, generating reports and scheduling.

In other words, keeping track of materials, ordering and specifying, counting, figuring and record-keeping often consume more than twice as much time as does the actual drawing! Although the ratio varies by discipline and project, it's clear that many designers and managers need to be free of all that paperwork, and nongraphic database management offers that break!

INCREASED PRODUCTIVITY

CAD has been widely credited with enhancing production, making revisions easier and decreasing errors and omissions. Clearly, a computer-aided drafting program can cut back on mistakes because it cannot forget to record changes the designer makes. And it's easier and faster to make changes on a computer screen — then have the machine implement the revisions — than to change all those paper drawings manually.

However, even with those advantages, a CAD program alone doesn't address the area of specification and administration of materials. While the drawing and drafting area of the project have been streamlined, the overwhelming amount of paperwork — coupled with documenting time, money and materials — still presents the same old grind.

You can realize a significant design advantage when you integrate drafting/design and data management. Written specifications, job-costing and project management can be developed simultaneously and automatically as products and materials are inserted into the design drawing.

Furthermore, the earliest design can become the skeleton of the following stage (and so on) without redrawing. Typically, a designer may have to estimate costs based on square footage and building type, a very generalized procedure. Good information management makes it possible to develop early cost estimates based on actual design quantities. The generic door, window, electrical outlet or service pump type can be easily replaced by specific products as they're selected and the estimate becomes progressively more accurate.

Productivity increases realized with CAD alone rarely exceed two or three times manual output. Effective management of CAD database information can result in big productivity leaps and eliminate tedious and time-consuming project tasks.

ENHANCED QUALITY

Productivity increases alone aren't the only justification for using alphanumeric design systems for your document production. The arduous and error-prone job of developing project specifications can be greatly relieved, allowing the designer or project manager to focus on the exciting and creative part of a design project—developing the actual design—while streamlining the management process.

The use of electronic catalogs and project scheduling software to select and track products and contractors is just one way to save time and avoid headaches. Many more design alternatives become possible, more time for checking and evaluating delivery and pricing strategies is allowed, and a greater percentage of the project time can be allotted to client development. Imagine actually being able to practice design as you dreamed you could in school!

NEW SERVICES TO OFFER

Ever-increasing competition in the business of design, engineering and architecture, combined with dwindling profits, makes it important to find new services to offer your clients. Those services can become both profit centers and ways to get an edge on the rest of the pack.

Engineering cost studies and product evaluations become feasible with good database management. A renewed emphasis on the design process is possible when the cost of contract documents can be proportionally decreased.

More advanced database management and document systems can allow you to offer facilities management services that continue beyond the installation phase. Many firms are maintaining product inventory and helping clients reallocate resources. This can give you an inside edge on future business and bring in additional revenues.

The possibilities are nearly limitless — and all make good business sense.

HOW TO USE THIS BOOK

The AutoCAD Database Book is a learning tool for CAD users interested in extending their knowledge and increasing the power and versatility of their graphic CAD programs. The book also serves as a reference for CAD users, managers and consultants who need to know how CAD can be extended into the full range of production applications in a design or engineering office.

The AutoCAD Database Book shows you several distinct techniques for working with CAD database information. Skim Chapters 1 through 3 and introductory pages of Chapters 4 through 9 to become acquainted with those techniques and decide what's best for your projects and applications.

The book should be used in close conjunction with your computer. We suggest you actually key the tutorial sections and sample programs — that's the quickest way to learn techniques for CAD database management and utility programming. The first chapters are tutorialized to get you started; programs in later chapters are well explained and documented.

Though the longer programs in Chapters 6 through 9 are more advanced, they offer you a unique opportunity to understand how AutoCAD's database works, and how AutoLISP, dBASE, BASIC and other languages can greatly enhance CAD information management.

For those who would rather "plug in and go," the programs will work either by keying them in from the book or loading them from the optional diskette.

Finally, Appendices A, B and C provide valuable reference material not currently available elsewhere for working with **DXF**, and attribute exchange and manipulation files.

HOW WELL SHOULD YOU KNOW AUTOCAD AND PROGRAMMING?

We assume you have a basic knowledge of MS/PC DOS and AutoCAD or your CAD system. However, we explain the specific topics, commands and techniques related to data handling and extraction. If you haven't read your *AutoCAD Reference Manual* recently, you should at least skim it before beginning the exercises in this book. Keep the manual handy for reference as you use this book and extend or design your own CAD database programs.

Although programming knowledge isn't necessary to use this book, the more you know, the better. You can key in the programs or buy the companion diskette and use the programs without even reading the programming section of the book.

The AutoCAD Database Book will also be useful to readers working with a programmer to develop a database system. The book will help you understand how to develop program specifications, and give you a good working knowledge of the many techniques involved with CAD database management.

SOFTWARE AND HARDWARE REQUIREMENTS

The AutoCAD Database Book can be used with any version of AutoCAD later than 2.18. Source code for all the AutoLISP routines are included on the companion diskette. dBASE III is required to run the dBASE code throughout. A compiled version of the bill of materials program, which will run without dBASE, is included on the companion diskette. We have also included information on Releases 9 and 10 when differences apply.

A GWBASIC or BASICA interpreter is required to run the BASIC programs in the book. Generally, those programs are included with an IBM or compatible PC. If you don't have either of those, any compatible BASIC interpreter will suffice.

In most cases, the programs can be compiled for easier use. The source code for the programs is included on the diskette along with compiled versions of the programs.

No hardware is required other than that required to run AutoCAD or your CAD system.

CONVENTIONS AND NOTATIONS

To be sure we're all speaking the same language, the items below serve as a guide to the naming and notational conventions used consistently throughout the book. These rules must be followed carefully.

1. 0's and O's; 1's and I's — These are noticeably different in the text and cannot be used interchangeably. O's must be typed as letters, and 0's as numerical values. The same is true of 1's and I's. Your routines won't work if these aren't entered correctly.

2. < ENTER > and < RETURN > — The < ENTER > is used interchangeably with < RETURN > or Carriage Return or [CR]. Throughout this book, < RETURN > will be used.

During an AutoCAD drawing session, a space bar can be substituted for < RETURN > when entering a command or an option. Until < RETURN > is hit, you can change what's on your screen by using the back space key and retyping the command.

3. Type: — Whenever you see this word in the page margins, type exactly what's shown in the proper case, including brackets, parentheses, forward and backward slashes, colons, semicolons, commas, spaces, etc. After **Type:**, explanations, reminders and other information will sometimes appear in parentheses. Don't type those notes.

4. Response: — Following **Response:** you'll see the computer's response as it appears on the screen. This may be a close approximation because of differences in your software version, computer brand and how your files have been created.

5. FILENAME.EXT — Several generalized names for files and directories are used throughout the book. You're expected to supply your actual filename and extension or directory required. For example, ACAD refers to the directory where you save AutoCAD files. Your actual name may be different. Remember that AutoCAD automatically places a **.DWG** extension on your drawing files. A **.DWG** extension is assumed if it's in the AutoCAD program.

6. Directories—You always should be in the same sub-directory as the current step in the exercises.

7. CTRL-X—Where **X** can be any other key, **CTRL-X** indicates that the **CTRL** (Control) key should be held down while you tap the designated letter key. Control <**CTRL**> keys used throughout this book include:

CTRL-S and CTRL NumLock—Freezes the display and the scrolling of a directory or other information.

CTRL-C—Cancels or aborts an action, such as a directory.

CTRL-Q—Toggles the printer on and off, valuable for printing directories and **README** files.

8. Command:—The AutoCAD Command: prompt indicates you should be in AutoCAD to take the next step.

Many other helpful rules and tips are prominently featured throughout the book.

YOU'RE ON YOUR WAY...

...to explore a largely untapped area of AutoCAD's power. You'll begin working with CAD database information in the next few pages. You'll be challenged to find creative solutions to suit your particular needs. And you'll learn just how important the non-graphic part of CAD can be in your daily work. Let's get started.

chapter 2
DATA BASICS

IN THIS CHAPTER

This chapter introduces you to the basic concepts of databases, how AutoCAD stores information and structures its data, and how you can access that information and use it to make your job easier. This chapter hits just the high points and leaves the finer details to later chapters.

Some users may be surprised to learn that AutoCAD isn't just a drafting program but is also a database manager. Most of you have heard of database managers, such as dBASE II, RBASE and others. Perhaps you've also heard of Dialog or other "online" databases. But AutoCAD as a database manager?

In fact, AutoCAD users can manage data in three ways. The first is with graphic information managed with the AutoCAD editor itself—this is the drafting function. The second is with AutoLISP, a programming language within AutoCAD that lets you write programs that will manage and manipulate graphic and non-graphic data in ways that are impossible to do with AutoCAD alone. The third way is to actually extract the desired data from the drawing file and organize it outside of AutoCAD with external data management programs, such as dBASE or Lotus 1-2-3. These last two techniques will be covered in great detail throughout this book.

Our first task is to understand graphic and nongraphic databases and what they do. What are the differences and how can they help us?

WHAT IS A DATABASE?

A database is a collection of information about a subject, organized to make it readily accessible by the user. The Source, for instance, is a public database on various financial and academic topics. A mailing list is also a database. A database doesn't even need to be computerized. An index card file or book of addresses is, in fact, a database.

A database manager, on the other hand, is a computer program that lets you create, organize and access all the data contained in an electronic database. dBASE, for example, can be used to create, organize and access a database such as a mailing list.

AutoCAD is also a database manager. You can use it to create, organize and access graphic data — this is called *drafting*. What is more important, and perhaps less obvious, is how AutoCAD can manage the nongraphic information about a drawing. Not only can AutoCAD keep track of your project's pictures, it can also keep track of the text and numeric or alphanumeric data associated with them. Anything you can draw with AutoCAD — from a mechanical assembly to a toaster to a building — can be tracked as a drawing, as text description, or as specifications within the AutoCAD database.

Designed to support a specific purpose, a database must be organized so that it will contain the necessary information to achieve that purpose.

A mailing list, for example, can be used to send announcements to all the people on the list. To do that, the database must be structured so it contains enough information about each person to ensure that the announcement reaches them.

A raw printout of a simple computer mailing list database might look like this:

```
#  <NAME>        <ADDRESS>        <CITY>        <ST> <ZIP>
1  JONES, JOHN   1234 MAIN ST     PALO ALTO     CA   94291
2  SMITH, MARY   4567 FRONT ST    SANTA CRUZ    CA   95060
```

This database is called a *file*, which consists of all the records that might be related by specific criteria. In this simple example, the criterion is a mailing list.

Each line in the file shown above is called a record, which contains the name and address of each person in the file, and is indexed by a unique record number. The record number is contained in the first column.

Each record in this mailing list file contains five pieces of information, each of which is contained in a field, which is simply a location within a record. The fields in this example are **NAME**, **ADDRESS**, **CITY**, **STATE** and **ZIP**. These fields are defined in a column header with each name being set off as shown: < Field Name >.

In the above example, you know that you'll always find a name in the second column of each record.

The header is where general information about the fields and records in the files is stored. This header information informs the user or the computer before the data entered in the file is used.

An *entry* is a record or field that actually contains an instance of data.

A *report* is a printout of information derived from the data contained in the database file. A report can contain any or all of the information contained in the database and may be structured any way you want, to make the information useful.

A drawing database is, in principal, structured the same way as any other database. Its purpose is to describe a drawing in a nongraphic way. A drawing database file consists of records of alphanumeric descriptions of *drawing primitives* (AutoCAD calls these *drawing entities*).

A drawing entity is a basic shape or form used in a drawing, such as a **LINE**, **ARC**, **CIRCLE**, **POINT** and **TEXT**. When you draw a line in AutoCAD, you're actually calling up an entity called **LINE** and defining its starting and ending points. AutoCAD then places a description of that entity in its database, and a graphic representation of that database record is displayed on the screen.

Entities, or primitives, are labeled this way because they're the most basic or primitive form of data accessible to the user from the drawing database.

Let's look at an example of a simplified drawing database:

<NAME>	<TYPE>	<LAYER>	<START>	<END>
0001	LINE	0	0,0	0,2
0002	LINE	0	0,2	2,2
0003	LINE	0	2,2	0,2
0004	LINE	0	0,2	0,0
0005	CIRCLE	6	1,1	1

This database describes a square, 2" per side with a circle of 1" radius inscribed in the square. All the drawing primitives (**LINE** and **CIRCLE**) reside on Layer **0**, except for the circle, which resides on Layer **6**.

Figure 1

Notice how much this database looks like the mailing list example shown earlier. The biggest difference between this sample and AutoCAD's drawing database is that the latter contains more fields. Let's quickly compare them.

NONGRAPHIC DATABASE

#	‹NAME›	‹ADDRESS›	‹CITY›	‹ST›	‹ZIP›
1	JONES, JOHN	1234 MAIN ST	PALO ALTO	CA	94291
2	SMITH, MARY	4567 FRONT ST	SANTA CRUZ	CA	95060

HYPOTHETICAL GRAPHIC DATABASE

‹NAME›	‹TYPE›	‹LAYER›	‹START›	‹END›
60000014	LINE	8	1,4	6,6
60000015	LINE	8	0,2	2,2

ACTUAL AUTOCAD GRAPHIC DATABASE EXCERPT

((-1. y name:60000014) (0."LINE") (8."0") (10 1.000000 4.000000) (11 6.000000 6.000000))

This example contains the same information as the first record in the hypothetical example above. We can now point out the similarity between the two types of databases. You will learn how to create this example yourself in the following section.

At this point, the biggest difference between the hypothetical graphic database and the AutoCAD drawing database example below is the names for the fields. Ignore the fact that they don't seem to be in columns and have parentheses; computers don't need to "visualize" the way humans do — in fact, they recognize both examples as lists or tables.

In the hypothetical example:

NAME is the field name; 1 is the value.
TYPE is the field name; LINE is the value.
LAYER is the field name; 0 is the value.
START is the field name; 0,0 are the values.
END is the field name; 0,2 are the values.

In the AutoCAD database example:

NAME equals -1; the value is 60000014.
TYPE equals 0; the value is LINE.
LAYER equals 8; the value is 0.

START equals 10; the values are 1.000000 and 4.000000.
END equals 11; the values are 6.000000 and 6.000000.

AutoCAD's field names are numbers. Numbers are used in place of text characters because a computer can access information more quickly that way. The field names are the first numbers given in the example above; the field name in the first field is "-1." A field name also looks like this: ((-1.<Entity name:60000014>). These numbers are called group codes (defined in more detail in Appendices A and B).

LOOKING AT THE DRAWING DATABASE

When working with AutoCAD, you're automatically adding, changing and deleting information in the database. This is the first type of CAD data management.

The second type, mentioned earlier in this chapter, involves AutoLISP. Below we will show you how to create the database sample we looked at above—this will show you what an actual AutoCAD drawing database readout looks like, and also give you a taste of AutoLISP.

Enter AutoCAD's drawing editor and draw one line from **1,4** to **6,6**. Press the **F1** key to put the screen into text mode.

At the **Command** prompt:

Type: `(setq a (entget (entlast)))` `<RETURN>`

AutoCAD should return a list that looks like this:

Response:
```
((-1 . <Entity  name : 60000014>)
(0 . "LINE">)
(8 . "0") (10 1.000000 4.000000) (11 6.000000
6.000000))
(-1 .  <Entity  name: 60000014>)
```

That's the **ENTITY NAME**—and the unique index number for the entity. The AutoLISP function **entlast** retrieved this number from the drawing database. Notice the group code, **-1**. That means "entity name."

```
(0 . "LINE")
```

That's the **ENTITY TYPE**, in this case, a line. The "**0**" is the group code for entity type and **LINE** is the type.

```
(8 . "0")
```

That's the name of the LAYER on which the entity was drawn; in this case, layer "**0**." The "**8**" is the group code for LAYER.

```
(10 1.000000 4.000000)
```

The **1.000000** is the absolute **X** coordinate and the **4.000000** is the absolute **Y** coordinate of the starting point of the line. The "**10**" is the group code for START.

```
(11 6.000000 6.000000)
```

Those are the absolute **X Y** coordinates of the ending point of the line. The "**11**" is the group code for END.

The length of the database record will vary, depending on the type of entity described.

Appendices A and B of this book describe all the group codes (or field names) assigned to different entity types.

Next, we'll look at a special entity called an *attribute*.

WHAT ARE ATTRIBUTES?

An *attribute* is a drawing entity designed to hold textual data and to link that data to graphic objects in the drawing database. Each time you insert one of these graphic objects (called a *block*) into a drawing, if that block has an attribute attached to it, you will be prompted by that attribute to add textual information to that block. This information will remain with that block forever. Later on, you can extract the data contained in these attributes and use that information to keep track of the objects in your drawing. Let's see how attributes work.

The best way to demonstrate how attributes work is by an example. Let's say you just got the contract to supply the entire Pentagon with new chairs. That's a lot of chairs. Since you were the low bidder, you have to make sure you don't order too many chairs or you'll lose money. You also learn that each chair is assigned a specific location within the building. Then you find out that there are 12 different kinds of chairs because the generals have to have better chairs than the colonels and so on down the line.

Easy, you say — just have twelve different chair symbols, insert the appropriate symbol in the proper location and then count all the different chair symbols. But we're talking thousands of chairs here. Actually, we're just talking thousands of chair *symbols*. What if you miscount? What would happen if a general had to sit in a private's chair? Would you be held responsible for upsetting the balance of world power? Never fear, because here is where attributes will save your day.

The solution to your dilemma is to add attributes to your chair symbols. If your chair symbols had attributes for chair type and location, it would be a simple matter to extract all this information from your drawing once the symbols have been inserted. Then you would have a list that would contain the exact quantity for each chair type and the location for each chair and you wouldn't have to count a single chair.

SYMBOL: ATTRIBUTE: VISIBLE
CHAIR TYPE: EXECUTIVE
LOCATION: GENERAL SMITH'S OFFICE

This is just one example of how you can manipulate the information behind the drawing to accomplish a number of important tasks. Here are a few more.

You can make a block or symbol automatically generate manufacturer's part numbers and prices. A subdivision map can display descriptions and addresses of each house shown. Electronic schematics can contain the values and ratings of resistors and ICs.

AutoCAD database functions can make the alphanumeric data in attributes visible or nonvisible, to extract complete lists of parts with quantities, and to calculate the cost of a design automatically as the drawing is created. Attributes are the building blocks of dynamic alphanumeric information, made into or linked to a graphic block. They also can be free-standing entities not linked to graphic elements.

ATTRIBUTE BLOCKS

You can create "talking" symbols for your drawings with attributes. When a graphic block that has an attribute linked to it is selected and inserted into an AutoCAD drawing, the block "talks" by prompting the user for associated information.

You can make the block "ask" for the name of the person assigned to a desk when a desk block is added to a furniture layout. The price of an electronic part can be added when that part is selected for a circuit diagram. The manufacturer's catalog number and associated colors and prices can be requested when adding products to an interior design drawing.

Any or all of the text information linked to a block can be made visible or be hidden from view. Both the visible and nonvisible information, however, is available to the computer for detailed reports and bills of materials.

Blocks of information can be created independently of graphic information. A tag can be created that links information on wallpaper, carpet, paint or other products; materials or services related to the drawing but not represented by a drawing symbol. That can be done completely nongraphically or can be linked to bubbles, arrows or tags for location identification.

By adding attributes to existing blocks, you can make a "nested" block out of a text attribute block and a graphic block. The new, combined block will have the characteristics of both. This means that attributes can be added to graphic information initially or at any time required.

Each instance of a block is unique, but contains the same structure of information. For example, a **CHAIR** symbol can prompt for the catalog number each time, or even automatically supply a default one. As each one is selected and inserted, a different color fabric can be chosen. That feature, called "instance attributes," is extremely useful in data management. (The above techniques are covered in greater detail in Chapter 3.)

DEFINING AND STORING ATTRIBUTE STRUCTURES

What information do you want to store? When you add attribute definitions to drawing blocks, you're really creating a database within the drawing itself. As we mentioned, your attribute database can be linked to a more sophisticated and extensive database outside the drawing. That outside database can allow the storage of more detailed information about items referred to in the drawing, so don't feel compelled to store every possible bit of information in the drawing itself.

The Release 10 feature, entity handles, enhances this capability and is covered in Chapter 3. In Chapter 4, you'll learn how to both link and design an external database management program that works with AutoCAD.

OUTPUT TO REPORTS

Your AutoCAD drawing and its associated database are useful only when you can print or plot reports from them. For graphic data, that can be done by using the **PLOT** command. When you want nongraphic data to be printed or sent to external database manager programs, you can use the **ATTEXT** command to create reports or transfer files to access, print or use that data. Reports can also be developed using external programs, such as dBASE, linked to **DXF** files.

SUMMARY

In this chapter, you've been introduced to graphic and nongraphic databases and the three basic ways they're used in and with AutoCAD and other CAD applications. In Chapter 3, you'll focus on attributes, and how to use them to generate bills of materials and other reports.

ATTRIBUTES

chapter 3

IN THIS CHAPTER

In this chapter, you'll learn the basic attribute commands and how to use them to create intelligent symbols. Next, you'll insert these "talking symbols" into a drawing and find out how to extract the data contained in the symbols. Finally, you'll see how this extracted data can be used to produce a simple bill of materials.

THE ATTRIBUTE COMMANDS

Five attribute commands let you create, edit, extract and format attribute text:

- **ATTDEF** is the **ATT**ribute **DEF**ining command. This is the basic AutoCAD command you'll use when you define attributes. There are many options within this command for formatting the way your attribute text will look. You can also specify the prompts for data that will come up when you use the attribute.

- **ATTDISP** is the **ATT**ribute **DISP**lay command. **ATTDISP** can be used in your drawing to make the normally visible attributes invisible or to make the normally invisible attributes visible. You'll use **ATTDISP** if you want to see all of the attributes in your drawing.

- **ATTEXT** is the **ATT**ribute **EXT**raction command. You'll use **ATTEXT** when you want to extract all or some of the information from the attributes in your drawing to use for creating reports about your drawing.

- **ATTEDIT** is the **ATT**ribute **EDIT** command used to change the values of existing attributes in your drawing. This editing function is similar to the **CHANGE** command for non-intelligent text.

- **DDATTE** is the command used to edit attributes by using dialogue boxes in Release 9. This method of editing attributes is much easier than using the **ATTEDIT** command, but isn't available on earlier versions or on many graphics cards which do not support the new Advanced User Interface with pull-down menus and dialogue boxes. We'll discuss the use of dialogue boxes later in this chapter.

Let's work with a simple example to see how these commands work. Get into AutoCAD and draw a 2" square, with the lower left corner at **3,3**. Now, inscribe a 2" circle inside the square. Let's say the drawing is a chair.

Now you are going to take this "dumb" chair drawing, add some attributes to it and save it as a block — the next time you see this "chair" it will talk to you.

CREATING ATTRIBUTES WITH ATTDEF

ATTRIBUTE FORMATS

The first thing you have to do is to decide how you want your attributes to look when you insert your chair symbol into a drawing. As you recall from Chapter 2, attributes are primarily carriers of textual data — so all the formatting possibilities that exist for ordinary text in your drawings are available for use with attributes as well.

You can have attributes displayed in any text style that you have available — at any size you desire. Attribute text can be formatted to be flush left, flush right, centered, aligned, fit, middle and style. You can even specify that you want your attribute text to be invisible so it won't clutter up your drawing. It all depends on how you want your finished symbol to look.

For the sake of this example, you will be adding three attributes to your chair drawing: A *visible* attribute, a *constant* attribute (which will also be visible) and an *invisible* attribute. This way, you'll have a chance to work with each different type of attribute.

Here are the three different attributes that you'll be working with for your chair symbol:

ATTRIBUTE TAG	DISPLAY	CONSTANT
TYPE	Invisible	yes
NAME	Visible	no
LOCATION	Visible	no

The text for your attributes will be 3/8" high and centered.

When you finish creating your attributes, your "chair" should look like the one in Figure 1.

The first attribute that you'll be creating will be the *constant* attribute.

THE CONSTANT ATTRIBUTE

There are two types of attributes: *variable* attributes and *constant* attributes. Every time you insert a block with a variable attribute in it, you'll be prompted by that attribute to type in a value. A constant attribute, on the other hand, always carries the value that was assigned to it when it was created with the **ATTDEF** command.

You won't be prompted for a value when you insert a constant attribute. The constant attribute is used when the same attribute information needs to be *constantly* associated with the same block. For example, if you wished a particular chair symbol to always represent a Steelcase Executive Chair, you could assign the product number as a constant attribute and you wouldn't have to type it in every time you inserted the block. So, let's create the first attribute.

Figure 1: The chair symbol with attribute tags and as it is inserted into a drawing.*

At AutoCAD's **Command** prompt:

Type: ATTDEF <RETURN>

**Response: Attribute modes Invisible:N Constant:N
        Verify:N Preset:N
    Enter (ICVP) to change, <RETURN> when done:

This is the main **ATTDEF** prompt. Upon selecting the **ATTDEF** command, your first prompt is "**Attribute modes.**" The system wants to know how you want the attribute field being created to appear. The **Invisible** option defaults to **No** and controls whether the text appears on the screen and in your graphic plot.

The **Constant** option which defaults to **No** is a non-editable value. This can be used for item titles and other non-changeable information. If you wish to be able to edit the field information, don't answer **Yes**.

Verify lets you edit the changeable attribute data before inserting it into the drawing. If this option is chosen, you can verify your answers to the prompts and respond to AutoCAD's **O.K.** query before accepting the entry in your database. This is important if you occasionally need to change attribute information.

---

*   We're going to continue using the chairs in the Pentagon example from Chapter 2.

**   The PRESET attribute type occurs only in Release 9 and later. No reference to PRESET will occur in earlier versions.

It's easy to get into the habit of automatically striking the **RETURN** key to accept the defaults, particularly when you usually do accept them. The verify option makes you stop and think about the data.

The **PRESET** mode in Release 9 and greater will be discussed later.

You can select **Yes** or **No** for any combination of the modes you want. AutoCAD also lets you change your mind about the mode of any field at a later time by typing **I**, **C**, **V** or **P** and then **<RETURN>** before entering data into the field. Because you want this first attribute to be constant:

Type: C <RETURN>

Response: Attribute modes Invisible:N Constant:Y
             Verify:N Preset:N
Enter (ICVP) to change, <RETURN> when done:

Notice that the letter after the word **Constant** is now a **Y**. This indicates that AutoCAD accepted your last response and changed the attribute mode to **Constant**. You will now see that the letter after the word **Invisible** is an **N**. This means that an attribute created at this point would be *not* **Invisible**. Since this first attribute is supposed to be **Invisible**, you must:

Type: I <RETURN>

Response: Attribute modes Invisible:Y Constant:Y
             Verify:N Preset:N
Enter (ICVP) to change, <RETURN> when done:

The letter after **Invisible** is now **Y**.

Now that the attribute mode is the way you want it, you'll be creating an **Invisible Constant** attribute. Next:

Type: <RETURN>

Response: Attribute tag:

Now, you can type in the attribute tag for this attribute:[*]

Type: TYPE <RETURN>

AutoCAD then prompts:

Response: Attribute value

Let's make this chair symbol represent the type of chair that will be ordered for the generals.

Type: EXECUTIVE <RETURN>

Now AutoCAD will prompt for the type of text formatting that you want to use on this attribute.

Response: Start point or Align/Center/Fit/Middle/Right/Style:

Because you want to **Center** this attribute in the chair symbol:

Type: C <RETURN>

Response: Center point:

AutoCAD is prompting for the **Center** point for the attribute:

Pick: a point with your pointing device on the screen at about the middle of the top line of your chair.

Response: Height <0.2000>:

---

* An attribute tag can be a string of characters or numbers, but it **must not** contain blanks. All characters are changed automatically to uppercase. The tag becomes the identifying code for every occurrence of this attribute in your drawing.

Now you can enter the **Height** of the attribute text, in this case **3/8** or **.375** inches:

Type: .375 <RETURN>

Finally, you will be prompted for the **Rotation angle** for this attribute:

Response: Rotation angle <0>:

Type: <RETURN>

Response: The word **TYPE** should appear centered just above your chair symbol. This is the first attribute tag for your chair symbol.

Now let's create the next two attributes for your chair.

VARIABLE ATTRIBUTES

The other two attributes to be added to your chair drawing will be *variable* attributes. When you insert a block into a drawing that has a variable attribute attached, you'll be prompted to type in a value from the keyboard and that instance of that attribute tag will contain whatever variable you typed. Where does this prompt come from?

When you create the attribute, tell AutoCAD how you want it to prompt you when inserting the block with the linked attribute. If you press <RETURN> without entering any text, AutoCAD automatically uses the attribute tag as the prompt. So let's see how that works.

If you haven't used an AutoCAD command since you created your last attribute, all you have to do is[*]:

Type: <RETURN>

---

[*] If you have used other AutoCAD commands since creating the last attribute, then the ATTDEF command dialog will prompt you through the text formatting and the text insertion point again. If this happens, you'll have to pick a new starting point for your next line of text by eye.

And AutoCAD will already be set up to create your next attribute one line down from your last one with the same text size and formatting:

Response: `Attribute modes Invisible:Y Constant:Y`
`    Verify:N Preset:N`
`Enter (ICVP) to change, <RETURN> when done:`

The next attribute will be a visible (**Not** Invisible) variable (**Not** Constant) attribute, so first:

Type: `I <RETURN>`

Response: `Attribute modes Invisible:N Constant:Y`
`    Verify:N Preset:N`
`Enter (ICVP) to change, <RETURN> when done:`

To change the attribute mode to **Visible**, and then:

Type: `C <RETURN>`

Response: `Attribute modes Invisible:N Constant:N`
`    Verify:N Preset:N`
`Enter (ICVP) to change, <RETURN> when done:`

Now you have the mode you want:

Type: `<RETURN>`

Response: `Attribute tag:`

AutoCAD prompts for the attribute tag. The next tag for this chair is **LOCATION**:

Type: `LOCATION <RETURN>`

Response: `Attribute prompt:`

This is where you add the attribute prompt. AutoCAD lets you create your own prompts or instructions for entering data in the field you create. For example, a prompt for entering a chair location might be: **"Enter chair location now..."** or **"Please enter a room number for this item."** This is optional if the attribute tag is sufficient for you to know what response to give or data to enter.

If you want to use just the attribute tag (in this case, the prompt would be **LOCATION**:) then simply:

Type: `<RETURN>`

If, on the other hand, you would like the prompt to be less cryptic, then make up your own:

Type: `Location for this chair <RETURN>`

Response: `Default attribute value:`

Finally, **"Default attribute value"** allows automatic entry of text or a number if you type nothing and just press **<RETURN>**. The default value can be nothing or anything at all. For example, the default value of **Quantity** could be **1**, the default value of **Chair** could be **Executive, swivel**.
For no default value:

Type: `<RETURN>`

Response: `Start  point or Align/Center/Fit/ Middle/Right/Style:`

Type: `<RETURN>`

The word **LOCATION** will now appear centered directly under the word **TYPE** on your chair drawing.

Creating the third and final attribute for this chair is done exactly the same way as the last one, but we'll walk you through it anyway, without comments:

Type: `<RETURN>`

Response: `Attribute modes Invisible:N Constant:N`
`        Verify:N Preset:N`
`Enter (ICVP) to change, <RETURN> when done:`

Type: `<RETURN>`

Response: `Attribute tag:`

Type: `NAME <RETURN>`

Response: `Attribute prompt:`

Type: `Name of occupant <RETURN>`

Response: `Default attribute value:`

Type: `<RETURN>`

Response: `Start point or Align/Center/Fit/Middle/`
`Right/Style:`

Type: `<RETURN>`

Response: The third attribute tag NAME appears underneath the previous one.

PRESET ATTRIBUTES

To establish the preset attribute mode, use the **ATTDEF** command, just as with CONSTANT and VARIABLE. In a sense, it gives you the advantages of both constant and variable attributes. When you insert a block with a preset attribute, the value is not requested but is set to the default value. If no value was specified, a null is entered into the database.

When you use dialogue boxes for attribute entry or editing, the preset attributes will show up in the dialogue box along with any other non-constant attributes.

We've found preset attributes to be extremely valuable. The value for a constant attribute doesn't appear in the entity section of the drawing database; so you're unable to edit it. The attribute always retains the value assigned to it when the attribute was created. The default value of a preset attribute will appear in the entity section of the drawing database, but you won't be prompted for the attribute value when you insert the symbol using the normal prompt method.

Let's say, for example, you have a symbol for a chair that contains a constant attribute with a value or **CHAIR** (which would never change), a variable attribute for color (which may be different for each instance of that symbol) and a preset attribute for a stock number of **CH1** (which would remain the same 99 times out of 100). When you insert this symbol, you would be prompted only for the color of the chair. If you decide at some later time to change all of the **CH1** chairs to **CH2** chairs, you can globally change every instance of **CH1** to **CH2** with one command. This method could save you a considerable amount of time when many blocks are to be inserted.

LINKING ATTRIBUTES TO A BLOCK

Now that you've created an attribute, you can easily save it along with the block drawing it relates to, with AutoCAD's **BLOCK** command.

Be sure to save your block to disk file with **WBLOCK** if you plan to use it again in another drawing.

If you're using attributes by themselves to tag parts of your drawing (rather than as part of a graphic symbol), you can save just the attributes as a block with the **BLOCK** command.

Type: BLOCK <RETURN>

Response: Block name (or ?)

Type: CHAIR-G <RETURN>

The -G differentiates the general's chair from the private's chair.

Response: Insertion base point:

Pick: The point on your drawing where you want to put the insertion point of your symbol.

Response: `Select objects:`

At this point, you can select the objects you want to include as part of your symbol (including attributes and other entities) by using any or all of the AutoCAD entity selection methods, including **Window**, **Crossing**, **Last** and **Pick**.

After you've picked all the desired objects on the screen, press **< RETURN >** and the objects will disappear, indicating that your block has been saved. If you wish to keep the objects you defined your block with on the screen,

Type: `OOPS <RETURN>`

Response: All of the objects that disappeared when you created the block will return to your screen.

After you've saved your symbol block, you can insert it anywhere in your drawing with AutoCAD's **INSERT** command. Once you've picked the insertion point for your symbol and have entered the **SCALE** and **ROTATION** angle, you'll be prompted for the attribute values for that block.

Type: `INSERT <RETURN>`

Response: `Block Name (or ?):`

Type: `CHAIR-G <RETURN>`

Response: `Insertion point:`

Pick: the desired insertion point.

Response: `X scale factor<1>/Corner/XYZ:`

Type: `1 <RETURN>`

Or any other appropriate scale factor.

Response: `Y scale factor (default=X):`

Type: `<RETURN>`

Or another scale factor, if it is different from the **X** scale.

Response: `Rotation angle <0>:`

Type: `90 <RETURN>`

The attribute prompts will now appear on the **Command** line.

Response: `Name of Occupant:`

Type: `General Jones <RETURN>`

Response: `Location for this chair:`

Type: `100 <RETURN>`

Response: The chair symbol will appear at the spot you indicated, with the words **General Jones** and **100** on the symbol.

At this point, you'll notice that the attribute prompts will be returned to you in the reverse order in which they were created. This is because AutoCAD stores all the data for the block definitions in reverse order. If it's important that the attribute prompts for a block appear in a particular order, then you must write the attribute definitions in the opposite order that you want them to appear.

Project: Now that you've created your first block with attributes and have played around with it a bit, here's a little project for you. Make a chair symbol for privates. Draw a square like those you did for the generals' chair, only leave out the circle.

Now create the same three attributes that you used for the first chair but use the value **PRIVATE** for the constant attribute tag **TYPE**. Finally, save this chair symbol under the name **CHAIR-P.** You will be using both of these chair symbols in an example at the end of this chapter.

TIP: Here's a method we've developed for quickly creating a large number of blocks with attributes. This tip will work only if all the symbols have the same attributes.

Let's say that you need to create a library of fifty different furniture symbols with attributes.

First, start an AutoCAD drawing, and draw all fifty pieces of furniture in that drawing.

Using **ATTDEF, DEF**ine a series of **ATT**ributes for this furniture in the order you wish to see the prompts.

Create and save a block that consists of only the attributes you've just produced. For example, let's call this block **ATT**.

INSERT the block **ATT** into all the furniture symbols using the following form:

Type: INSERT <RETURN>

Response: Block name (or ?):

Type: *ATT<RETURN>

After the **INSERT** prompts appear, the **ATT** block will be inserted into the drawing, exploded into its component parts.

Save each furniture drawing with the **BLOCK** command.

Save each of the blocks to your hard disk with the **WBLOCK** command.

Now when you **INSERT** one of those furniture symbols, the attribute prompts will appear in the order in which they were first written when you created the block called **ATT**.

USING THE ATTDISP COMMAND

The **ATTDISP** command turns the attribute block on and off to view. When the attributes aren't activated, it speeds up **REDRAW** and presents a more pristine view of the drawing data. When you wish to view or plot the text data, merely activate them.

The default setting for attributes is visible unless **Invisible** is turned on. Entering **N** selects the normal mode. Entering **ON** makes all visible and **OFF** makes all invisible. Changing any display mode automatically regenerates the drawing unless **REGENAUTO** isn't activated.

Type: ATTDISP <RETURN>

Response: Normal/On/Off <Normal>:

Type: OFF <RETURN>

Notice the results of changing the parameters.

Type: ATTDISP <RETURN>

Response: Normal/On/Off <Off>:

Type: N <RETURN>

Now we're back where we started.

EDITING AN ATTRIBUTE WITH ATTEDIT

Often you'll discover that the values of a particular attribute have changed and the data entered must be changed to reflect the new condition. The **ATTEDIT** command lets you edit the values. The first thing to do if you wish to edit an attribute is to select an object for editing using **Object/Window/Last**. Select one of your chair symbols. Then call the **ATTEDIT** command.

Type: ATTEDIT <RETURN>

Response: Edit attributes one at a time? <Y> <RETURN>
Block name specification <*>: <RETURN>
Attribute tag specification <*>: <RETURN>
Attribute value specification <*>: <RETURN>
Select Attributes:

If you enter **Y**, you can edit attributes individually. This mode will edit only those attributes currently visible on the screen. Any of the properties of the attribute being edited, including placement and values, can be changed.

If you select **N,** you can do global editing. That is, you can change all instances of a value within a given attribute tag. For example, say you have 500 chair symbols in a drawing, and one of the attribute tags is for MANUFACTURER. At the last minute, you find that you can get a better deal with a different chair manufacturer. You could use the **ATTEDIT** command to change the name of the manufacturer for all chair symbols.

SINGLE CHANGES

When editing attributes individually, you may select the attributes by **tag**, **value** or **blocks**. The first prompt is:

```
Select attributes:
```

Selection may occur by **P**ointing, **W**indowing or **L**ast. Defaults may be selected by entering < **RETURN** >. Selected attributes are marked by an **X**. Use the pick box and touch the text "**General Jones**."

Response: `Value/Position/Height/Angle/Style/Layer`
`        /Color/Next  :`

If you select **V**alue, you may change the attribute's value. You are prompted:

Response: `Change or Replace?`

Type: `C <RETURN>`

Response: `String to change:`

Enter name of the string you wish to change.

Type: `Jones`

Response: `New string:`

Type: `Smith`

Notice that "**General**" is unchanged and the name "**Jones**" has been replaced with the name "**Smith**."

Response: `New attribute value:`

Selecting < RETURN > automatically enters blanks.

If **POSITION** is selected, you're asked for a new Starting, Center or End point. If Height, Angle, Type or Layer are selected, they may be appropriately edited. **Color** lets you select any color number from **1** to **255** or standard color names such as **White**. Special colors such as **BYLAYER** or **BYBLOCK** also can be entered.

GLOBAL CHANGES

When you're doing global editing, AutoCAD prompts:

Response: `Global edit of Attribute values.`

Response: `Edit only attributes visible on screen? <Y>`

Selecting **N** changes AutoCAD to text mode and prompts:

Response: `Drawing must be regenerated afterwards.`

Changes made in the drawing will be affected only after the drawing is regenerated. If you're editing visible attributes, you're prompted:

Response: `Select attributes:`

Attributes can be selected by Pointing, Windowing or Last. Entering < RETURN > edits all attributes.* An **X** is drawn at the starting point of all selected attributes, and you're prompted:

Response: `String to change:`
`New string:`

If you're editing visible and invisible attributes, there are no **X** marks for the screen in text mode. For example:

---

* **CTRL-C** terminates the command if you wish to stop.

Response: `String to change:CHAIR-TYPE`
`New string:TABLE-TYPE`

Tip: Refer to the **CHANGE** command in your *AutoCAD Reference Manual* for more ways to edit attribute values and parameters.

USING THE DDATTE COMMAND

Probably the two most obvious new features in AutoCAD Release 9 and later are the pull-down menus and the dialogue boxes. The only problem is that these features are available, at present, only for a limited number of graphics systems. Although dialogue boxes have a number of uses, we'll address only the ways in which they're used for adding and editing attributes.

Dialogue boxes can be used for both attribute data entry and for editing existing attributes.

USING DIALOGUE BOXES FOR ATTRIBUTE DATA ENTRY

If you have the Advanced User Interface option available on your system, there are now two ways that you can be prompted for attribute information when you insert a block: (1) you can set a system variable so that either the standard attribute prompts are issued at the bottom of the screen, or (2) so that a dialogue box will appear on the screen with a list of all of the non-constant attribute prompts. Figure 2 is a dialogue box that shows the two non-constant attributes used in our chair example.

If you want to use dialogue box attribute prompts, you must set the system variable **ATTDIA** to **1** with the **setvar** command (**setvar "ATTDIA" 1**). To return to using the Command Line Attribute prompt method, you must set the variable **ATTDIA** to **0**.

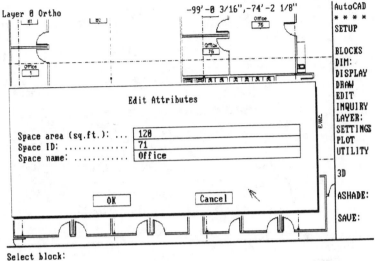

Figure 2: Dialogue box.

USING DIALOGUE BOXES FOR ATTRIBUTE EDITING

Attribute editing is probably the slickest new use for dialogue boxes. Now, instead of having to struggle with remembering the name of the attribute you want to edit, all you have to do is

Type: DDATTE <RETURN>

Response: Select Block:

select the block that contains the attributes you want to edit (see Figure 3), and a dialogue box will appear that contains all of the non-constant attributes and their current values for the block you just selected. Now you can simply point to the attribute value you wish to change, type in the new value and pick the **OK** button at the bottom of the dialogue box. The new attribute value will be saved in the inserted block.

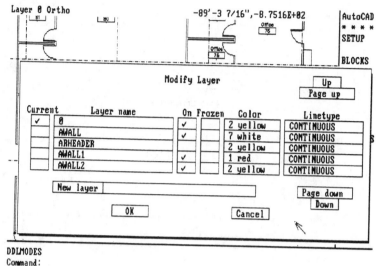

Figure 3: Dialogue boxes and attribute editing.

ATTRIBUTE SYSTEM VARIABLES

Three system variables, which are set by using the **setvar** command, affect the way that attribute is presented when you insert a block that contains attributes. They are **ATTDIA**, **ATTREQ** and **TEXTEVAL**.

If the **ATTDIA** variable is set to **1**, and you can use the Advanced User Interface, all the attribute prompts will be presented in a dialogue box, as explained earlier. If **ATTDIA** is set to **0** or the Advanced User Interface is not available, the attribute prompts will be issued in the normal fashion, one at a time on the command line.

If the **ATTREQ** variable is set to anything other than **0**, you will not be prompted for any attributes when you insert a block. All the attributes will be set to their default values that were determined when they were created. They can, however, be edited at a later time.

If you've written a function in AutoLISP that inserts a block with attributes and you want to have it pause so that you can type in attribute values (by using either the command **PAUSE** or a \), then the system variable, **TEXTEVAL**, must be set to a non-zero value. Otherwise AutoCAD will assume that the **PAUSE** command is the attribute value and will not pause for user input. This is also true for any AutoLISP **COMMAND** function in which your input is expected.

Release 9 has sample drawings that demonstrate the dialogue boxes and the new attribute types. (See the "counter" drawing on the "Sample Drawings" disk.)

USING THE ATTEXT COMMAND

Attribute data extraction and reporting are done by invoking the **ATTEXT** command, which stands for **ATTribute EXTract**. At AutoCAD's **Command** prompt,

Type: ATTEXT <RETURN>

Response: CDF, SDF, or DXF attribute extract
        (or Entities)?

If you pick **CDF**, AutoCAD produces a standard **Comma Delimited File** format. That file contains, at most, one record for each block reference in the drawing file. Each field of each record is separated by a comma, with character fields enclosed in quotes. dBASE can read these files directly using the **APPEND FROM . . . DELIMITED** command. For more information on **CDF**, see Chapter 4.

If you pick **SDF**, a **Space Delimited File** is created, which is the most standard file and is basically a columnar list of information. dBASE reads this file using the **APPEND FROM . . . SDF** command. Here, one record is written for each block reference. Fields are affixed so your program knows where one stops and the other starts. Again, see Chapter 4 for more on **SDF**.

If **DXF** is selected, AutoCAD creates a subset of the **DXF** file with only **Block References**, **Attribute** and **End of Sequence** entities. If **Entities** is selected, you'll be prompted to select the objects whose attributes you want to extract. You then must select **CDF**, **SDF** or **DXF** for the format of the file you wish to create. More on this in Chapter 9.

DEFINING ATTRIBUTE AND DATABASE STRUCTURES

When you add attribute information to a block, you're actually creating an alphanumeric database within the drawing database. This database within a database can act as a link between the graphic information in the drawing and a more sophisticated and extensive database outside the drawing.

The outside database lets you store more detailed information about items referred to in the drawing. For example, a block for a chair may have only two attributes linked to it (such as **TYPE** and **LOCATION**). These two attributes are all that are necessary to identify any chair symbol as a unique item. For example, there would be only one chair **TYPE** *general* in **LOCATION** *100*. All these attribute values can be extracted and used as an index to a much larger outside database, which could contain details about each chair symbol that would be impractical to keep in the AutoCAD drawing database.

Even though there doesn't seem to be a theoretical limit to the number of attributes that can be linked to an individual block, there does seem to be a practical limit.

You've probably noticed that the larger and more detailed your drawings get, the more sluggishly your computer seems to operate. This is because when you increase the size of your drawing database, AutoCAD has more records to search through before it can find a specified record—with really large drawings, this can slow things down to a crawl.

If you create a block with ten attributes linked to it and insert that block just once, you've added twelve records to the drawing database. Each record takes up about the same amount of storage space, whether it's a text attribute or a complex graphics block. If you insert a block into your drawing only 10 times, that adds 120 records to your drawing file.

The consequence of this information inflation is a huge, slow drawing. A better strategy would be to track only identification and quantity data in your drawing and link that information to more detailed data in dBASE II or III, Lotus 1-2-3 or other external database managers. So don't feel compelled to store all the information you might ever wish to know about a symbol in your drawing.

At this point, the first question you must ask is, what data do I want to track? When you select the data to store, make a list of needed information. Be thorough and don't worry about what will be in the drawing and what will be external to it. It's easier to add data structure in the beginning than to go back and edit a large drawing database.

Once you've made your list, flag all the things you need to see on the drawing itself, or what would be appropriate to decide during the drawing process.

TIPS

It's often easier to use a code to assign an attribute tag to a symbol representing an object. For example, a chair could have a code like CH1 and a generic description like Executive Chair. The CH1 serves as a place marker, or "alias," which can later be expanded with more specific and detailed information once design decisions have been made.

This will also make it easier to revise the drawing and the database than it would if the extra detail were linked to the graphic block itself. The designer can later go to the catalog and select color, finish, casters, etc. This process is also easier than loading your desk with catalogs and cluttering the database during the drawing or designing process. It's better to store this kind of information externally.

On the other hand, if you were inserting a door into a wall, it might be better to get the designer to choose whether the door is fire-rated. That not only creates a more accurate door schedule but also ensures that the details related to building codes aren't left out during the specification process.

While it's wise to store most of your data in an external database, don't be shy about storing attribute data in the drawing file, particularly information that is best decided upon when the drawing is made—this is what the attribute is designed for. Just be realistic about what large amounts of internal data will do to **REDRAW** time. Your drawing rhythm might be impeded by having to stop and answer multiple questions on inserting each attribute-linked block.

Once you've compiled your list and decided what's appropriate for both the drawing and for the external database, make a separate list for each type of data. Next, determine the amount of space needed on each data "line" and what each line is to be called. Finally, create the attributes and data linkages appropriate for your design needs.

DEFINING THE DATABASE FIELD

It's important to review the terms *field* and *record*, which were first introduced to you in Chapter 2. Each group or line of data information, such as manufacturer number and price, is called a *field*, and each block of data, including one or more fields linked to an attribute block, is called a *record*.

AutoCAD and other database systems require you to indicate the maximum amount of information you intend to store in a field so the program can identify and retrieve it in the future. The database also requires you to give each field an ID code so it understands what it's looking at later.

Estimate the maximum number of characters each field should contain and assign each a brief **ID** code. For example, **MFGNO, 30 CHARACTERS**, might represent the manufacturer's catalog number and would allow a maximum of 30 characters.

In addition to giving each field a size and **ID** code, you also will be required to determine whether the field is to contain alphabetical or mathematical data. If it's to contain values upon which a mathematical operation, such as pricing, must be performed, then the field is **Numeric**. If it's text or nonmathematical (numbers requiring no calculation), then **Character** is appropriate.

A field can be **V**isible or **N**onvisible on an AutoCAD drawing. If you need to see the information all the time, or for block **ID** purposes, designate the field **V**isible; otherwise, select **N**onvisible. Too much text data on a drawing becomes cluttered and difficult to handle, so work sparingly on the visible data.

Much of the information and advice given here about formatting your AutoCAD internal database will also apply to the external databases you create later. If you plan to use both, plan them early so that they're compatible and efficient. Thinking ahead as much as possible eliminates tedious, time-consuming and often tricky database structural conversions.

PROCESS

- Make your data list.
- Know how the information is to be used. Will it be best inserted at drawing time or later?
- Define your field sizes and types.
- Assign ID codes.
- What data needs to be Visible and what Nonvisible?

ATTRIBUTE TEMPLATE FILES

Before we go back and create an extract file we must create a *template* file, which contains the desired structure for your attribute extract file. It tells the **ATTEXT** command which attribute tags to look for, and in what order to place the information contained in those attributes. Below is a simple template file that tells **ATTEXT** to extract any values associated with attribute tags **ROOMNO** and **EMPNAME** from any blocks named **ROOMTAG**:

```
BL:NAME  C008000    (Block name, 8 chars)*
ROOMNO   C005000    (Room number, 5 chars)
EMPNAME  C020000    (Employee name, 20 chars)
```

The database file produced by using this template file should look like this:

```
ROOMTAG 100 John Smith
ROOMTAG 102 Bill Johnson
ROOMTAG 105 Mary Hartman
```

Let's try it. Exit AutoCAD** and create a template file named **CHAIRS.TXT** with your text editor that looks like this:

---

*   Do not add the text in parentheses to your template file; these are just comments.

** Or if you have set up your **ACAD.PGP** file as suggested in Appendix E you can just type EDIT at the AutoCAD command line to enter your favorite text editor.

```
BL:NAME    C008000
TYPE       C012000
LOCATION   C008000
NAME       C020000
```

It's important not to add spaces to the file you created above with the editor's **TAB** key. Use the space bar. AutoCAD doesn't recognize tabs.

Save the file and make sure it is in the same directory as your AutoCAD drawings. Restart AutoCAD and load your **CHAIR** drawing[*].

If you haven't already done so, get out your Pentagon plans and insert both of your chair symbols (**CHAIR-G** and **CHAIR-P**) into your drawing, using different values when you are prompted for name and location. Insert these symbols at least twice for each chair type.

You are now ready to continue creating your extract file.

Type: ATTEXT

Response: CDF, SDF or DXF Attribute extract (or Entities)? <C>

Type: S <RETURN>

Response: Template file <default>

Type: CHAIRS <RETURN>

Then:

Response: Extract file name <default>

---

[*]   Or simply exit the text editor.

Pressing < **RETURN** > selects the default setting, which is usually the name of the current drawing file (to which AutoCAD adds a **.TXT** extension), for the name of your data extract file — or you could type in a name of your own choosing. (Leave off the **.TXT** extension. AutoCAD will automatically append it.) If you type **CON**, the output is sent to the screen; typing **PRN** at this prompt will send it directly to a printer.

Response: Here is what we got when we tried this example:

```
CHAIR-G  EXECUTIVE   100    MACARTHUR
CHAIR-P  PRIVATE     234    CHAPLIN
CHAIR-G  EXECUTIVE   345    JONES
CHAIR-G  EXECUTIVE   201    CLARK
CHAIR-P  PRIVATE     394    HAWKINS
CHAIR-G  EXECUTIVE   239    RIDDLEY
```

BILL OF MATERIALS

You can easily make a bill of materials by sending an **SDF** file associated with an appropriate template file to your disk. That file can be quite sufficient for a basic materials list. Of course, a more sophisticated report or database can be created by linking an AutoCAD **SDF** or **CDF** file with a database manager like dBASE. We'll show you how that's done in Chapter 4.

ENTITY HANDLES

One of the most exciting additions to the Release 10 version of AutoCAD is the *entity handle*. This may seem like a minor addition, but it has powerful possibilities for linkages to external databases, as well as for text-oriented databases such as master specifications and material standards.

The linkages to information outside the AutoCAD datafile could include electronic photographs, "hypertext," spreadsheets, educational programs or CDROM disks, just to name a few.

WHAT IS AN ENTITY HANDLE?

AutoCAD has included a way to assign a special and unique identifier to each entity in the drawing. You can add it automatically to the entity as you are drawing, or add it later. The entity handle is permanently assigned to an entity and remains with it unless you actively remove it or unless you copy part of the drawing to an external file using the **WBLOCK** command. If you delete an entity from a drawing, its entity handle is never used again in that drawing. This keeps external databases from making a data error by mistaking a new entity with an old entity handle for the old entity.

HOW CAN ENTITY HANDLES BE USED?

In computer programming terms, an entity handle is a "pointer." This simply means that the numbers or characters contained in the entity-handles field in the database "point" to an identical number or character string in another area of the database file or in another file. For example:

```
File A
Record 1        #164890   ◄──────────┐
Record 2        #790438              │
Record 3        #987657              │
Record 4        #652307              │
Record 5        #937895              │
                                     │
File B                               │
Record 1        #872747              │
Record 2        #688866              │
Record 3        #321790              │
Record 4        #164890   ◄──────────┘
Record 5        #191993
```

This pointer relationship allows two different data records or fields to be linked together logically. In other words, if a program wants to know what additional information is related to File A/Record 1, it simply looks in the linked File B until it finds a record with a entity handle value identical to that in File A/Record 1. In the illustration above, the record in File B is Record 4.

The ability to relate two different records means that you can create more complex models of architectural and design projects. An example of linked data information would be the simple linkage of a block representing a chair to an external bill-of-materials database that contains costing information. This is what we showed you in the prior example of linkage to external databases.

The big difference is that an attribute with a tag code or link/pointer doesn't need to be assigned to the block—AutoCAD can now do this automatically. The most important feature of this new way to link to external database files is that you're no longer limited to linking attributed blocks–now you can easily link almost any entity to external files. Futhermore, through the use of DXF files and AutoLISP, the external links can be bi-directionally linked to the drawing. The drawing, in other words, can react to changes in the external data as well as the external data reacting to changes in the drawing. For example, an external database can contain deleted records that were linked to now-deleted drawing entities.

External databases of textual information, like master specifications, can be keyed to related graphic entities in the drawing to more fully describe a graphic object when it's used in a specification. You can link external video images with external programs to display more information about the product or material the drawing entity represents. The uses of entity handles to better record information about a design are limitless.

WHAT AutoCAD FUNCTIONS ALTER HANDLES?

1. When an entity is erased, the handle is never again used in that drawing. A new handle is assigned to an entity when it is added to the drawing.

2. When the **SAVE** command is used, entity handles are retained in the saved file even if the handle's name is changed.

3. When the **WBLOCK** command is used, handles are removed from the entities written to the external file. The system variable **HANDLES** in the external files is set to off (0).

4. When the **INSERT** command is used to import fragments of external drawings into an existing drawing, existing handles contained in the external fragment are replaced in the new drawing. The handles in the external file aren't changed. The data added to the active drawing are treated as if they were newly created.

5. When **DXFIN** (full) is used, all handles are retained and assigned to the recreated entities.

6. When **DXFIN** (partial, entities only) is used, the existing handles contained in the **DXF** file are replaced in the newly recreated drawing file with new handle values.

HANDLES COMMAND – CONTROLLING THE ENTITY HANDLE

The AutoCAD **HANDLES** command has two functions: It either causes the system to assign a unique pointer or identifier to every entity in the drawing, or it deletes all such handles contained in the drawing. You invoke it this way:

Type: HANDLES

Response: ON/DESTROY

If you select **ON**, AutoCAD assigns a unique value to every entity in the drawing and then continues to assign handles to every subsequent entity added to the drawing. The system variable **HANDLES** is also set to on **(1)**.

If you select **DESTROY**, all handles in the drawing database are deleted. The system variable **HANDLES** is set to off **(0)**.

When you pick the **ON** option, every entity is assigned a handle even if it had none before. This includes all entities listed by the **DBLIST** command, including blocks, attributes, polyline vertices and sequence ends. Entities contained in a block definition are *not* assigned handles, since they're considered part of a larger entity.

Note: Counts created from a drawing using entity handles for identifiers will be inaccurate if you expect subassembles of components within blocks to be treated as separate entities.

When the **LIST** and **DBLIST** commands report the value of entity handles, they're presented as hexadecimal numbers or strings.

When you pick the **DESTROY** option, there are several safeguards presented to avoid destroying important external database links by mistake. You must type the entire word "DESTROY" without any abbreviation. When you select **DESTROY**, AutoCAD displays a warning message:

```
         * * * * * WARNING * * * * *

Completing  this  command  will  destroy  ALL
database  handle  information  in  the  drawing.
Once  destroyed,  links  into  the  drawing  from
external  database  files  cannot  be  made.

If  you  really  want  to  destroy  the  database
handle  information,  please  confirm  this  by
entering  "message"  to  proceed  or  "NO"  to  abort
the  command.

Proceed with handle destruction <NO> :
```

"Message" is a randomly selected "key" that must be typed in order to destroy the handles. This prevents absent-minded entering of a destroy "key" without thinking about the consequences. It also prevents a macro from being created to delete handles not intended for deletion.

The system variable **HANDLES** contains a value of **1** if handles is on and **0** if it's off. This system variable can be read by the **SETVAR** command or by an AutoLISP program. Only the **HANDLES** command can change the value of the variable — it is read-only.

The entity handles feature, as mentioned above, is one of the most powerful features of the latest AutoCAD product. We can expect important program links to be provided through this feature by both Autodesk and third-party developers. See page 138 for an example of an AutoLISP function to work with the entity handle. An explanation and example of its use is the **DXF** file in Chapter 7.

SUMMARY

The basic commands and techniques learned here are some of the most important in the AutoCAD program. They make it easy for you to add intelligence to your drawing and to share that information with a host of other programs.

As you'll learn in later chapters, it's possible to make more sophisticated links to the outside and extract more detailed information using **DXF** and AutoLISP.

chapter 4 CREATING A BILL OF MATERIALS PROGRAM

IN THIS CHAPTER

In the last chapter, you learned how to create attribute blocks and export attribute information from AutoCAD to other programs. In this chapter you'll go on to create a simple dBASE program to manage and print bills of materials based on information extracted from your AutoCAD drawing. To do this, you'll use the **ATTEXT** command, discussed in the previous chapter.

A bill of materials is basically a list of the products, materials or parts that make up a building, engineering project or design. A bill of materials may contain product descriptions, catalog numbers, quantities, prices and other such information. When this information is carried inside the drawing as attributes, your drawing file quickly becomes cumbersome, and your computer's performance slows.

A better way to manage such information is to assign a minimum number of attributes to desired drawing symbols or blocks (see Chapter 3), then create your list with an outside database manager or spreadsheet linked to the attributes in your drawing.

The bill of materials program in this chapter is comparable to some that might cost you hundreds of dollars. It's a relatively simple program, but based on a sophisticated concept. If you don't want to type in all the code, an optional diskette contains the dBASE II and dBASE III Plus versions of this program. If you don't want to use dBASE, the diskette also includes a compiled, or stand-alone, version of the program in this chapter. The program is commented throughout, so that you can revise it to suit your application. Or, you can create your own bill of materials program based on techniques outlined in this chapter.

AUTOCAD BILL OF MATERIALS DATA

Let's create the AutoCAD attribute data structure you'll use in the Bill of Materials (BOM) program. Refer to Chapter 3 for a refresher course in creating attribute fields and data extract files to use with your database program. The structure of the attributes for this program is slightly different than the one in Chapter 3.

In this case, we're more interested in the products and materials being specified in a design of new buildings; in Chapter 3, we were doing a facilities management task.

We'll create the attribute data fields and develop a test database to be used in a short dBASE tutorial that demonstrates how an external database system can import, manipulate and report on data assigned to an AutoCAD block. The same database will be used with the actual bill of materials program that follows.

Enter AutoCAD and begin a drawing called TEST. Then create a sample block of a chair. For our purposes, it can be the same 2" square with a 1" circle that we used in Chapters 2 and 3.

When you assign attributes to blocks in AutoCAD, remember to predefine them, using the **ATTDEF** command with the following setup:

1. The attribute ITEMNO should be visible. Other attributes can be visible or invisible.

2. Attribute tags and prompts should be:

TAG:	PROMPT:
STATUS:	STATUS (NEO or C)
ITEMNO:	ITEM NUMBER
QTY:	QUANTITY **(default value of 1)**
CTGRYNO:	CATEGORY
DESC:	DESCRIPTION
IORA:	ITEM OR ASSEMBLY **(default of I)**
CLASS:	CLASS

These fields correspond to those used with the ei:IntelliFile CDROM electronic product catalogs produced by the authors' company. The fields work with their ei:MicroSpec and Turbo-Designer products.

ATTRIBUTE TAG DEFINITIONS

STATUS records the status of the product represented by the block it links to. Status could define whether a product is on order or on the construction site ready for installation.

ITEMNO is the identifier or item number, such as CH1 or EX-ECHAIR for Executive Chair. This is the "pointer" that links the object in the drawing to the record in the external database.

QTY records the quantity of the products or materials the block represents. In the case of a chair it would probably retain the default value of 1. If it represented carpet, it might become 38 for 38 yards.

CTGRYNO stands for category. This can record the location relationship of the block or entity. For example, the chair represented by the block might reside in Office 100; if so, CTGRYNO should be 100.

DESC is a description field. It might contain "Executive Office Chair"; this is more descriptive than CH1, which might be the ITEMNO.

IORA indicates whether the attribute is linked to a simple or nested block. This is useful to know in recording accurate product or material counts.

CLASS can represent a group of objects or products, such as chairs or windows. A one- or two-character code represents this; for example, CH for chairs or WD for windows.

Any other fields you add won't be reported to the BOM program. When you've defined the block attributes, **INSERT** several blocks into the drawing and answer the prompts. Then extract the data once with the **ATTEXT** command, using the **CDF** file option, and again using the SDF option. The **CDF** file should be named **TEST.CDF** and the **SDF** file **TEST.SDF**. Use the following template file in both cases:

BOMACAD.TXT

```
STATUS        C001000
ITEMNO        C010000
QTY           N009002
CTGRYNO       C010000
DESC          C030000
IORA          C001000
CLASS         C002000
```

The files you just created will be used in the next section as samples.

WHY USE dBASE?

dBASE II and its big brother, dBASE III-Plus, are database management programs published by Ashton-Tate, Inc. Because of their power, flexibility and popularity, those programs have become the database standard for personal computers.

Like AutoCAD, those programs contain a built-in language styled after the general purpose language, Pascal. What most differentiates dBASE from other database management programs is the ease with which database files and reports can be created. Pascal or BASIC require many more pages of code to do those chores. In fact, dBASE makes it so much easier to create custom database programs that it's become vital to any CAD user wanting to manage complex information with a minimum of effort.

This book isn't meant to teach you dBASE, but rather to give you enough information to use it to create a small custom program. More experienced users will learn the essential CAD interfaces from which they can build more complex systems.

dBASE, like BASIC and AutoLISP, can be run from AutoCAD's **Command** line. In the case of dBASE, it runs from the "dot" prompt. That's the way the input line is identified when dBASE is started. You can easily create, edit, query and format files directly from the dot prompt; that will often be the best way to use dBASE.

You don't need a special program like the bill of materials program included in this chapter to use dBASE. In fact, dBASE in its "natural" state lets you change, modify and add many different structures of attribute data "on the fly." A customized program like BOM, which takes advantage of the dBASE progamming language, is highly structured and requires some time and programming knowledge to create or modify.

However, a task that's repeated often and/or is done by people with less familiarity with the basic dBASE system can benefit from a structured approach. Also, you'll need to perform complex functions that can be accomplished only with dBASE. Examples are highly formatted reports, custom input screens and complex conversion routines.

First, let's learn how to work with AutoCAD data directly from the dBASE dot prompt. We'll learn how to:

1. Create a database file to which you'll add or import data from AutoCAD.

2. Import data from AutoCAD to dBASE.

3. Edit the new dBASE file.

4. Add additional data directly into the dBASE file.

5. Create and print a report on the data in your file.

Let's take a minute to load dBASE and create a mini-demonstration bill of materials with the dot prompt. First, get into the directory in which you've loaded dBASE. Then:

Type: DBASE <RETURN>

Response: (A copyright message appears.)

Type: <RETURN>

Response: A small period appears at the upper left-hand edge of the screen. This is the dot prompt. If your version is set up for assist mode, dBase will display the **ASSIST** mode menu. Press the **ESC** key to exit the assist menu.

The first step in any dBASE program is to create the database file. With a structured file and basic dBASE, you can manage a sophisticated bill of materials database without any other programming. Let's create our own file now.

CREATING A DATABASE FILE

At the dBASE dot prompt:

Type: `CREATE <RETURN>`

Response: `Enter the name of the new file:`

Type: `ITEMDB <RETURN>`

Response: (dBase will display the table creation screen.)

You will now fill the blank fields with a field name, field type, width and (if type is numeric) number of decimal places.

Type: `STATUS <RETURN> C 1 <RETURN>`

Response: `002`

Type: `ITEMNO <RETURN> C 10 <RETURN>`

Response: `003`

Type: `QTY <RETURN> N 7 <RETURN> <RETURN>`

Response: `004`

Type: `CTGRYNO <RETURN> C 10 <RETURN>`

Response: `005`

Type: `DESC <RETURN> C 30 <RETURN>`

Response: `006`

Type: IORA <RETURN> C 1 <RETURN>

Response: 007

Type: CLASS <RETURN> C 2 <RETURN>

Response: 008

Type: MISC1 <RETURN> C 40 <RETURN>

Response: 009

Type: MISC2 <RETURN> C 40 <RETURN>

Response: 010

Type: MISC3 <RETURN> C 40 <RETURN>

Response: 011

Type: MISC4 <RETURN> C 40 <RETURN>

Response: 012

Type: MISC5 <RETURN> C 40 <RETURN>

Response: 013

Type: COST <RETURN> N 9 <RETURN> 2 <RETURN>

Response: 014

Type: <RETURN>

Response: (Press < RETURN > to confirm and any other key to resume.)

Type: <RETURN>

Response: Input data records now? (Y/N)

Type: N

Response: .

IMPORTING DATA FROM AutoCAD TO dBASE

The next step in using data from AutoCAD is to import the data output—the **CDF** or **SDF** file—you created with AutoCAD's **ATTEXT** command above. That's done by using the **APPEND** command in dBASE. At the dBASE dot prompt:

Type: USE ITEMDB <RETURN>

Response: .

Type: APPEND FROM TEST.CDF DELIMITED <RETURN>

Response: Three (Or number of records added.)

If you're using an **SDF** file:

Type: APPEND FROM TEST.SDF SDF <RETURN>

Response: Three (Or number of records added.)

EDITING YOUR NEW dBASE FILE

When you've added the AutoCAD data to your dBASE file, you then may edit it in several ways, including **EDIT** and **BROWSE**. The most common is **EDIT**, if you know the record you want to edit, or **BROWSE** if you want to start at the beginning of the file and scroll through it at will. Let's use **BROWSE** to view and change existing data.

At the dBASE dot prompt:

Type: `USE ITEMDB <RETURN>`

Type: `BROWSE <RETURN>`

Response: (You're given a columnar list of the data file to view or edit.)

CURSOR MOVEMENTS WHEN EDITING A FIELD IN dBASE III-PLUS

You now can see the data file and can modify it using some of the edit commands in the **BROWSE** mode. Here's a summary of the commands:

- **END** takes you to the first character in the next field.
- **HOME** takes you to the first character in the previous field.
- The **UP ARROW** takes you to the first character of the field directly above the current field.
- The **DOWN ARROW** takes you to the first character of the field directly below the current field.
- **^HOME** displays a menu at the top of the screen that lets you rapidly move to the **TOP** (beginning) or **BOTTOM** (end) of the database.
- **^Y** deletes the rest of the current field.
- **^C** moves the cursor down one screen.
- **^R** moves the cursor up one screen.
- **^U** marks a record for deletion but won't delete it until the file is packed.
- **ESC** aborts **BROWSE** mode.

ADDING NEW DATA TO YOUR dBASE FILE

You may want to add data to the existing file. This is done with the **APPEND** command, which opens the file and lets you add one or more records to the end.

At the dBASE prompt:

Type: `USE ITEMDB <RETURN>`

Type: `APPEND <RETURN>`

Response: (dBASE opens the file)

Enter three new items into the database; for example, a **Chair with Arms**, a **Leather Chair** and a **Side Chair**.

PRINTING REPORTS FROM dBASE

Data are useful only when put to work. Printing a report is the most common use. You can print an entire data file by using the **LIST** command.

Type: `USE ITEMDB <RETURN>`

Type: `LIST <RETURN>`

This displays the entire file to the screen.

Type: `SET PRINT ON <RETURN>`

Type: `LIST <RETURN>`

This prints everything. Or, you may set up a sort-by-parameter and print a selected report from the data. For example:

Type: `USE ITEMDB <RETURN>`

Type: `LIST ALL FOR QTY<1 <RETURN>`

Response: (dBASE lists items whose quantity field exceeds 1.)

You can create a more sophisticated report by using a report form. It works this way:

Type: CREATE REPORT BOM <RETURN>

Response: (Options menu displayed.)

Use the down arrow to move the highlight bar to **Page Title**.

Type: <RETURN>

Response: (Text box appears with cursor.)

Type: Bill-of-Materials Report ^END [Hold down "Ctrl" key and strike "End" key.]

Response: (Text box disappears.)

Use right arrow to move to the **Columns** pull-down menu.

Response: (The **Columns** pull-down menu is displayed, with **Contents** highlighted.)

Type: <RETURN>

Type: ITEMNO <RETURN>

Use the down arrow to move to **Heading**.

Type: <RETURN>

Type: TAG CODE ^END

You've now finished creating column one of the report. Use the **PgDn** key to set the menu for inputting information for the second column.

Type: PgDn

Response: (**Contents** is highlighted.)

Type: < RETURN >

Type: DESC < RETURN >

Use the cursor to move to **Heading**.

Type: < RETURN >

Type: DESCRIPTION ^END

Type: PgDn

dBASE is now ready for the third column.

Type: < RETURN >

Type: CTGRYNO < RETURN >

Use the cursor to move to **Heading**.

Type: < RETURN >

Type: CATEGORY ^END

Now that you've finished creating three columns, use the right arrow to move to the **EXIT** pull-down menu. Be sure the highlight bar is on **SAVE**, then press

Type: < RETURN >

You've created your report form. Now you can send the output to the screen or a printer using the **REPORT** command. To send output to the printer:

Type: SET PRINT ON < RETURN >

Type: USE ITEMDB < RETURN >

Type: REPORT FORM BOM < RETURN >

Response: (dBASE prints your report.)

If you want to sort by a parameter, use the **REPORT** command as follows:

Type: USE ITEMDB <RETURN>

Type: REPORT FORM BOM ALL FOR QTY>1 TO PRINT
<RETURN>

Response: (dBASE prints only items with quantities greater than 1.)

USING THE dBASE PROGRAMMING LANGUAGE

Using the dBASE commands at the dot prompt limits you to one command at a time, which makes many things impossible to do, such as heavily formatted reports. That makes the dBASE programming language important, particularly because it lets you create an input screen, won't intimidate a novice user, and will create fancy formatted reports.

In the final version of the bill of materials, you'll concentrate on creating a program that runs under dBASE, but doesn't depend on the user to type in commands. You'll see menus and input lines much like any other application program. To demonstrate this, let's illustrate the principle of a **Command** file or dBASE program.

At the dBASE dot prompt:

Type: MODIFY COMMAND TEST <RETURN>

Response: (dBASE briefly displays **NEW FILE**, then gives you a blank screen on which to type.)

Type: CLEAR <RETURN>

Type: ?"I am a test program" <RETURN>

Type: CTRL-W (Hold down the control key and type W.)

You've created your first dBASE program! Now

Type: `Do Test <RETURN>`

Response: `I am a test program`

You can use a text editor to easily write or key in your programs from the listings in this book. Although dBASE includes a built-in editor, Wordstar or the CAD-Edit programs on *The AutoCAD Database Diskette* are much easier to use and are less limiting.

BILL OF MATERIALS PROGRAM STRUCTURE

The bill of materials program you'll work with is based on the files used by the ei:MicroSpec and Turbo Designer systems, developed by the authors to provide a sophisticated CAD database management system linked to AutoCAD. The program structure is valid for many general-purpose applications and, of course, can be modified easily or used as a model for a program of your own design.

The data structure is a single dBASE file linked to a universal AutoCAD attribute structure. The attribute structure contains codes that uniquely identify each typical item in the drawing, and that link to a larger, more fully defined data form in your dBASE program.

The two-tiered data structure allows as much information as you want to be linked to the block, but leaves a minimum amount in the drawing itself to prevent slow **REGEN** times and inflated file sizes.

The dBASE file structure is defined below. Let's look at a flow chart of the program.

FLOW CHART

> **AUTOCAD:** *create an attribute with a fixed-structure link to an extract file with a .txt template file, created with the **ATTEXT** command.*

> **SDF file:** *created from **ATTEXT**.*

> **dBASE:** *create programs with menus and procedures designed to make linking, editing and reporting easy for the user. Append the **SDF** file to the **DBF** file.*

> **DBF file:** *(itemdb.dbf) with expanded information structure. Append the **SDF** file to the **DBF** file.*

> **BOM.PRG:** *the main menu program that controls the link to AutoCAD and lets you select a sub-program for adding data, editing and reporting.*

> **BOMADD.PRG:** *the sub-program for adding new data to the dBASE data file.*

> **BOMED.PRG:** *the sub-program for editing data in the dBASE data file.*

> **BOMRPT.PRG:** *the sub-program for creating and printing reports.*

dBASE FILE STRUCTURE

The dBASE file, shown below with the fields defined, has the same structure as the one you created in the tutorial section above. Now you're already starting to write your bill of materials program!

DATABASE STRUCTURE:ITEMDB.DBF

FLD	NAME	TYPE	WIDTH	DEC
001	STATUS	C	001	
002	ITEMNO	C	010	
003	QTY	N	007	000
004	CTGRYNO	C	010	
005	DESC	C	030	
006	IORA	C	001	
007	CLASS	C	002	
008	MISC1	C	040	
009	MISC2	C	040	
010	MISC3	C	040	
011	MISC4	C	040	
012	MISC5	C	040	
013	COST	N	009	002

ITEM FIELD DESCRIPTIONS

We discussed these fields earlier, when we created the attribute definitions and the attribute extract file. The same field names you used there are repeated here, but we've added several new ones. The information from the attribute fields in your drawings will be imported into the fields of the same name in the dBASE program. The new ones will be entered from within the dBASE program itself. That's how we expand and link the two databases.

STATUS: Is this item New (N) or Existing (E), On Order (O) on in the Construction Yard (C)?

ITEMNO: The ID tag of the block or item.

QTY: How many does each instance of the block represent?

CTGRYNO: In what category does the item belong? It might be a room number or other grouping.

DESC: Describe the item.

IORA: Identifies the block as an item, assembly of parts, or a simple or nested block.

CLASS: Identifies the grouping of items this item belongs to.

MISC1: A user-definable field. This is one place where you can enter additional information outside the drawing file.

MISC2: A user-definable field.

MISC3: A user-definable field.

MISC4: A user-definable field.

MISC5: A user-definable field.

COST: The cost, value or price of the item.

The next step is to write your own program or key in the programs included in this chapter.

HOW TO KEY IN A LISTING

When you key in the program listings included here, use EDLIN, Wordstar in non-document mode, the dBASE screen editor, or any text editor in non-document mode. The indentation doesn't have to be exactly as the listing shows, but everything shown on a line must remain on the same line. dBASE reads the code one line at a time and requires that a semicolon end any line wrapped to another line. The lines that begin with asterisks indicate notes; dBASE ignores these. So it's okay for you to add your own notes. Just remember to begin the line with one or more asterisks.

HOW TO DEBUG YOUR LISTING

The most critical aspect of writing any computer program is the debugging process. If you key in code from a book, be careful to type the code exactly as it appears in the listing (with the aforementioned exception of the indenting).

If the program doesn't run, it's probably due to a typing error. Check everything with your text editor and try again. If you need extra help, a number of debugging techniques can be used.

If something's wrong, dBASE generally repeats the command line containing the error and lets you change it. You must make a note of the error and then go into the code to correct it.

If the error is more serious, you can interrupt the program by pressing < ESCAPE > or CONTROL-C. In the worst case, start over. Nothing bad will happen — reboot the computer and start again.

Several dBASE commands will help you find a bug. If you add the TALK, STEP and ECHO commands to the first line or two of your programs, dBASE will help debug itself. When you've found the problem, delete those commands and your program returns to normal.

TALK automatically displays the result of every dBASE operation on the screen. The programs in this book all set TALK OFF. Just add the line SET TALK ON, and do your debugging. Then set TALK OFF before saving your program for later use.

ECHO is similar to TALK. It prints every command line on the screen as it happens. The result is gibberish on your data screen. This command is a powerful way to see what's going right as well as what's going wrong. Add the line SET ECHO ON to the beginning of your programs, and run them.

STEP is the most powerful tool. When you set TALK ON and ECHO ON, as well as STEP ON, the computer will execute one line at a time, and stop and wait for you to press < RETURN >.

Now, set the added debugging commands OFF and you're in business. Let's begin.

PROGRAM LISTINGS

The first module in the set of programs that make up the bill of materials program is the main menu program, which calls all the other options. When a subprogram has finished running, control of the program is returned to the master menu BOM.PRG for further instructions. The code listings below contain detailed comments the first time a procedure is used. This should help you learn what the program is doing and can also help you translate the program design into other database languages.

MAIN MENU

BOM.PRG — This is the main menu program for your bill of materials system. It presents the basic options, calls other programs, contains a routine to import data from an AutoCAD file, and performs other housekeeping functions. This is the database structure for the **ITEMDB.DBF** file, which contains the bill of materials information:

```
*** DATABASE STRUCTURE:ITEMDB.DBF
*** FLD   NAME      TYPE WIDTH DEC
*** 001   STATUS         C    010
*** 002   ITEMNO     C   010
*** 003   QTY            N    007  000
*** 004   CTGRYNO        C    010
*** 005   DESC           C    030
*** 006   IORA           C    001
*** 007   CLASS          C    002
*** 008   MISC1          C    040
*** 009   MISC2          C    040
*** 010   MISC3          C    040
*** 011   MISC4          C    040
*** 012   MISC5          C    040
*** 013   COST       N   009  002
SET TALK OFF
CLEAR ALL                 @ 0,0 CLEAR
*** The following commands set the dBASE environment.
STORE 'Y' TO run
@ 5,22 SAY 'AUTOCAD BILL OF MATERIALS PROGRAM'
@ 16,19 SAY "Copyright 1986, Frederic H. Jones, Ph.D."
@ 24,22 SAY "DO YOU WISH TO CONTINUE ?";
    GET run PICTURE '!'
READ
*** This writes a message to the screen and waits for a
*** response from the keyboard.. The "@5,22" means
*** at line 5 and column 22 display the message "AutoCAD
*** bill of materials program." The quote marks tell
*** dBASE that it is a line of text, not commands.
  IF run = 'Y'
*** An IF sequence must end with a related ENDIF.
    @ 0,0 CLEAR
    ELSE
```

```
    CLEAR
    CANCEL
  ENDIF
*** The next function writes the main menu to the screen
*** and waits for a response.  Depending on the response,
*** the program runs the appropriate subprogram or
*** function.
DO WHILE .t.
*** A DO WHILE sequence must end with an ENDDO.
 @ 0,0 CLEAR
 CHOICE = " "
 @ 3,34 SAY "MAIN MENU"
 @ 5,24 SAY "(0) Exit to operating system"
 @ 7,24 SAY "(1) Add new items to Item List"
 @ 9,24 SAY "(2) Edit records in Item List"
 @ 11,24 SAY "(3) Print A Report"
 @ 13,24 SAY "(4) Append from AutoCAD SDF file"
 @ 15,24 SAY "(5) Return to Dot Prompt"
 @ 17,24 SAY "Enter Desired Action" GET CHOICE
READ
   DO CASE
*** A DO CASE must end with an ENDCASE.
     CASE choice = '0'
       @ 0,0 CLEAR
       QUIT
     CASE choice = '1'
       DO BOMADD
     CASE choice = '2'
       DO BOMED
     CASE choice = '3'
       DO BOMRPT
     CASE choice = '4'
 @ 0,0 CLEAR
     STORE .t. TO a
 DO WHILE a
 STORE '               ' TO sdfile
*** The next sequence  prompts you to specify the
*** name of the file to read into the dBASE program from
*** AutoCAD.
     @ 5,15 SAY 'What SDF file do you wish;
         to append?';
   GET sdfile PICTURE '!!!!!!!!!!!!!'
```

```
           READ
IF sdfile = '                    '
   STORE .f. TO a
      ELSE
```
*** The next sequence trims the blanks from the file and
*** stores it in a temporary file.
```
         STORE TRIM(sdfile) TO tsdfile
         USE itemdb
```
*** The USE command activates the item database file.
*** The APPEND command adds the AutoCAD information to
*** a temporary file, then to the main item database file.
```
         APPEND FROM &tsdfile SDF
```
*** The next sequence creates a new index file for dBASE.
*** The index helps dBASE more quickly find a data record
*** without searching through unorganized data.
```
         INDEX ON itemno TO Nitem
         RELEASE sdfile
         RELEASE tsdfile
         @ 0,0 CLEAR
      ENDIF
  ENDDO
    CASE choice = '5'
      CANCEL
      OTHERWISE LOOP
  ENDCASE
ENDDO t
```

SPECIFYING AND EDITING RECORDS

BOMED.PRG — This next module lets you easily specify and edit the bill of
materials files one record at a time. It lets the user access files by their item
codes rather than by record numbers, as with the dBASE dot prompt.

```
*** Procedure BOMED.PRG
SET SAFETY OFF
USE ITEMDB INDEX NITEM  && Index allows direct access to desired record.
STORE .T. TO MORE
DO WHILE MORE && Loop until user indicates no more.
   CLEAR
```

```
*** This sequence asks the user which item number to edit.
STORE .T. TO RIGHT && This loop lets the user inspect record before editing
    DO WHILE RIGHT
        CLEAR
      STORE 'Y' TO YA,MOR
      STORE '            ' TO MITEMNO
        @ 2,0 SAY 'Which Item Code do you wish to edit?  ' GET
         MITEMNO
        READ
        IF MITEMNO = '             '
            RETURN
        ENDIF
        STORE MITEMNO TO TOKEN
        SET EXACT ON
        FIND &TOKEN && Go find the desired record.
        IF EOF()
            @ 24,0 SAY 'That Item Code does not exist - try again? ';
                            GET YA PICTURE '!'
            READ
            IF YA = 'Y'
                LOOP                  && Go try again.
            ELSE
                STORE 'N' TO MOR       && Set up exit conditions.
                STORE .F. TO MORE
            ENDIF YA = 'Y'
        ENDIF EOF
        SET EXACT OFF

*** Now display the data from the record to be edited.
*** This does not yet allow modifying the data.
        IF YA = 'Y'
            @   4, 0 SAY 'Item Code'
            @   4,25 SAY ITEMNO
            @   5, 0 SAY 'Status'
            @   5,25 SAY STATUS
            @   6, 0 SAY 'Quantity'
            @   6,25 SAY QTY
            @   7, 0 SAY 'Category'
            @   7,25 SAY CTGRYNO
            @   8, 0 SAY 'I or A'
            @   8,25 SAY IORA
            @   9, 0 SAY 'Class'
```

```
@    9,25 SAY CLASS
@   10, 0 SAY 'Description'
@   10,25 SAY DESC
@   11, 0 SAY 'Misc1'
@   11,25 SAY MISC1
@   12, 0 SAY 'Misc2'
@   12,25 SAY MISC2
@   13, 0 SAY 'Misc3'
@   13,25 SAY MISC3
@   14, 0 SAY 'Misc4'
@   14,25 SAY MISC4
@   15, 0 SAY 'Misc5'
@   15,25 SAY MISC5
@   16, 0 SAY 'Cost'
@   16,25 SAY COST
```

*** Now ask the user if this is the record to be modified.
```
    STORE 'Y' TO YES
    @ 22,0 SAY 'Is this the record you are looking for? ';
GET YES PICTURE  '!'
    READ
    IF YES = 'Y'
        STORE .F. TO RIGHT
    ENDIF YES = 'Y'
ELSE
    STORE .F. TO RIGHT
ENDIF YA = 'Y'
ENDDO RIGHT
```

*** We have the right record so let's modify it.
```
IF YA = 'Y'
    STORE .T. TO ALLOK
    DO WHILE ALLOK
        @ 22, 0 CLEAR && Get rid of messages at bottom of screen.
```

*** Set up a work area in memory to receive input.
```
        STORE ITEMNO TO MITEMNO
        STORE STATUS To MSTATUS
        STORE QTY TO MQTY
        STORE CTGRYNO TO MCTGRYNO
        STORE IORA TO MIORA
        STORE CLASS TO MCLASS
```

```
          STORE DESC TO MDESC
          STORE MISC1 TO MMISC1
          STORE MISC2 TO MMISC2
          STORE MISC3 TO MMISC3
          STORE MISC4 TO MMISC4
          STORE MISC5 TO MMISC5
          STORE COST TO MCOST
```

*** Read new data into memory instead of into database.
```
          @    4,25 GET MITEMNO
          @    5,25 GET MSTATUS
          @    6,25 GET MQTY
          @    7,25 GET MCTGRYNO
          @    8,25 GET MIORA
          @    9,25 GET MCLASS
          @   10,25 GET MDESC
          @   11,25 GET MMISC1
          @   12,25 GET MMISC2
          @   13,25 GET MMISC3
          @   14,25 GET MMISC4
          @   15,25 GET MMISC5
          @   16,25 GET MCOST
          READ
```

*** Is the user satisfied with the accuracy of this data?
```
          STORE 'Y' TO YA
          @ 22,0 SAY 'Are these changes correct?  ' GET YA PICTURE '!'
          READ
          STORE YA  'Y' TO ALLOK
     ENDDO ALLOK
```

*** OK, move the data from the work area to the database.
```
        REPLACE ITEMNO WITH MITEMNO, DESC WITH MDESC
        REPLACE STATUS WITH MSTATUS, QTY WITH MQTY
        REPLACE CTGRYNO WITH MCTGRYNO, IORA WITH MIORA
        REPLACE CLASS WITH MCLASS, MISC1 WITH MMISC1
        REPLACE MISC2 WITH MMISC2, MISC3 WITH MMISC3
        REPLACE MISC4 WITH MMISC4, MISC5 WITH MMISC5
        REPLACE COST WITH MCOST
     ENDIF YA = 'Y'
```

```
*** Now find out if there are more items to be updated.
    IF MOR = 'Y'
      @ 23,0 SAY 'Is there another Item Code to edit (Y/N)?  ';
       GET MOR PICTURE '!'
       READ
       STORE (MOR = 'Y') TO MORE
    ENDIF MOR = 'Y'
ENDDO MORE
RELEASE ALL
RETURN
```

ADDING NEW RECORDS

BOMADD.PRG — **BOMADD.PRG** lets you add new records to the database file from the keyboard rather than from an AutoCAD file. This way, you can create and extend a specification instead of depending on the drawing database to access your project data.

```
*** Procedure BOMADD.PRG
SET SAFETY OFF
USE ITEMDB INDEX NITEM  && The index allows checking for duplicates.
STORE .T. TO MORE
DO WHILE MORE  && Continue adding until user indicates no more.

*** The next sequence creates an empty work area in memory.
    STORE '              ' TO MITEMNO
    STORE ' ' TO MIORA
    STORE '   ' TO MCLASS
    STORE ' ' TO MSTATUS
    STORE 0 TO MQTY
    STORE '          ' TO MCTGRYNO
    STORE '                           ' TO MDESC
    STORE '                              ' TO MMISC1
    STORE '                              ' TO MMISC2
    STORE '                              ' TO MMISC3
    STORE '                              ' TO MMISC4
    STORE '                              ' TO MMISC5
    STORE 0.00 TO MCOST
```

*** The next sequence displays the field titles and asks for an item code.

```
CLEAR
@ 24,0 SAY 'Enter blanks for Item Code when you want to quit.'
@ 2,25 SAY '    MASTER ITEM FILE   '
@  4,0 SAY 'Item Code                 ' GET MITEMNO
@  5,0 SAY 'Status'
@  6,0 SAY 'Quantity'
@  7,0 SAY 'Category'
@  8,0 SAY 'I or A'
@  9,0 SAY 'Class'
@ 10,0 SAY 'Description'
@ 11,0 SAY 'Misc11'
@ 12,0 SAY 'Misc12'
@ 13,0 SAY 'Misc13'
@ 14,0 SAY 'Misc14'
@ 15,0 SAY 'Misc15'
@ 16,0 SAY 'Selling Price'
READ
IF MITEMNO = '              '
    STORE .F. TO MORE      && If the item code is blank set up exit
ENDIF                      && conditions.
```

*** Now check for the existence of the record.

```
STORE .F. TO FOUND
IF MORE
    STORE TRIM(MITEMNO) TO TOKEN
    SET EXACT ON
    FIND &TOKEN
    IF .NOT. EOF() && If record not found EOF() will be true
        @  5,25 SAY STATUS  && Display contents of found record.
        @  6,25 SAY QTY
        @  7,25 SAY CTGRYNO
        @  8,25 SAY IORA
        @  9,25 SAY CLASS
        @ 10,25 SAY DESC
        @ 11,25 SAY MISC1
        @ 12,25 SAY MISC2
        @ 13,25 SAY MISC3
        @ 14,25 SAY MISC4
        @ 15,25 SAY MISC5
        @ 16,25 SAY COST
```

```
      @ 22,0 SAY 'The above Item Code already exists.' + ;
      ' Duplicates not allowed.'
      WAIT
      STORE .T. TO FOUND     && Force skipping this record.
   ENDIF EOF
ENDIF MORE
SET EXACT OFF
```

*** The next sequence is used to enter data into the blank work area.

```
IF MORE .AND. .NOT. FOUND     && Skip this code if record exists.
   STORE .T. TO AGAIN
   DO WHILE AGAIN  && This loop allows correcting the data.
      @  5,25 GET MSTATUS
      @  6,25 GET MQTY
      @  7,25 GET MCTGRYNO
      @  8,25 GET MIORA
      @  9,25 GET MCLASS
      @ 10,25 GET MDESC
      @ 11,25 GET MMISC1
      @ 12,25 GET MMISC2
      @ 13,25 GET MMISC3
      @ 14,25 GET MMISC4
      @ 15,25 GET MMISC5
      @ 16,25 GET MCOST PICTURE '99999999999.99'
      READ
      STORE 'N' TO OK
      @ 23,0 SAY SPACE(79)     && Clear the previous message on this line.
      @ 23,0 SAY 'Do you want to change anything? ' GET OK PICTURE '!'
      READ
      IF OK = 'N'
         STORE .F. TO AGAIN     && No need to repeat the input steps.
      ENDIF OK
   ENDDO AGAIN
```

*** The data in the work area is now moved into a blank record in the database.

```
   IF MITEMNO '            '
      APPEND BLANK
   REPLACE ITEMNO WITH MITEMNO, DESC WITH MDESC
   REPLACE STATUS WITH MSTATUS
   REPLACE MISC1 WITH MMISC1, MISC2 WITH MMISC2
   REPLACE MISC3 WITH MMISC3, MISC4 WITH MMISC4
   REPLACE MISC5 WITH MMISC5, COST WITH MCOST
```

```
        REPLACE CLASS WITH MCLASS
        REPLACE QTY WITH MQTY, CTGRYNO WITH MCTGRYNO, IORA WITH MIORA
     ELSE
        STORE .F. TO MORE && For blank item number set up exit conditio
     ENDIF MITEMNO  '            '
   ENDIF .NOT. FOUND
ENDDO MORE
RELEASE ALL
RETURN
```

CREATING REPORTS

BOMRPT.PRG — Predesigned reports are important for the casual dBASE user not familiar with the dot prompt, and are essential for a complexly formatted report. This module is the most likely candidate for customization and expansion. You should be able to pick up the basic principles from this module for extension.

```
*** Procedure BOMRPT.PRG
SET HEADING OFF
SET SAFETY OFF
*** Ask the user to supply a header for the report.
CLEAR
STORE '                      ' TO HEADER HEADER TO BE PRINTED';
      GET HEADER PICTURE'!!!!!!!!!!!!!!!!!!!!!!!!!!!!!!!!!!'
READ
STORE TRIM(HEADER) TO THEADER

*** Be sure that the printer is ready to go.
@ 10, 10 SAY 'TURN ON PRINTER AND LINE UP PAPER'
@ 12, 10 SAY 'PRESS ANY KEY TO CONTINUE......'
WAIT
CLEAR
SET DEVICE TO PRINT
SET CONSOLE OFF
SET TALK OFF
STORE 99 TO LINECNT
STORE 1 TO PAGENO
```

```
USE ITEMDB INDEX NITEM  && The items are listed in index order
```

*** Now print each item in the file .
```
DO WHILE .NOT. EOF()
```

*** This section of commands starts a new page and prints a suitable header.
```
    IF LINECNT > 48
       EJECT
       @ 1,20 SAY 'YOUR COMPANY NAME'
       @ 3,25 SAY 'MASTER ITEM LIST'
       @ 3,65 SAY 'DATE  ' + DTOC(DATE())
       @ 4,20 SAY THEADER
       @ 4,65 SAY 'PAGE  ' +STR(PAGENO,3)
       STORE 6 TO LINECNT
       STORE PAGENO+1 TO PAGENO
    ENDIF
```

*** This is the body of the report.
```
    @ LINECNT,   1 SAY ' '
    @ LINECNT+1, 1 SAY 'ITEM NO:      ' + ITEMNO
    @ LINECNT+2, 1 SAY 'STATUS:       ' + STATUS
    @ LINECNT+3, 1 SAY 'QTY USED:     ' + STR(QTY,7)
    @ LINECNT+4, 1 SAY 'CATEGORY:     ' + CTGRYNO
    @ LINECNT+5, 1 SAY 'I OR A:       ' + IORA
    @ LINECNT+6, 1 SAY 'CLASS:        ' + CLASS
    @ LINECNT+7, 1 SAY 'DESCRIPTION:  ' + DESC
    @ LINECNT+8, 1 SAY 'MISC1:        ' + MISC1
    @ LINECNT+9, 1 SAY 'MISC2:        ' + MISC2
    @ LINECNT+10,1 SAY 'MISC3:        ' + MISC3
    @ LINECNT+11,1 SAY 'MISC4:        ' + MISC4
    @ LINECNT+12,1 SAY 'MISC5:        ' + MISC5
    @ LINECNT+13,1 SAY 'COST:         ' + STR(COST,9,2)

    STORE LINECNT + 14 TO LINECNT
    SKIP
ENDDO EOF
```

```
*** The report is done.
EJECT
SET DEVICE TO SCREEN
SET CONSOLE ON
RELEASE ALL
RETURN
```

HOW TO RUN BOM.PRG

Type: dBASE bom <RETURN>

Response: screen shot of main menu (see Figure 1).

```
MAIN MENU
(0) Exit to operating system
(1) Add new items to Item List
(2) Edit records in Item List
(3) Print a Report
(4) Append from AutoCAD SDF file
(5) Return to Dot Prompt
Enter Desired Action
```

Figure 1: Main menu for the Bill of Materials program.

SUMMARY

This concludes the lesson in using dBASE to edit and print a bill of materials and to create a program to maintain a bill of materials database. Of course, you can create far more complex programs. A number of third-party bill of materials programs also have been developed to work with AutoCAD and other CAD systems. Such programs can result in productivity gains limited only by your imagination.

chapter 5 AUTOLISP PROGRAMMING

IN THIS CHAPTER

In Chapters 3 and 4, you learned the basics of attributes and how to create a simple bill of materials program. In this chapter, you'll learn some of the basic concepts of LISP and how to write programs in AutoLISP so that you can extract and use data from AutoCAD drawings. These data include the blocks and attributes you've learned how to create in the previous chapter. When finished, you'll have learned just how simple LISP really is and how easy it is to understand and write AutoLISP programs.

AUTOLISP OVERVIEW

LISP stands for **LIS**t **P**rocessing, a simple, yet powerful language for handling symbolic data (words instead of numbers).

Because it's such a versatile and powerful language, LISP is the language of choice among Artificial Intelligence researchers.

If computer programming were like sculpture, then LISP would be like a sculptor's clay to most other computer language's stone. With LISP you can add a little piece here and a little dab there until you get a result that works. If you don't like the result, you can remove pieces and squeeze other parts around until the work pleases you—this is a modeling concept. Many programming languages use the building block concept where you must add building blocks and chisel away at them. If the result doesn't work, then too bad. You have to throw away a lot of what you did and start over—just as if you were carving in stone.

AutoLISP is a subset of common LISP with many additional built-in graphics handling functions. AutoLISP was designed by Autodesk to extend AutoCAD's power by allowing you great latitude in creating an even more powerful drafting package for specific applications.

Because AutoCAD was designed to be a powerful general purpose drafting system, it wasn't possible, or practical, to include every type of useful feature for each drafting discipline. AutoLISP was created to fill that gap. For example, AutoCAD has no command for drawing parallel lines simultaneously—a useful feature for drawing walls on building plans. However, several AutoLISP programs make drawing double wall lines as easy as drawing ordinary lines[*].

But what will AutoLISP do for you? Why should you spend a lot of time learning an obscure specialized computer language? The answer is in two words—power and money.

First, the power. Even very simple AutoLISP functions add more power to AutoCAD. Imagine if everything that you put into your drawing was tracked automatically? Later in this chapter, you'll learn how to keep track of any item that you specify in a drawing with only ten simple lines of AutoLISP code.

And, of course, there's money. You can save by doing your drafting faster with the aid of AutoLISP routines and you can *earn* by being more productive. The next four chapters will show you how AutoLISP can save hours every week by eliminating repetitive, error-prone tasks.

Of course, you can skip the explanation of how AutoLISP works, and just use the examples, which were designed to allow you to modify and build on them to suit your own purposes. However, that would be impossible to do without some basic understanding of AutoLISP. We encourage you to plow ahead and

---

[*]   For example, the wall drawing routines in TURBO DESIGNER™ and AutoCAD AEC®.

gain some facility for using AutoLISP. A good place to start is by reading *AutoLISP in Plain English*, by George O. Head (Ventana Press). You will find it well worth the effort.

This chapter presents the basics of AutoLISP in a practical, hands-on fashion with many useful programming examples that will help you to understand and use AutoLISP effectively in your own work.

LEARNING ABOUT AUTOLISP

LISP is probably one of the simplest, yet most powerful programming languages around. However, the general consensus is that LISP is very difficult to learn, when quite the opposite is often true.[*] LISP is simple because it's a language that consists of only three elements: the *atom*, the *list* and the *function*.

The best way to start learning AutoLISP is to sit down and start playing with it on your computer as you follow along with the examples in this chapter. The first few one-line examples can be typed directly on AutoCAD's **Command** line and the result will be displayed as soon as you press < RETURN >.

The longer examples can be typed into any text editor or word processor, saved under any filename (with an **.LSP** extension) and loaded into AutoCAD and executed.

To simplify matters even further, see Appendix E, which will teach you to set up a text editor to use while you're running AutoCAD to simplify program writing and debugging.

You also can use SideKick™ or one of the other memory resident text editors for writing your AutoLISP code, but remember to always use the **F1** key to flip your screen out of the graphics mode before you call any of those programs. Otherwise, you may lock up your computer.

---

[*] LOGO, the computer language developed to teach young children programming, is a subset of LISP.

BASIC CONCEPTS

ATOMS: The basic unit of any LISP program is called the **ATOM**. Just as atoms were once thought to be the smallest possible units of matter, a LISP atom is simply the smallest possible unit in a LISP program. An atom can be a word, a symbol* or a number. It can have a meaning assigned to it (in which case the atom can also be called a variable or a function name) or it can simply stand for itself (with no other meaning assigned it). For example, consider the following lists:

```
'(furniture chairs tables desks lamps beds)


'(chairs side-chairs easy-chairs typing-chairs)


'(77 83 5.25678 44 33 1)
```

All the words or numbers (such as chairs, easy-chairs or 44) in the above lists are atoms, and because each of those lists begins with a quote (the list is called a "quoted list"), the atoms are called literals (i.e., they hold no additional value other than that of the word itself).

Think of an atom as being the same thing as a variable name in another computer language, such as BASIC. An atom usually acts the same way as a variable does.

For many purposes, you can use an atom like you would use a variable name in another language. But an atom can be much more than a variable name, because, while you can only assign a *value* to a variable name, you can *bind* almost anything to an atom. Not only can you assign a simple value to an atom, such as **(setq a 6)**, you can bind lists to atoms like this:

Type: (setq b '(furniture chairs tables desks))

Response: (furniture chairs tables desks)

---

*   An atom is often referred to as a SYMBOL.

In addition, when you assign a value to an atom, you can assign a different value to that atom within a function, and when that function is finished, the atom is rebound to the value it was set to before that function was run.

LISTS: A **LIST** is simply a group of atoms (or even a single atom) that is contained within a pair of parentheses. Lists must be constructed in a particular way to make sense to the LISP Interpreter. A list can be made up of other lists or combinations of lists and atoms as in the examples below:

```
()
```

This list is called an empty list or a **nil** list. Even though the list has nothing in it (which is why it's called a **nil** list), it's still a list because it's set off by a pair of parentheses.

```
'(table)
```

This list consists of a single atom surrounded by parentheses.

```
'(desks files)
```

This list contains two atoms.

```
'((desks files) (chairs stools))
```

This list contains two **SUBLISTS** each of which contains two atoms. A sublist is simply a list contained or nested inside another list. Lists can be nested inside other lists to almost any depth.

```
'(furniture (chairs stools side-chairs))
```

This list contains an atom and a sublist that consists of three atoms.

```
'((beds (single-bed murphy-bed)) (lamps) 97)
```

This list contains two sublists and an atom. The first sublist contains an atom and another sublist inside it that contains two atoms.

As you can see from the examples above, lists can be nested to great depths, and be quite complex — that may be why a lot of people think LISP is a difficult language.

AutoLISP programs will run much faster if complex, nested lists are used. However, for the purposes of illustration, you'll only be working with simple lists in these examples.

FUNCTIONS: A **FUNCTION** is a LISP program[*] that may be called by another LISP program and executed, or it can be executed directly from the **Command** line in AutoCAD.

Functions are similar to programs, functions, procedures or subroutines in other computer languages.

A function always returns a *result*. Think of a function as a black box, with a hole in either end, that performs a process. You stick the raw materials in one end of the black box, and the finished product comes out the other end. If you want to add the numbers **2** and **4**, you stick those numbers (called arguments) in the black box called + (**PLUS**) and the result, **6**, comes out the other end.

Many functions are already built into AutoLISP, such as the common math functions + - * / and the logical operators <, >, =, /=.[**] LISP's real power, however, is its ability to let you define your own functions to suit a specific application. Below is an example of a simple AutoLISP function that takes any number given to it and multiplies it by **10**.

Let's try it — hit the **F1** key, get into AutoCAD's text mode and:

Type: `(defun tentimes (number) (* number 10))`

Response: `TEN TIMES`

---

[*] In various books about LISP, there's some disagreement about the definition of a function. Some books call functions **procedures**. Other books call a function a type of **procedure** that does not have a side effect. Because the *AutoLISP Programmer's Reference* only talks about functions, we'll refer to everything as a function regardless of side effects. We'll discuss side effects a little later in this chapter.

[**] Those built-in functions are called LISP **primitives**.

This function can be called from another function with the following function call (which is simply another list that contains the name of the function and the value from which the function will derive an answer):

Type: (tentimes 2) <RETURN>

Response: 20

AutoCAD should print **20** on the next line. If not, retype the function.

If you got **20**, then congratulations. You've just successfully written your first AutoLISP program! Now, let's call the new function using other numbers as arguments:

Type: (tentimes 20) <RETURN>

Response: 200

Type: (tentimes 3.7) <RETURN>

Response: 37.0

Let's look at that function in detail to see how it works. Here's the same function formatted to conform to accepted LISP programming practices:[*]

```
(defun tentimes (number)
 (* number 10)
)
```

The function is just a list that contains two atoms, defun and **tentimes**; a sublist that contains the atom **number** and another sublist that contains the three atoms *****, **number** and **10**.

---

[*] You don't have to follow the indenting conventions you find in this function or any other function in this book. The only spacing that's absolutely necessary in LISP code is one space to separate each atom in a list. We do, however, think that following standard conventions of indention helps enormously in making the code more readable, clarifying the programmer's intent and making the code easier to debug.

What does all this mean? The first atom, **defun**, is a built-in LISP function that indicates this list will be a definition of a **function**. The next atom, **tentimes**, is simply the name you've chosen to call the function that you're defining.

The first sublist that contains the single atom **number** is called the *argument list*. In this case, our function will take only one argument. An *argument* is an independent variable that takes the value given it when the function is called, and uses that value within the function.

The argument can be named anything. You could call it **Ralph**, but the word **number** was used as a reminder of the type of variable that would be used in that function.

The next line in that function contains the actual formula for multiplying a given number by 10. That formula could be expressed in algebra as:

```
answer=number * 10
```

But in LISP it's expressed as:

```
(* number 10)
```

That is, multiply the variable called **number** by **10**.

Isn't it easy? And that's all there is to LISP. You now know almost everything there is to know about the structure and syntax of LISP.

Now that you've gotten your feet wet with a simple LISP function, let's take a little closer look at the mechanics of the LISP Interpreter. Other computer languages have many different grammatical forms, called syntax, that vary with the type of operation you want to perform. LISP, on the other hand, has only one syntactical form—the function call. For example, if you want to say **x = 2 + 4** in LISP, you would:

Type: (setq x (+ 2 4))

Response: 6

Let's examine the above list or expression more closely. If you understand how it works, you'll have a better grasp of how LISP actually works.

First, look at the list **(+ 2 4)**. This is called a sublist. Inside the LISP Interpreter is a section called the List Evaluater.[*] Whenever the List Evaluater sees a list that doesn't have a single quote in front of the list, it tries to evaluate that list. The List Evaluater takes the atom of the deepest sublist (in this case the symbol **+**) and checks to see if there is a function available called **+**. If it finds a function called **+**, it then will pass the numbers **2** and **4** (called *arguments*) to that function and the function called **+** will be evaluated. The function called **+** will probably say:

```
TAKE THE VALUE OF THE FIRST ARGUMENT AND
    PLACE IT IN
A LOCATION IN MEMORY CALLED "a"
    WHILE THERE ARE MORE ARGUMENTS
        INCREMENT THE VALUE OF LOCATION "a"
            BY THE VALUE OF THE NEXT ARGUMENT
RETURN THE VALUE OF LOCATION "a" TO THE
    EVALUATER
```

In this case, the value returned from evaluating the function called **+** is **6**. When the first sublist has been evaluated, the sample expression now looks like this to the List Evaluater:

```
(setq x 6)
```

The List Evaluater now looks for function, **setq**, which says:

```
SET THE VALUE OF THE ATOM NAMED IN THE FIRST
ARGUMENT TO THE VALUE OF THE SECOND ARGUMENT.
```

AutoLISP will always return the value of the last evaluated function to the **Command** line. In order to check the value of **x**, you can type this on the **Command** line:

Type: !x <RETURN>

Response: 6

---

[*]   An EVALUATER is a machine that evaluates; an EVALUATOR is a person who evaluates.

AutoLISP will print 6 on the next line. Typing **!** (an exclamation point) followed by the name of any atom on the **Command** line will display the value that has been bound to that atom by a function. Try typing **!y**. AutoLISP should display **nil**, which means that there is no value bound to the atom called **y**.[*]

Let's see what happens when you quote a list. Type the same list into the **Command** line, but put a quote in front of the sublist like this:

Type: `(setq x '(+ 2 4)) <RETURN>`

Response: `(+ 2 4)`

If you type **!x**, **(+ 2 4)** will be displayed. That means that because the list **(+ 2 4)** was quoted, it wasn't evaluated by the List Evaluater and it simply set the value of **x** to the list.[**] To see what a really long list looks like, press **F1** to flip the screen to text mode and:

Type: `!ATOMLIST`

That **ATOMLIST** is the list of all the atoms that have some value attached to them. Most of those atoms are names of the built-in AutoLISP functions.

---

[*] Actually there's no atom called **y** because **y** was never defined as an atom. If at one time you had assigned a value to **y** using the **setq** function and then later set the value of **y** to nil, then the atom called **y** would still exist in the computer's memory.

[**] If, at a later time, you wanted the value of 2 + 4, you could say **(EVAL X)** and then the List Evaluater would evaluate the list that is bound to the atom **x**.

SOME RULES ABOUT CONSTRUCTING LISTS

In LISP, a list can either be part of the program or data to be operated on by the program. The same list can even be data and part of the program simultaneously. Certain rules, however, must be observed to properly operate lists when you construct them for a LISP program.

Atoms within lists and lists should always be separated by one or more spaces.

The first atom of any list that may be evaluated must be the name of a valid function.* The list

```
(1 2 3 4 5)
```

will not evaluate unless there is a function called **1**. On the other hand, the list:

```
(+ 1 2 3 4 5)
```

will evaluate to **15**, but it's still a useless list, because the result of this evaluation hasn't been passed to either an atom or another list for further evaluation, as it has in the following two examples:

```
(setq answer (+ 1 2 3 4 5))
```

```
(setq answer (* 10 (+ 1 2 3 4 5)))
```

which brings us to the next rule.

You must always pass the result of a function evaluation to be the argument of another function or to an atom, unless the purpose of the evaluated function is its side effect.

What is a side effect? Common LISP doesn't have side effects. You normally pass arguments to a function such as **(setq c (+ a b))** and the result of evaluating that function is returned.

---

* Either the name of a built-in function or a function that has been previously defined by **defun**.

AutoLISP has many functions that are evaluated solely for their side effects and the result of the evaluation is often ignored. For example, when the function

```
(command "line" pt1 pt2 "")
```

is evaluated, the purpose is to invoke the AutoCAD command processor to draw a line between **pt1** and **pt2**—that's the side effect of the function called **command**. However, the result returned by this function (**nil**) is always ignored.[*]

If you don't want a list to be evaluated, quote the whole list and then **setq** that quoted list to an atom such as:

```
(setq ylist '(89 121))
```

so that when you want to look at that list, it has been defined as **ylist**.

That's really all you need to know about the structure and syntax of LISP and AutoLISP. The only other important thing to know about AutoLISP is how the various built-in functions work and how to write your own functions to solve your particular application problems.

PRACTICAL TIPS ON USING AUTOLISP'S BUILT-IN FUNCTIONS

This section features practical exercises on using some of the more common AutoLISP functions. You should follow along by typing in these examples on AutoCAD's **Command** line so you can see the actual results. You're encouraged to experiment with the structure and variables to see what other kinds of results are possible with some of these functions.

---

[*] To better illustrate a side effect, think of your digestive system as a LISP function. The raw material your digestive system operates on is food (the arguments passed to the function). The direct result produced by the function of your system digesting this food and converting it into energy is waste (the value of which is nil). The side effect of this function, however, is to produce the energy to operate your body.

The first thing to do is to **setq** the values to a few atoms so that you can use the values bound to those atoms instead of having to retype them each time. These atoms will be reused for the rest of the examples in this section. Type the following line at the **Command** line:

Type: `(setq a 1.0 b 2.0 c 3.0 d 4.0 e 5.0)` `<RETURN>`

Response: `(5.0)`

You'll notice that here you've set the value of several atoms with one **setq** function. Many of the built-in AutoLISP functions, such as **setq** and most of the arithmetic functions, allow the use of multiple arguments.

The advantage of **setq**ing several atoms with one function call is that it's much faster for the List Evaluater to evaluate five pairs of arguments in one function call than to evaluate five separate function calls.

Now let's explore how some of those functions function!

ARITHMETIC FUNCTIONS

AutoLISP has many built-in math functions, and in this section you'll play with some of the basic arithmetic functions, such as add, subtract, multiply and divide.

In math, there are basically three kinds of notation:

1. Algebraic or infix notation, the one you learned in high school algebra, in which the operator symbol is in the middle of the expression (i.e., $2 + 2$).

2. Postfix notation, in which the operator symbol appears at the end of the expression (i.e., 2 2 +), as used in Hewlett-Packard calculators and Forth.

3. Prefix notation, in which the operator symbol appears at the beginning of the expression: (+ 2 2). LISP appears to use prefix notation in its math operations, but the math symbol is merely the name of the function called when that particular list is evaluated, as it is the first element in the list. Keeping this fact in mind, you'll see how easy it is to set up complex math formulas in LISP. Take this simple list to evaluate:

Type: (+ 2 4) <RETURN>

Response: 6

    If you think like the List Evaluater, you'll say "**ADD** to **2** the value of **4**," or if you use the atoms that you've previously **setq**ed, the list will read:

Type: (+ b d)

Response: 6.0

    or "**ADD** to the value of **b** (**2**) the value of **d** (**4**)." With all the arithmetic functions, we can pass an almost unlimited number of arguments and the List Evaluater will evaluate all the atoms down to a single result. For instance, the following list:

Type: (+ a b c d e)

Response: 15.0

    will be evaluated as "**ADD** to the value of **a** the value of **b** and to that result **ADD** the value of **c** and keep repeating that until there are no more arguments in the list."
    The **SUBTRACT** function operates the same way:

Type: (- e a)

Response: 4.0

    The List Evaluater says "**SUBTRACT** from the value of **e** (**5**) the value of **a** (**1**)" and returns the result of **4**. More complex subtraction is evaluated the same way:

Type: (- e a b a)

Response: 1.0

The List Evaluater says "**SUBTRACT** from the value of **e** (5) the value of **a** (1) and then from that result **SUBTRACT** the value of **b** (2) and keep repeating that until there are no more arguments."

If only one argument is given to the **SUBTRACT** function, it will subtract the value of that argument from **0**:

Type: (- e)

Response: -5.0

"**SUBTRACT** the value of **e** from **0**" will return a **-5**.

MULTIPLICATION and **DIVISION** functions are evaluated in exactly the same way:

Type: (* e c)

Response: 15.0

"**MULTIPLY** the value of **e** (5) by the value of **c** (3)."

Type: (* e c d b)

Response: 120.0

"**MULTIPLY** the value of **e** (5) by the value of **c** (3) and **MULTIPLY** that result by the value of **d** (4) and keep repeating that until there are no more arguments in the list."

Type: (/ e b)

Response: 2.50

"**DIVIDE** the value of **e** (5) by the value of **b** (2)"

Can you evaluate the following list by yourself?

Practice: (/ e b d c)

Hint: the answer is 0.20833.

Now, let's try playing List Evaluater and evaluate more complex lists. Remember, you always evaluate the most deeply nested list first. (See if you can figure out this one before you type it in):

```
(setq answer (- (* (/ e b c) (* c a e) b)
   c (+ e d c b a)))
```

Evaluate the deepest level of sublists and you get this:

```
(setq answer (- (* 0.833333 15 2) 3 15))
```

Evaluate the next level of lists for this:

```
(setq answer (- 25 3 15))
```

LIST MANIPULATING FUNCTIONS

This section briefly explains how several important list manipulation functions work, and then shows how they can be used to build and access a database made up of lists.

As mentioned earlier, a list can either represent a program or data. Because this book is about linking AutoCAD with databases, we'll be concerned mostly with lists as data or databases in this section.

TAKING THINGS APART WITH CAR AND CDR

car and **cdr** are LISP functions that take apart a list. **car** will return the first element of any list to which it's applied:

Type: `(car '(furniture (chairs tables)))`

Response: `furniture`

Type: `(car '((chairs tables) furniture))`

Response: `(chairs tables)`

cdr will return *all but* the first element of a list:

Type: `(cdr '(furniture (chairs tables)))`

Response: `((chairs tables))`

Type: `(cdr '((chairs tables) furniture))`

Response: `(furniture)`

You can also combine **car** and **cdr** to extract other elements of a list:

Type: `(car (cdr '(furniture (chairs tables))))`

Response: `chairs`

Many other functions related to **car** and **cdr** will extract other elements of a list.

For example, the function **cadr** will extract the second element of a list:

Type: `(cadr '(furniture tables chairs))`

Response: `tables`

There are actually a lot of functions, such as **caadr, caaadr, caaaadr, caddr, cadddr,** or **caddddr** for extracting various elements of a list. These can be dangerous functions to use, because often in LISP you may not know the exact order of the elements of a complex list and you can end up extracting the wrong element. It's been found that by using only the functions **car, cdr, cadr** and **caddr** you can do an adequate job of taking a list apart.

Here's an example of how to extract the **X, Y** or **Z** element of the following entity, list which is returned by **entget** and assigned to **a**:

```
((-1 <Entity name: 60000014>) (0 . "LINE")
    (8 . 0) (10 1.0 3.4 5.0) (11 9.0 1.0 5.0))
```

Car will return the **X** coordinate:

Type: `(car (cdr (assoc 10 a)))`

Response: `1.0`

Cadr will return the **Y** coordinate:

Type: `(cadr (cdr (assoc 10 a)))`

Response: `3.4`

And finally, **caddr** will return the **Z** coordinate:

Type: `(caddr (cdr (assoc 10 a)))`

Response: `5.0`

LAST

last is a handy function, because it will return the last element in a list, as in:

Type: `(last '(furniture tables chairs))`

Response: `chairs.`

last is not used for disassembling a list because there isn't a corresponding function that will return *all but the last* element of a list.

REVERSE

reverse will return the list in reverse order:

Type: `(reverse '(furniture tables chairs))`

Response: `(chairs tables furniture).`

PUTTING THINGS TOGETHER WITH LIST, APPEND AND CONS

Now that you know how to take lists apart with **car** and **cadr**, let's learn how you can make lists with **list**, **append** and **cons**. Each of those functions will return a different type of list, so it's important to know the difference in how each of them operates. Many hours have been wasted trying to track down a problem in a LISP function, only to find that the wrong function had been used to build a list.

These explanations and words of caution should save you at least a few sleepless nights. Try typing these examples, along with your own variations, into AutoCAD's **Command** line so you can see the results yourself.

The first thing you'll do is **setq** some variables to use in the following examples:

Type: `(setq fruit '(apples oranges))`

Response: `(apples oranges)`

Type: `(setq vegetables '(carrots peas))`

Response: `(carrots peas)`

Type: `(setq nuts '(walnuts almonds))`

Response: `(walnuts almonds)`

LIST

The **list** function will take any number of elements (either atoms and/or lists) and string them together into one list. For example:

Type: `(list fruit nuts)`

Response: `((apples oranges) (walnuts almonds))`

Type: `(list 'fruit 'nuts)`

Response: `(fruit nuts)`

Type: `(list fruit 'fruit)`

Response: `((apples oranges) fruit)`

If you want to get fancy and create a list that contains apples and peas, all you have to do is:

Type: `(list (car fruit) (cadr vegetables))`

Response: `(apples peas)`

This list contains the first element (**car**) of the list bound to the atom fruit and the second element (**cadr**) of the list bound to the atom vegetables.

What do the following lists return?

```
(list 'fruit (car fruit) (cadr fruit))


(list (car vegetables) (cdr nuts))


(list (cadr fruit) '(car nuts))


(list (list 'fruit (car fruit) (cadr fruit))


(list 'vegetables (car vegetables) (cdr
    vegetables)) (list 'nuts (car nuts)
    (cadr nuts))
```

APPEND

The **append** function takes only lists as arguments and strings the elements of those lists together as in the following examples:

Type: `(append fruit nuts)`

Response: `(apples oranges walnuts almonds)`

Here, you make a list using **list**:

Type: `(setq newlist (list fruit nuts))`

Response: `(fruits nuts)`

Then use **append** to append **newlist** to **vegetables**:

Type: `(append newlist vegetables)`

Response: `((apples oranges) (walnuts almonds) carrots peas)`

As you can see from the above example, **append** will only go one level deep into a list. That is, it will only strip off the top level of parentheses of each list before appending the lists together into a new list.

If you want a simple list that just contains the six atoms, do this:

Type: `(append fruit nuts vegetables)`

Response: `(apples oranges walnuts almonds carrots peas).`

CONS

The function **cons** is short for **cons**truct. **cons** will add a new element (atom or list) to the front of a list — one element at a time. For example:

Type: `(cons fruit nuts)`

Response: `((apples oranges) walnuts almonds)`

or:

Type: `(cons 'vegetables vegetables)`

Response: `(vegetables carrots peas)`

cons will only accept two arguments—the new first element and the list to which it will be added. Notice that unlike **list** and **append**, **cons** doesn't create a new list. That's important when you want to create a list while in a loop, as shown in the following example (see complete example on page 96).

Say you want to create a loop that will execute ten times, and each time the loop executes you want to add a number to a list called **numberlist**. Starting with the number **1**, each number in the list will be twice as big as the previous number. The result of this function will be a list that looks like this:

```
(512 256 128 64 32 16 8 4 2 1)
```

Start out by defining **numberlist** as an empty or **nil** list:

```
(setq numberlist ())
```

Now set a counter variable to **1** for the first pass in the loop:

```
(setq count 1)
```

Then set up the loop to **repeat** ten times:

```
(repeat 10
```

The first thing to do in the loop is to **cons** the value of the atom **count** to the list **numberlist**:

```
(setq numberlist (cons count numberlist))
```

Now double the value of the atom **count**:

```
(setq count (* count 2))
```

Now, to display the lists of numbers,

```
(print numberlist)
```

Finally, close the loop with a closing parenthesis to balance the open one in front of the function **repeat**:

The **numberlist** will look like this the first four times the loop repeats:

1.   (1)
2.   (2 1)
3.   (4 2 1)
4.   (8 4 2 1)

And so on...

THE DIFFERENCES BETWEEN LIST, APPEND AND CONS

list, **append** and **cons** build lists in different ways, and unless you clearly understand the differences between those functions, you'll have difficulty in writing code that will build and manipulate lists in a predictable way.

The next example illustrates a function that's too long to type on the AutoCAD **Command** line; now is a good time to learn how to save, load and call LISP functions.

Type the following function in a text editor in a non-document mode:

```
(defun makelist ()
  (setq numberlist ())
  (setq count 1)
  (repeat 10
    (setq numberlist (cons count numberlist))
    (setq count (* count 2))
    (print numberlist)
```

Next, save this file in your AutoCAD subdirectory under the filename **MAKELIST.LSP**.

Enter the AutoCAD drawing editor, and at the **Command** line:

Type: (load "makelist") <RETURN>

Response: MAKELIST

If you've correctly typed in this function, AutoCAD will print MAKELIST on the next line, which means your function has properly loaded. To call and execute this function:

Type: (makelist) <RETURN>

Response: **numberlist** should print ten times rapidly on the screen, growing longer each time. That means the loop is executing properly. When **numberlist** stops flashing it should read:

    (512 256 128 64 32 16 8 4 2 1)

This is a simple list of ten atoms. If you substituted the line:

    (setq numberlist (list count numberlist))

for:

    (setq numberlist (cons count numberlist))

in our **makelist** function, **numberlist** would look like this:

    (512 (256 (128 (64 (32 (16 (8 (4 (2 (1
        ()))))))))))

That would be a difficult list to manipulate. If you substituted the line:

    (setq numberlist (append count numberlist))

you would get an error message because **append** can only append a list to another list, and you've tried to append an atom called count to the list.

If, however, you add a line before the **append** function to change the atom count to a list, then the function will work:

```
(setq countlist (list count))
(setq numberlist (append countlist
   numberlist))
```

Now **numberlist** will look like this:

```
(512 256 128 64 32 16 8 4 2 1)
```

Exactly the same form of list you used with **cons** in the first example. And finally, if you **cons countlist** to **numberlist** in the example, **numberlist** will look like this:

```
((512) (256) (128) (64) (32) (16) (8) (4) (2)
   (1))
```

Now you know how to take apart and build lists. What's the point of all of this? Because all the data you'll be gathering, manipulating and changing will be contained in lists of various types, you must have a good grasp of how those lists are constructed. Then you'll be able to write AutoLISP code that can access and manipulate the information.

ASSOCIATION LISTS AND ASSOC

An association list is a list structured so that it can be accessed by the **assoc** function. Let's play with the association list:

Type:
```
(setq food '((fruit apples oranges)
      (vegetables carrots peas) (nuts walnuts
      almonds)))
```

Response:
```
((fruit apples oranges) (vegetables carrots
      peas) (nuts walnuts almonds))
```

Let's examine the structure of the list. The whole association list is **setq**ed to the atom called **food**, consisting of three sublists, each containing three atoms. The first atom in each sublist is called the *key* or *index*, and in this particular association list, the second and third atoms in each sublist relate to the first atom. Apples and oranges are fruits; carrots and peas are vegetables; and walnuts and almonds are nuts.

Type: `(assoc 'fruit food)`

Response: `(fruit apples oranges)`

If you want to just retrieve the data in the association list:

Type: `(cdr (assoc 'fruit food))`

Response: `(apples oranges)`

Think of the association list as a database and each of the sublists as individual records in that database. The first atom in the sublist would be that record's index and any other atoms that follow the index atom in that sublist would be individual data fields.

That's exactly how AutoCAD's drawing database is structured. Each drawing entity, whether it be a **LINE**, **ARC**, **CIRCLE**, **TEXT** or **BLOCK**, is structured as an association list that, in turn, is indexed by an entity name.

SUMMARY

This chapter covered a lot of new territory. You discovered the power of using AutoLISP for customizing AutoCAD applications. You learned the basic underlying principles of LISP and AutoLISP, and how LISP functions work. You actually used some of the built-in AutoLISP functions, and put lists together and took them apart. You added and extracted data from a list, and began to write and execute AutoLISP programs.

In the next chapter, you'll look at the structure of AutoCAD's database and how it relates to AutoLISP. You'll also learn how to write some simple practical programs that allow you to extract and organize meaningful information about your drawings.

<table>
<tr><td>chapter
6</td><td># THE DRAWING
DATABASE AND
AUTOLISP</td></tr>
</table>

IN THIS CHAPTER

In Chapter 5, you learned the basic concepts of AutoLISP and gained some hands-on experience in how it actually works. This chapter will give you an overview of how the AutoCAD drawing database is constructed and how to write simple AutoLISP routines to extract usable information from that data. You'll also expand your knowledge of how some of the more advanced AutoLISP functions work, and how you can take a simple AutoLISP function and expand it into a very useful application. Let's get started.

ANOTHER LOOK AT AUTOCAD'S DATABASE STRUCTURE

To see what an association list for an AutoCAD drawing entity looks like, you'll do the same exercise used in Chapter 2, but this time in a new context. Enter the AutoCAD drawing editor and draw one line from **1,4,0** to **6,6,4**. Press the **F1** key to put the screen into text mode. Then, at the **Command** prompt:

Type: (setq a (entget (entlast))).

AutoCAD should return with a list that looks like this:

Response: ((-1 . <Entity name : 60000014>) (0 . "LINE")
(8 . "0") (10 1.0 4.0 0.0) (11 6.0 6.0 4.0))

This is an association list that contains five sublists. Each sublist contains three atoms. The first atom in each sublist is called a *Group Code*. Each item of information about a drawing entity has its own unique Group Code. For example, the Group Code for entity type is **0** and the code for layer name is **8**.

You may notice in some of the sublists that the second atom is only a dot "." The second and third atoms in those lists are known as dotted pairs. All you need to know about a dotted pair is that the dot acts only as a place holder, and when you access a sublist with a dotted pair like this:

Type: (cdr (assoc '0 (entget (entlast))))

Response: "LINE"

only the atom **line** is returned.

What it all means:

(-1 . < Entity name: 60000014 >)

This is the **ENTITY NAME**. It has a Group Code of **-1** and it's the unique index number for this drawing entity. The functions **entnext** and **entlast** will retrieve this number from the drawing database.

(0 . "LINE")

This is the **ENTITY TYPE**, in this case a line. Entity type has a Group Code of **0**.

(8 . "0")

This is the name of the **layer** on which the entity was drawn, in this case Layer **0**. The layer name has a Group Code of **8**.

(10 1.0 4.0 0.0)

This is the absolute **X Y Z** coordinate of the starting point of the line. It has a Group Code of **10**.

(11 6.0 6.0 4.0)

This is the absolute **X Y Z** coordinate of the ending point of the line. It has a Group Code of **11**.

The size of the entity association list will vary, depending on the type of entity it describes.

Appendix C in the *AutoCAD Reference Manual* describes all the Group Codes assigned to different entity types. Those are the same numbers used as keys in the entity association list. Appendices A, B and C in this book offer complete, fully commented drawing databases with all the Group Codes, showing where they go and what they mean.

Here's a simple AutoLISP function that will list all the entity association lists in a drawing:

```
(defun c:entlst ()
  (setq e (entnext))      :Set e to the first entity name.
  (while e                ;Loop as long as there are entities.
    (print (entget e))      ;Print the entity list.
    (terpri)                ;New line.
  (setq e (entnext e))      ;Set e to next entity.
  )
)
```

If you like, you can press **Control Q** to turn on the printer echo so you can print the drawing database to study its structure. (This is for use only in a small drawing; otherwise, the information will scroll off the screen.)

The AutoLISP program, **c:entlst**, is a basic loop structure that will look at every item in the drawing database. By inserting certain control statements in the middle of this loop structure, you can cause the program to look only for drawing entities that meet certain criteria.

For example, the following function called **blkcnt** counts the total number of blocks that have been inserted into a drawing.

Type the following function into your favorite text editor (ignoring any line that starts with a semicolon) and save it with the filename **BLKCNT.LSP**.

```
(defun blkcnt ()
;Resets the counter variable to 0.
  (setq cnt 0)
;Set E to the first entity in the drawing database
  (setq e (entnext))
;Begin the loop that looks at every drawing Entity
  (while e
;Set ENTTYP to the entity type of the current entity.
    (setq enttyp (cdr (assoc 0 (entget e))))
;If the current entity is a block INSERT then
    (if (equal enttyp "INSERT")
;Add one to the counter variable.
      (setq cnt (1+ cnt))
    )
;Set E to the value of the next entity in the database.
    (setq e (entnext e))
;Continue with the loop until there are no more entities.
  )
;After all of the entities have been looked at, print the
;total number of block insertions found in the drawing
  (princ "\nThere are ") (princ cnt)
  (princ " blocks in this drawing")
)
```

The function **blkcnt** has the same loop structure as the function **c:entlst**. However, their primary difference can be found in the conditional structure inside the loop, which states that if the entity type (Group Code **0**) is named "**INSERT**," to count that entity as an inserted block and to add one to the counter variable. A simple routine at the end of the function prints out the total of **cnt** after that function has gone through the whole drawing database.

Now try running **blkcnt** on any drawing file containing blocks that you have by loading your desired drawing file and at the **Command:** prompt,

Type: `(load "blkcnt")` `<RETURN>`

Response: BLKCNT

Type: `(blkcnt)` `<RETURN>`

The function **blkcnt** can be further refined to only count blocks with a certain name. **blkcnt1** will only count blocks named **desk**. To use this example, you must have some blocks named **desk** in your drawing file. You could change the word **desk** in this function to the name of another block.

```
(defun blkcntl ()
 (setq cnt 0)
 (setq e (entnext))
 (while e
;Set blknm to the value of Group Code 2 for the current entity.
    (setq blknm (cdr (assoc 2 (entget e))))
    (setq enttyp (cdr (assoc 0 (entget e))))
;If entity type is INSERT and if the block name is desk
;for the current entity then
    (if (and (equal enttyp "INSERT")
         (equal blknm "DESK"))
;Add 1 to the counter variable.
      (setq cnt (1+ cnt))
    )
    (setq e (entnext e))
 )
 (princ "\nThere are ") (princ cnt)
 (princ " desks in this drawing")
)
```

The only change in this function is that now the entity type has to equal **insert** and the block name has to equal **desk** before the counter is incremented.

You could refine this function even more, and have it prompt you for the name of the block to count:

```
(defun blkcntla ()
 (setq cnt 0)
```

```
;String input with prompt for the name of the block.
  (setq blk (getstring
      "\nName of the block to count: "))
;The function strcase turns a string into all upper case
;letters.  That ensures that you'll be matching an upper case
;word to an upper case block name in the database
  (setq blk2 (strcase blk))
  (setq e (entnext))
  (while e
     (setq blknm (cdr (assoc 2 (entget e))))
     (setq enttyp (cdr (assoc 0 (entget e))))
     (if (and (equal enttyp "INSERT")
          (equal blknm blk2))
       (setq cnt (1+ cnt))
     )
     (setq e (entnext e))
  )
  (princ "\nThere are ") (princ cnt)
  (princ " ") (princ blk)
  (princ "s in this drawing")
)
```

When you run that version of **blkcnt1**, you'll first be asked for the name of the block you wish to count in the drawing.

Suppose you want to count both desks and chairs in a drawing. All you need are a separate counter for desks, a separate counter for chairs, and another **IF** statement to look for chairs, as in the function **blkcnt2**:

```
(defun blkcnt2 ()
;Set counter for desk to 0
  (setq deskcnt 0)
;Set counter for chair to 0
  (setq chrcnt 0)
  (setq e (entnext))
  (while e
     (setq blknm (cdr (assoc 2 (entget e))))
     (setq enttyp (cdr (assoc 0 (entget e))))
;If the current entity is a block insertion, and it's a desk then
     (if (and (equal enttyp "INSERT")
          (equal blknm "DESK"))
```

```
;add one to the desk counter.
      (setq deskcnt (1+ deskcnt))
    )
;If the current entity is a block insertion, and it's a chair then
    (if (and (equal enttyp "INSERT")
             (equal blknm "CHAIR"))
;add one to the chair counter.
      (setq chrcnt (1+ chrcnt))
    )
    (setq e (entnext e))
  )
;Print the total number of desks and chairs to the screen.
  (princ "\nThere are ") (princ deskcnt)
  (princ " desks and ") (princ chrcnt)
  (princ " chairs in this drawing")
)
```

You can set up any type of conditional statement to look for almost any type of entity in a drawing file. Using the structure presented here, you could even write a function that would delete all lines on **Layer 53** that are less than 2" long.

Since Version 2.6, there's a much faster way to extract data from the drawing database than by looking through each entity record with AutoLISP. Use the **ssget** function with the "**X**" option. **Ssget "X"** will take a list (called a filter list) containing sublists that contain the specific information you're interested in, and will return a selection set that contains the entity names all of the entities that match the filter list.

For example, if you wanted to look at all of the block insertions of a block called "DOOR" on a layer called "FLOOR3," then you could call **ssget** this way:

```
(setq ss (ssget "X" (list (cons 0 "INSERT")
    (cons 2 "DOOR") (cons 8 "FLOOR3"))))
```

The selection set **ss** would then contain the entity names of all insertions of the block "DOOR" that occur on the level FLOOR3. **Ssget "X,"** however, will not create a selection set that contains all of the doors on layers FLOOR2 and FLOOR3 in one pass, nor will it return attribute values or specific text strings.[*].

For a single-instance search, **ssget "X"** will work about ten times faster than stepping through each record in the database.

Here's an example of an AutoLISP routine that will search the drawing database for instances of certain blocks and report the quantity found.

```
(defun ssblkcnt ( / blklst curblk ss)
;List containing the names of blocks being searched for.
  (setq blklst '("ID1" "ID2" "SPACEID")).
;Start of loop.  This loop repeats only once for each block
;in the blklst.
  (while blklst
;Get the first block name of blklst.
    (setq curblk (car blklst) blklst (cdr blklst))
;Build the selection using curblk as the block to search.
    (setq ss (ssget "X" (list (cons 0 "INSERT")
      (cons 2 curblk))))
;Print the report to the screen.
    (princ "there are ")
    (princ (sslength ss))
    (princ " blocks named ")
    (princ curblk)
    (princ " in this drawing")
    (setq ss nil)
    (terpri)
  )
  nil
)
```

You can easily modify this routine for any number of purposes.

---

[*]   See Section 5.2.1 of the *AutoLISP Programmer's Reference* for specific limitations.

BLKWRITE

The last example is a program that automatically writes out all the defined blocks in a drawing to the hard disk as drawing files, first checking to make sure the file isn't already there. That program performs many error-trapping functions and even writes files to disk that list which drawing files were copied and which blocks were duplicates of drawings already on the hard disk.[*]

blkwrite is significant because it demonstrates a fairly large, complex and complete AutoLISP program with several interesting programming techniques. The first technique checks your disk to see if a particular file exists:

```
(if (equal (setq l (open (strcat
      blkname ".dwg") "r")) nil)
  (<WRITES THE BLOCK>)
  (<DISPLAY MESSAGE THAT FILE EXISTS>)
)
```

The second routine will only accept certain characters from the keyboard for user input:

```
(setq a nil)
;creates lists of acceptable character codes
;these can be any ASCII codes that you desire.
;This list is for codes for RETURN button on
;cursor, RETURN on keyboard, space, N, Y,
;n and y.  One of these keys must be
;pressed to end the loop.
(setq ynlst '(0 13 32 78 89 110 121))
;If a key in this list is pressed, then
;the user has indicated a desire to continue
;with the routine.
(setq ylst '(0 13 32 89 121))
(terpri)
(prompt"\nDo you wish to write the block
      list out to a file?<Y>: ")
;this loop will continue until an acceptable key,
```

---

[*] This program will work only with AutoCAD Version 2.6 and later.

```
;listed in ynlst, is pressed
  (while (equal (member a ynlst) nil)
    (setq a (last (grread)))
  )
;If any key in ynlst is pressed, then the loop will end.
  (if (member a ylst)
;if Y or space or <RETURN> is pressed, then the
;next function will be called
    (<CALL NEXT FUNCTION>)
  )
```

You should find this last routine particularly valuable. This is a technique for displaying a default value with the user prompt. AutoCAD will accept that displayed default value if you press **<RETURN>** without entering anything. That default routine looks like this:

```
(setq fname (getvar "dwgname"))
(princ "\nEnter file name <")
(princ fname) (setq fname (getstring ">: "))
(cond ((equal fname "") (setq fname
    (getvar "dwgname"))))
```

INTRODUCTION TO BLKWRITE

This routine searches the block table section of a drawing file, using the AutoLISP function **tblnext**, for all defined blocks and writes them out to a disk file if a drawing file of the same name doesn't already exist. A list of all the blocks written to disk will be generated and written to a disk file—with the same filename as the drawing file with the extension **.BLK**. If any duplicate filenames appear, another file will be written that lists all blocks in the drawing file that were *not* written to disk due to name duplication. That file will have the extension **.BEX**.

```
(defun C:blkwrite ( / e blocklist blkcnt a
       ynlst ylst l excptlist blk)
;finds the first block definition in the block table
  (setq blk (tblnext "BLOCK" T))
  (setq blocklist () excptlist () blkcnt 0)
```

```
;begins the search loop through the block table
  (while blk
;finds the name of the current block
    (setq blkname (cdr (assoc 2 blk)))
;The body of this program is inside this conditional
;statement. It will only execute if all of the following
;conditions are true for the current entity: 1. It is a block
;insertion. 2. The block hasn't been saved before. 3.
;The block isn't an "anonymous" block such as a hatch
;pattern. 4. A drawing doesn't exist on the hard disk
;with the same name as the block.
      (cond
        (
         (and
;Is current entity a block definition?
          (equal (cdr (assoc 0 blk)) "BLOCK")
;has current entity been saved before?
          (equal (member blkname blocklist) nil)
          (equal (member blkname excptlist) nil)
;is current entity an "anonymous" block?
          (not (equal (substr blkname 1 1) "*")))
;does a drawing file exist with the same name as the
;current entity?
          (if (equal (setq 1 (open (strcat
              blkname ".dwg") "r")) nil)
            (progn
;if all conditions are met, write the block to the hard disk
              (command "wblock" blkname blkname)
;add the block name to the blocklist
              (setq blocklist (cons blkname
                  blocklist))
              (terpri)
;increment the number of blocks saved and
              (setq blkcnt (1+ blkcnt))
;Display message to screen
              (princ "Block ") (princ blkname)
              (princ " written to disk")
            )
            (progn
;if drawing file already exists on disk, display message and
              (princ "\nDrawing file ")
              (princ blkname)
```

```
                (princ " already exists...")
                (close 1)
```
;add the name of the block to the exception list
```
                (setq excptlist (cons blkname
                        excptlist))
              )
            )
          )
        )
```
;go to next block definition in the block table
```
    (setq blk (tblnext "BLOCK"))
  )
```
;The code in this section will only accept Y, N, space
;or <RETURN> from the keyboard. If Y or space or
;<RETURN> is pressed, the program continues. If N is
;pressed, then the program ends. This illustrates a
;good technique for error-trapping data entry.
```
  (setq a nil)
```
;creates lists of acceptable character codes
```
  (setq ynlst '(0 13 32 78 89 110 121))
  (setq ylst '(0 13 32 89 121))
  (terpri)
```
;Displays the total number of blocks written to the disk
```
  (princ "A total of " ) (princ blkcnt)
  (princ " blocks were written to disk from
  this drawing file.")
  (prompt"\nDo you wish to write the block
      list out to a file?<Y>: ")
```
;this loop will continue until an acceptable key is pressed
```
  (while (equal (member a ynlst) nil)
    (setq a (last (grread)))
  )
  (if (member a ylst)
```
;if Y or space or <RETURN> is pressed, then the function
;named wrtlist is called
```
    (wrtlist blocklist excptlist)
  )
  (terpri)
  (gc)
)
```
;End of main function

```
;Start of function that will write the block lists
(defun wrtlist (blocklist excptlist /
        blkfilename f g h excptfilename)
```
;reverses the lists so they'll be in the order the
;blocks were written
```
  (setq blocklist (reverse blocklist))
  (setq excptlist (reverse excptlist))
```
;this routine allows you to enter any filename for the block
;list file, with the default name the same as the current
;drawing name. This is a good example of how to set
;default values and have them appear on the prompt line.
```
  (setq fname (getvar "dwgname"))
  (princ "\nEnter file name <")
  (princ fname) (setq fname (getstring ">: "))
  (cond ((equal fname "") (setq fname
      (getvar "dwgname"))))
  (setq blkfilename (strcat fname ".blk"))
```
;if the block filename doesn't already exist, then
```
  (if (equal (setq g (open blkfilename "r"))
        nil)
```
;this section writes the .BLK file. This is how to write a
;text file with AutoLISP.
```
    (progn
      (setq f (open blkfilename "w"))
      (print "Blocks written to disk from
          drawing file " f)
      (princ (getvar "dwgname") f)
      (while blocklist
        (print (car blocklist) f)
        (setq blocklist (cdr blocklist))
      )
      (close f)
```
;this section writes the .BEX exception file
```
      (cond ((not (equal excptlist nil))
        (setq excptfilename (strcat
            fname ".bex"))
        (setq h (open excptfilename "w"))
        (print"Duplicate file name on disk for
            these blocks from " h)
        (princ (getvar "dwgname") h)
        (while excptlist
          (print (car excptlist) h)
```

```
            (setq excptlist (cdr excptlist))
        )
        (close h))
    )
)
```
;if a .BLK file exists with the chosen filename, then a
;message is displayed and this function will then call itself
;to give the user a chance to enter a new filename.
;This is called recursion.


```
(progn
    (close g)
    (princ "\nThis filename already exists, please redo")
    (terpri)
    (wrtlist blocklist excptlist)
  )
 )
)
```
;end of the block file list writing function

SUMMARY

In this chapter, you learned how AutoCAD's drawing database is structured and how to write programs in AutoLISP that can extract meaningful data from the drawing database. You've also modified and expanded a simple AutoLISP function to extract different types of information from the drawing database. You've learned what a more complex AutoLISP program looks like and how to add error-trapping and user interface routines to your AutoLISP applications.

In Chapter 7, you'll examine the drawing database in even more detail, and learn exactly how attributes are linked to blocks in the drawing. You'll learn how to extract attribute information from your drawings with AutoLISP. Finally, you'll see some practical examples of how AutoLISP drawing database programs are used in the real world.

chapter 7

UNDERSTANDING THE DRAWING DATABASE

IN THIS CHAPTER

In the last two chapters, you explored some of the basic principles of AutoLISP and learned how to access the drawing database. In this chapter, you'll examine AutoCAD's database structure in more detail and see just how powerful AutoLISP can be when it comes to extracting all types of information from an AutoCAD drawing database.

You'll learn more about how some of the advanced AutoLISP functions work, and you'll use those functions in writing your own database extraction routines. You'll also see how AutoLISP can be used in many different day-to-day applications.

Finally, you'll begin to write some advanced AutoLISP code to utilize some of those concepts in real world applications.

THE DRAWING DATABASE CONCEPT

In Chapter 6, you took a look at AutoCAD's drawing database when you ran the function **entlst**. What you saw was a database description of a drawing formatted as a LISP association list. What does that mean? To answer that, let's define some terms.

As explained in Chapter 2, a database is simply a collection of information about related subjects organized in a way that's accessible to the user. Let's look again at the conceptual drawing database in more detail.

A drawing database is structured exactly the same way as any other database. Its purpose is to describe a drawing in a non-graphic way. A drawing database file is made up of records of alphanumeric descriptions called *drawing primitives* (AutoCAD calls these *drawing entities*).

A drawing entity is a basic shape or form used in a drawing. **LINE, ARC, CIRCLE, POINT** and **TEXT** are all examples of drawing primitives.

When you draw a line in AutoCAD, you're actually calling up a primitive called **LINE** and then defining the starting and ending points of that primitive. AutoCAD then places a description of that primitive in its database, and a graphic representation of that database record is displayed on the screen.

Let's look again at our simplified *hypothetical* drawing database:

```
# <NAME    >   <START>    <END   >    <LAYER >
1 LINE         0,0,0      0,2,0       0
2 LINE         0,2,0      2,2,0       0
3 LINE         2,2,0      0,2,0       0
4 LINE         0,2,0      0,0,0       0
5 CIRCLE       1,1,0      1           6
```

This database describes a square 2" on a side with a circle of 1" radius inscribed in the square. Notice how similar the database looks to the mailing list example we showed you in Chapter 2. The only difference between this sample drawing database and AutoCAD's drawing database is that the latter contains more fields.

Now is a good time to look at the AutoCAD drawing database. To do that, get into AutoCAD's drawing editor and:

Draw a square, using the **LINE** command from **0,0** to **0,2** to **2,2** to **0,2**. Finally, type **C < RETURN >** to close the square.

Draw a 1" radius circle with the center of the circle at **1,1**. It looks like the chair from Chapter 2.

Now let's load and run our old friend **entlst** from Chapter 6. Press **F1** to enter text mode, and:

Type: (load "entlst")

Response: ENTLST

Type: entlst

But, now, when you run **entlst** to look at your drawing database, it doesn't look like our hypothetical example. That's because AutoLISP takes each database record and formats that record into an association list so the record can be used by AutoLISP. If you reorganize the *hypothetical* drawing database records into association lists, they'll look like this:

```
((# . 1) (NAME . "LINE") (START 0 0 0) (END 0
2 0) (LAYER . "0"))
((# . 2) (NAME . "LINE") (START 0 2 0) (END 2
2 0) (LAYER . "0"))
((# . 3) (NAME . "LINE") (START 2 2 0) (END 2
0 0) (LAYER . "0"))
((# . 4) (NAME . "LINE") (START 2 0 0) (END 0
0 0) (LAYER . "0"))
((# . 5) (NAME . "CIRCLE") (START 1 1 0) (RAD .
1) (LAYER ."6"))
```

The actual AutoCAD association list for the first record is:

```
((-1 . <Entity name: 60000014>) (0 . "LINE")
 (8 . "0")(10 0.0 0.0 0.0) (11 0.0 2.0 0.0))
```

Now you can begin to see the similarity. At this point, the only difference between our sample and AutoCAD's record for our chair drawing is the names for the fields. **#** is **-1**, **NAME** is **0**, **START** is **10**, **END** is **11** and **LAYER** is **8**. Those numbers are called *Group Codes*. The AutoCAD field names are numbers because they're faster and more efficient to access than names.

By using the **assoc** function (covered in Chapter 5), you can access any field (in this case, sublist) in this record. If you wanted to find out what layer this line was on, you would use the Group Code for "layer name" (which is **8**) as the association key to extract the layer name from the first record of the drawing database. This is how you would do it:

First, find the name of the first record in the database:

Type: `(setq e (entnext))`

Response: `<Entity name 60000014>`

The AutoLISP function **entnext**, if used without an argument, will retrieve the first record in the database.

Type: `(setq layer (cdr (assoc 8 (entget e))))`

Response: `"0"`

AutoCAD's record database structure is much longer than indicated here because many entity types require more information to describe them than a line does. A complete list and description of all the drawing database's field names or Group Codes can be found in Appendix A.

DXF FILES AND ASSOCIATION LISTS

The structure and manipulation of **DXF** files will be covered in detail in Chapter 9. However, it's important here to point out the similarity between the drawing database association list and the **DXF** file format.

Neither the drawing database association list nor the **DXF** file is the actual AutoCAD drawing database — they're merely specially formatted versions of that database. The actual drawing database is encoded in binary format and is proprietary. You can, however, infer that the actual drawing database is structured quite closely to those file formats.

The **DXF** file format looks quite different from the association list format, but as you can see, they are almost functionally identical. The entities section of a **DXF** file looks like this for the single line example you've been using:*

```
ENTITIES   ;Start of entities section
   0       ;Start of entity (entity name follows)
LINE       ;Name of entity
   8       ;Group code for layer (layer name follows)
0          ;Name of layer
   10      ;Start X coordinate follows (Group Code)
0.0        ;Start X coordinate
   20      ;Start Y coordinate follows (Group Code)
0.0        ;Start Y coordinate
   11      ;End X coordinate follows (Group Code)
0.0        ;End X coordinate
   21      ;End Y coordinate follows (Group Code)
2.0        ;End Y coordinate
   0       ;Start of file separator
ENDSEC     ;End of (entities) section
   0       ;Start of file separator
EOF        ;End of file
```

This format is used because the **DXF** file format is primarily designed to be read by another program, and the one line/one field format is the easiest to read from a disk file.**

---

* You can create this **DXF** file yourself by loading your previous drawing example into the AutoCAD drawing editor and typing **DXFOUT RETURN RETURN RETURN**. Now exit the drawing editor and load the **DXF** file into your text editor (the **DXF** file will have the same name as your drawing file with a .DXF extension).

** The two coordinates show up in a **DXF** file only if they are non-zero.

Notice that the entity type and layer field names are the same as in the association list format. Only the **START Y** and **END Y** coordinate fields are new here. Because the association list format can hold the **X Y** coordinates as pairs and **X** and **Y** can be individually addressed by using **car** and **cadr**, there's no need for separate **Y** fields in that format. The **DXF** format is designed to be read by such sequential file reading statements as **LINE INPUT** in BASIC and **READLN** in Pascal. In addition, an entity name isn't generated in the **DXF** file format, because it wasn't expected that a file search would be done on such files.

Now that you have a fundamental grasp of how AutoCAD's drawing database is structured, you'll be shown how to access and modify the drawing database with the help of AutoLISP.

THE PROGRAMMING ENVIRONMENT

If you haven't already done so, read the section in Appendix E about **ACAD.PGP** files. It describes how to set up a small text editor so you can write, test, run and edit your AutoLISP programs without ever having to leave the AutoCAD drawing editor. By spending ten minutes or so to set up this facility, you won't have to wait while you load or end AutoCAD just to re-edit your program.

GATHERING INFORMATION

First, take a look at the information you'll be modifying in the AutoCAD database.

Let's make a simple drawing block with attributes. Start a new AutoCAD drawing and make a block that consists of two attributes by following the directions in Chapter 3. Set the text to be 9" high and centered. The first attribute tag will be **ROOMNO** and should be visible with no default value. The second attribute tag should be **EMPNAME** and also should be visible, but with a default value of **VACANT**. Draw a box around the **ROOMNO** tag and save the block under the name **ROOMTAG**.

INSERT that block into the drawing three times, using different room numbers and names. Don't forget to save the sample drawing — you'll use it again in the next chapter.

Turn the printer on, press **Control Q** to turn the printer echo **ON** and load and run the **entlst** AutoLISP function from the last chapter. Your output should look like this:

```
(
(-1 . <Entity name: 600000a0>)   ;Unique ID number
0 . "INSERT")                    ;Entity type (Insert block)
(8 . "0")                        ;Layer Name
(66 . 1)                         ;Attributes follow flag
(2 . "ROOMTAG")                  ;Name of this block.
(10 58.0 129.0 0.0)              ;Insertion point for block
(41 . 1.0)                       ;X scale factor
(42 . 1.0)                       ;Y scale factor
(50 . 0.0)                       ;Rotation angle
(43 . 1.0)                       ;Z scale factor
(70 . 0)                         ;Column count for MINSERT
(71 . 0)                         ;Row count for MINSERT
(44 . 0.0)                       ;Clmn spacing for MINSERT
(45 . 0.0)                       ;Row spacing for MINSERT
)
```

Attribute records always immediately follow the "**INSERT**" or block record they're attached to if field **66** (attributes follow flag) has a value of **1**.

```
(
(-1 . <Entity name: 600000b4>)   ;Unique ID number
(0 . "ATTRIB")                   ;Entity type
(8 . "0")                        ;Layer name
(10 20.0 115.5714 0.0)           ;Insertion point for text(left)
(40 . 9.0)                       ;Height for attribute text
(1 . "John Jones")               ;Attribute value
(2 . "EMPNAME")                  ;Attribute tag
(70 . 0)                         :Column count for MINSERT
(73 . 0)                         ;Row count for MINSERT
(50 . 0.0)                       ;Attribute text rotation angle
(41 . 1.0)                       ;X scale factor for attrib text
(51 . 0.0)                       ;Obliquing angle for attrib text
```

```
(7 . "SIMPLEX")          ;Text STYLE of attribute *
(71 . 0)                 ;Text generation flag (normal)
(72 . 1)                 ;Text Justification type (centered)
(11 57.5 115.5714 0.0)   ;Alignment point for text
                         (centered)

)
```

The following list is the second attribute record attached to the block. Because that record is almost identical to the last record, you won't need the comments.

```
(
(-1 . <Entity name: 600000c84>)
(0 . "ATTRIB")
(8 . "0")
(10 46.7857 131.0)
(40 . 9.0)
(1 . "100")
(2 . "ROOMNO")
(70 . 0)
(73 . 0)
(50 . 0.0)
(41 . 1.0)
(51 . 0.0)
(7 . "SIMPLEX")
(71 . 0)
(72 . 1)
(11 57.5 131.0 0.0)
)
```

The record **seqend** (or **SEQuence END**) always appears at the end of a linked series of records. The purpose of this record is to signal that the end of a multiple record entity has been reached. The record also contains the entity name for the first entity in that series. Currently, only two types of entities consist of more than one record: **BLOCK** or **INSERT** with attached attributes; and **POLYLINES**.

---

* Not the name of the font file.

```
(
(-1 . <Entity name: 600000dc>)
(0 . "SEQEND")                          ;entity type (SEQuence END)
(8 . "0")                               ;layer name
(-2 . <Entity name: 600000a0>)          ;name of first entity in this series
)
```

ACCESSING THE DRAWING DATABASE WITH AUTOLISP

In Chapter 6, the first AutoLISP program example was a small function called **entlst**. **entlst** demonstrates the basic method that you'll be using to access and list the drawing database with AutoLISP. Let's examine **entlst** in greater detail so we can see what each line does:

```
(defun c:entlst ()
```

defun is the **def**ining **fun**ction. When the List Evaluater sees **defun** at the beginning of the list, it doesn't evaluate that list. The **defun** list is placed in memory and it's evaluated only when the name of the defined function is called by another function.

c:entlst is the name of this particular function. The **c:** before the function name means this function can be called from the AutoCAD **Command** line as if it were a regular AutoCAD command.[*] If this function were just called **entlst**, it could only be called from within a list, surrounded by parentheses, like this: **(entlst)**.

```
(setq e (entnext))
```

entnext is an AutoLISP function that will return the name of a drawing entity in the AutoCAD drawing database. **entnext** called without an argument, as in this case, will return the name of the first entity in the database. In this line, the atom **e** is set to the value of the first entity name in the drawing database. If an argu-

---

[*]   Contrary to popular myth, neither the **c:** nor the function name has to be typed in upper case letters.

ment is supplied with **entnext** (the argument must be a valid entity name), **entnext** will return the next entity name in the database after the argument name supplied.

If the end of the database is reached and there are no more entities, **entnext** will return **nil** (or no value).

```
(while e
```

while defines a basic while loop. While the atom **e** contains a value, the list that starts with the function **while** will continue to be evaluated. Because **while** will only operate as long as **e** has a value, when the end of the database is reached, the atom **e** will have no value (**nil**) and the **while** loop will no longer be evaluated.

```
(print (entget e))
```

entget retrieves the association list that contains all the information about the entity name represented by the atom **e**. The argument for that function must be the name of a valid entity retrieved by **entnext**.

print simply prints the list **entget e** to the screen.

```
(terpri)
```

terpri stands for **terminal print**, which prints a blank line on the screen. That function is used to increase the readability of the list.

```
(setq e (entnext e))
```

This line sets the value of **e** to the next entity name in the database so you can look at that entity when the **while** loop repeats. As mentioned above, the function **entnext**, when called with the name of a drawing entity as an argument, will return the name of the next entity in the database. If there are no more entities in the database, the atom **e** will have no value (or **nil**) and the loop won't continue.

```
    )
  )
```

Those two closing parentheses close the **while** loop and the function definition respectively.

FINDING BLOCKS WITH ATTRIBUTES

You've looked at the data structure of a block with linked attributes, and you've also examined in greater detail how the function **entlst** works. Now you'll modify and expand **entlst** to find only the blocks in the drawing database that have attributes. Remember: if Group Code **66** is set to **1** in an entity record of an **INSERT** entity type, that means the block has attributes attached.

Here's the new function:

```
(defun findatt ()
;Sets e to the first record in the database
  (setq e (entnext))
;Starts the loop to look at every entity in the database
  (while e
;Sets enttyp to Group 0 (Entity type) and blknm to the
;Block name for current entity
     (setq enttyp (cdr (assoc 0 (entget e))))
     (setq blknm (cdr (assoc 2 (entget e))))
;If current entity is a Block Insertion and the attributes
;follow flag is set then
     (if
       (and
         (equal enttyp "INSERT")
         (equal (cdr (assoc 66 (entget e))) 1)
       )
;The function progn is used here because normally only
;the first "result is true" list is evaluated in the IF function.
;We want every list within the progn function evaluated if
;the result is true.
        (progn
;Print the block name
           (print blknm)
           (terpri)
        )
     )
;Do the loop again if there are more entities.
  (setq e (entnext e))
  )
)
```

If you load and call the function, **findatt**, from within the sample drawing you did earlier in this chapter, you'll see that the name of every block that contains attributes is printed on the screen. **findatt** first looks only for "INSERT" records that contain the Group Code of **66** set to **1** (the attributes follow flag) then prints the name of the block it finds in that record.

This is interesting, but not very useful. You really would like to see the attribute tags and attribute values for each block. So, how do you do that?

Here's the strategy. When you've found an "INSERT" record that contains a Group Code of **66** set to **1**, you then know that, at least, the next record contains an attribute linked to that block. In fact, every record between "INSERT" and **seqend** will be an attribute linked to that block. Now, all you have to do is write a function that steps through and reads every record between "IN-SERT" and **seqend**. Again, you can use the basic structure of **entlst** to write this function.

```
(defun attriblst (ent name)
;Starts the loop to look at every entity until SEQEND is found
  (while (not (equal name "SEQEND"))
;go to the next record after "INSERT"
    (setq ent (entnext ent))
;reads the current entity type
    (setq name (cdr (assoc 0 (entget ent))))
;if the entity type is "ATTRIB"
    (if (equal name "ATTRIB")
      (progn
;get the value of the attribute tag
        (setq attag (cdr (assoc 2
            (entget ent))))
;get the value of the attribute value
        (setq attval (cdr (assoc 1
            (entget ent))))
;print the attribute tag and its value to the screen
        (princ "\nThe Value of attribute ")
        (princ attag)
        (princ " is ")
        (princ attval)
        (terpri)
```

```
      )
    )
  )
```
;return the name of the last entity read to the calling function
```
  (setq ent ent)
)
```

Now you must modify the function **findatt** so that it will call the function **attriblst**. **findatt** will now look like this:

```
(defun findatt ()
  (setq e (entnext))
  (while e
    (setq enttyp (cdr (assoc 0 (entget e))))
    (setq blknm (cdr (assoc 2 (entget e))))
    (if
      (and
        (equal enttyp "INSERT")
        (equal (cdr (assoc 66 (entget e))) 1)
      )
      (progn
```
;this is the only line changed. This line calls the function **attriblst**,
;passes the current entity name and the name of the current block to **attriblst** and then,
;when **attriblst** has finished it returns the name of the current entity to e.
```
        (setq e (attriblst e blknm))
      )
    )
  (setq e (entnext e))
  )
)
```

Type both of these functions together in a text editor in a non-document mode and save the file under the name **FINDATT.LSP**. To run this function:

Type: `(load "findatt")` ‹RETURN›

Response: ATTRIBLST[*]

Type: `(findatt)`

Response: The value of attribute ROOMNO is 100
The value of attribute EMPNAME is John Jones

and so on.

The function **attriblst** is a little different from the function **findatt**. You could have included the body of this function inside of the loop of **findatt** and achieved the same result, but this is an example of how to pass arguments back and forth between functions.

Following the function name **attriblst** is the sublist:

`(ent name)`

These are the arguments on which this function operates. When you call this function with:

`(setq e (attriblst e blknm))`

The atom **ent** takes on the value of the atom **e**, and the atom **name** takes on the value of the atom **blknm**. When the function is finished, it then returns the result of the last list in the function evaluated to the function that called it. In that function, the last list evaluated is:

`(setq ent ent)`

The result of that list is returned to **setq e** in the calling function.

---

[*]   The name of the last function in the file.

PRACTICAL APPLICATIONS

Now you know how to look at any piece of information in an AutoCAD drawing database. What are the practical uses for this? Remember, you now can extract just about any type of information contained in the drawing database. Below are a few ideas of how you can use the programming techniques and tools you've learned.

WALL QUANTITY TAKEOFF — If you wanted to calculate the lineal feet of wall in a building floor plan, you would draw walls, and only walls, on a layer reserved for walls. Call that layer **WALL**. Now, all you have to do is write a function that looks through the drawing database for all **LINE** entities on layer **WALL**; total up their lengths and divide that total by two (because it takes two lines to draw one wall). You could even draw different types of walls on different layers and keep track of the quantity of each wall type by layer.

Here's a simple example of an AutoLISP function that will find the total length of all walls drawn on a layer named **WALL**. This function is based on **entlst**.

```
(defun wallcnt ()
 (setq wlencnt 0)
 (setq e (entnext))
 (while e
   (setq enttyp (cdr (assoc 0 (entget e))))
   (setq layname (cdr (assoc 8 (entget e))))
   (if
     (and
       (equal enttyp "LINE")
       (equal layname "WALL")
     )
     (progn
       (setq stpt (cdr (assoc 10 (entget e))))
       (setq enpt (cdr (assoc 11 (entget e))))
       (setq wlen (distance stpt enpt))
       (setq wlencnt (+ wlen wlencnt))
     )progn
   )if
 (setq e (entnext e))
```

```
)
(princ "\nThere are ")
(princ (/ wlencnt 24))
(princ " Lineal feet of wall in this drawing")
)
```

A FASTER METHOD OF QUANTITY COUNT — In Chapter 3 you
learned how to extract attributes by using the **attext** command,
then reading the attribute file into a database program to produce
reports. If all you want is a quick count of, say, chips in a particular integrated circuit board, it would be much faster to use the
function blkcnt2 in Chapter 6. The blocks you count by using
that method don't even need attributes attached to them.

A QUICKER WAY OF PRODUCING REPORTS — If you were to
slightly modify our last function, **findatt**, to write the information
line to a disk file instead of to the screen, you would have a simple
report of all the attribute tags and their associated values. You
can, of course, format the output in different ways. You can write
the results of **attriblst** to a disk file by making the functions **attriblst** and **findatt** look like this:

```
(defun findatt ()
;User prompt for filename
  (setq filenm (getstring
      "\nEnter filename for report: "))
;Set the value of f to the filename of the file to be
;written to. "w" means to open the file in the write mode.
  (setq f (open filenm "w"))
  (setq e (entnext))
  (while e
    (setq enttyp (cdr (assoc 0 (entget e))))
    (setq blknm (cdr (assoc 2 (entget e))))
    (if
      (and
        (equal enttyp "INSERT")
        (equal (cdr (assoc 66 (entget e))) 1)
      )
      (setq e (attriblst e blknm))
    )
(setq e (entnext e))
)
```

```
;Close the file that you previously opened.
  (close f)
)


(defun attriblst (ent name)
  (while (not (equal name "SEQEND"))
    (setq name (cdr (assoc 0 (entget ent))))
    (if (equal name "ATTRIB")
      (progn
        (setq attag (cdr (assoc 2
            (entget ent))))
        (setq attval (cdr (assoc 1
            (entget ent))))
```
;These princ functions have been changed so that they
;will print to file f specified in the file OPEN function
```
        (princ "\nThe Value of attribute " f)
        (princ attag f)
        (princ " is " f)
        (princ attval f)
      )
    )
  (setq ent (entnext ent))
  )
  (setq ent ent)
)
```

NEW INFORMATION FROM THE DATABASE — We were asked by a geological engineering firm to develop a program that would list all the intersection points for an irregularly spaced grid. We did this by taking each gridline (a **LINE** entity on a layer named **GRID**) and comparing it with every other gridline for an intersection by using the AutoLISP function **inters**. We then put each coordinate into a list with **cons** and when the comparison was done, the list was sorted for order using the **min** function. Next, we saved the sorted list to a disk file so it could be processed by another program.

TRACK ENTITIES THAT ARE NOT BLOCKS — In another example, we were asked to develop a program that would check to see if all of the polylines in a drawing were closed properly; if they weren't, the program was to automatically close them. An example of the program can be found in *The AutoCAD Database Diskette*.

The applications are almost endless. Every bit of information contained in your drawing is now accessible and can be tracked. You're limited only by your imagination.

In the next chapter, you'll get to the good part — how to change the information in the database by using a powerful function called **subst**; and how to use that function to create an AutoLISP program that will automatically update your drawings from an outside database.

ACCESSING THE TABLE SECTIONS — If you have AutoCAD Version 2.6 or later, you can now access the information in the tables sections of the drawing database on a read-only basis. This means that you can now find out what layers, line types, text styles and views have been defined in a drawing with AutoLISP. More important, you can directly read the entity data that makes up a block definition. We have included complete information on how to access the tables sections, including AutoLISP examples, along with a commented listing of the association list format of these tables at the end of Appendix A.

USING ENTITY HANDLES

Entity handles are a powerful new way to access, organize and link information in the AutoCAD drawing database both within the database and with information in other databases. The concepts and implications of entity handles were covered in Chapter 3. In this section, you'll learn how to access the entity handles and learn some practical ideas for using them.

First, how do you find an entity's handle, or how do you find the entity if you have only its handle? Try this exercise. Start by loading one of your existing drawings into the drawing editor — make sure that it's Release 10. Next:

Type: HANDLES

Response: ON/DESTROY

Type: ON <RETURN>

Entity handles will now be generated for each entity in your drawing. Now you're ready to pick an entity and find its handle.

Type: (setq a (cdr (assoc 5 (entget (car (entsel))))))

Response: Select object:

Pick any entity on the screen, then,

Response: "30" (or whatever the handle is for the selected entity)

What you just did was to use the function **entsel** to select an entity and return the value of Group 5 (the entity handle) to the variable a.

Finally, you can use the function **handent** to find the entity that's associated with that handle. Then you can pass that entity name to the **redraw** function to highlight that entity (so you can see that it's the entity that you first picked) like this:

Type: (redraw (handent a) 3)

Response: The entity that was chosen in the previous example is high-lighted on the screen.

That's really all there is to accessing entity handles. Using entity handles in a significant application, however, requires a considerable amount of planning and programming. Here are a few practical application ideas.

RELATING BLOCKS TO ONE ANOTHER

You can use entity handles as pointers to show relationships among a series of blocks by placing them in attributes created for that purpose in other blocks. If, for example, you wanted to show which chair symbols belonged to which table symbols in a drawing, you could attach an attribute to each chair symbol that contained the entity handle of the table symbol with which the chair symbol was associated. Then you could write an AutoLISP routine so that when you picked a chair symbol, it would find the attribute that contained the table symbol entity handle, and it would use that handle to locate the proper table. The handle attribute in the table symbol could contain a list of all of the chair handles associated with that table.

RELATING AN ENTITY TO ANOTHER DATABASE

When an entity is created in a drawing and an entity handle assigned to it, that handle can also be assigned to information in another file that relates to that entity. The information in the outside file can be accessed by an AutoLISP routine that prompts you to pick an entity, find that entity's handle, search the file for the handle, and then read the associated data.

Here's a sample AutoLISP routine that will find the entity handle of a selected entity, search an outside file for a record that contains that entity handle, and then return the contents of that record. This program is designed to read comments that have been linked to entities by the next routine **comment**.

```
(defun c:rcomment ( / eh l fn s)
;Selects the entity and returns the handle to eh.
  (setq eh (cdr (assoc 5 (entget (car
      (entsel "\nPick Entity to search"))))))
;Highlights the selected entity by referring to its handle.
  (redraw (handent eh) 3)
;Looks for a data file with the same name as the current
;drawing with an extension of CMT and opens it for reading.
  (setq fn (open (strcat (getvar "DWGNAME") ".CMT") "r"))
;Read the first line of the file.
  (setq l (read-line fn))
```

```
;While there are lines in the file to be read
  (while 1
;compare line with entity handle.
    (if (equal 1 eh)
;If it's the same as the entity handle then
        (progn
;read the next line of the file that contains the desired
;comment and
          (setq s (read-line fn))
          (terpri)
;print the comment to the screen.
          (princ s)
;Set I to nil to end the loop when a match is found.
          (setq 1 nil)
        )
;If no match is found then keep reading the file.
    (setq 1 (read-line fn))
    )
  )
;Close the file.
  (close fn)
;This is used to prevent nil from showing up on the
;command line.
  (princ)
)
```

The above routine reads comments that are linked to the entities by the entity handle in another file. The file has the same name as the drawing file, with the extension **CMT**. The file that this sample program is designed to read is a simple two-line-pair ASCII file and it looks like this:

```
2
This is a line
7
This is an arc
```

```
6
This is a circle
A
This is a closed polyline
```

The first line of the pair contains the entity handle key, and the next line contains the data associated with that handle. This is a very simple file for AutoLISP to read and write. Many other data formats are possible, such as a space-delimited file, but the AutoLISP routines to read and write those files would have to be a bit more complex than this example.

This next routine adds comments to selected entities in a drawing and stores them in an outside data file, along with the entity handle associated with each commented entity.

```
(defun c:comment ( / eh l fn)
;Select the entity to comment and return the handle to eh.
  (setq eh (cdr (assoc 5 (entget (car
      (entsel "\nPick Entity to comment"))))))
;highlight the selected entity.
  (redraw (handent eh) 3)
;Open the data file to append mode.
  (setq fn (open (strcat (getvar "DWGNAME") ".CMT") "a"))
;Prompt for the comment to add to the entity.
  (setq l (getstring T "\nComment? "))
;Write the entity handle to the data file.
  (write-line eh fn)
;Write the comment to the data file.
  (write-line l fn)
;Close the data file.
  (close fn)
  (princ)
)
```

This last routine searches through the data file for all of the entity handle keys and highlights every entity in the drawing that had a comment attached to it by the last routine.

```
(defun c:shcomment ( / eh d fn)
;Open file to read data.
  (setq fn (open (strcat (getvar "DWGNAME") ".CMT") "r"))
;Read first handle in file.
  (setq eh (read-line fn))
;Read first comment line in file.
  (setq d (read-line fn))
;While there is data in the file
  (while eh
;highlight the entity if there is an associated handle.
    (if eh (redraw (handent eh) 3))
    (setq eh (read-line fn)) ;read a handle
    (setq d (read-line fn)) ;read a comment)
;Let the user know what happened.
  (princ "\nHighlighted entities have comments. ")
  (close fn)                          ;close file.
  (princ)
)
```

The above AutoLISP routines are small but useful examples of how you can use entity handles to link entities in a drawing to information contained in another database. The possibilities are almost unlimited.

MODIFYING THE DRAWING DATABASE

chapter 8

It's one thing to be able to write a program that reads and makes reports based on AutoCAD's drawing information. But actually being able to change that drawing with a program that you wrote is something else again.

In this chapter, you'll learn how to write AutoLISP functions that will actually change the contents of a drawing, based on information that isn't contained in that drawing. With a very powerful AutoLISP function called **subst**, those changes will be made automatically.

You'll also explore the LISP concept of property lists and how they can be used to extend the usefulness and utility of AutoCAD in many different applications.

Finally, you'll go step by step through an actual AutoLISP programming project recently completed by the authors.

CHANGING THE DATABASE WITH ENTMOD AND SUBST

subst will **subst**itute one expression (an atom or a list) for another expression in a list. The best way to explain how this function works is to try it:

Type: `(setq a '(fruit apples oranges)) <RETURN>`

Response: `(fruit apples oranges)`

Now:

Type: `(subst 'pears 'oranges a) <RETURN>`

Response: `(fruit apples pears)`

As you can see, **subst** substitutes pears for oranges in the list. If you

Type: `!a`

Response: `(fruit apples oranges)`

you get your original list back. In order to permanently change the list, set the value of the new list like this:

Type: `(setq a (subst 'pears 'oranges a))`

Response: `(fruit apples pears)`

Now

Type: `!a`

Response: `(fruit apples pears)`

You also can use multiple instances of **subst** to substitute expressions at almost any level of nesting in a list. However, it's a bit more complex. Let's try an example:

Type: `(setq b '((fruit apples oranges)`
`          (nuts walnuts almonds)))`[*]

Response: `((fruit apples oranges)`
`             (nuts walnuts almonds))`

---

* You should type all this on one line at the **Command** prompt. We have broken these lists into two lines because the pages of this book aren't wide enough.

Now substitute pears for oranges:

Type: `(setq c (subst (subst 'pears 'oranges`
`(car b)) (car b) b))`

Response: `((fruit apples pears) (nuts walnuts almonds))`

This looks a lot more complex than it actually is. Let's examine the list inside out. The inner list:

Type: `(subst 'pears 'oranges (car b))`

Response: `(fruit apples pears)`

That's easy enough: you're substituting **pears** for **oranges** in the first sublist **(car)** of list **b**. Now, take the new sublist **(fruit apples pears)**, and substitute it for the old sublist in the main list. Below is the same way of stating this:

Type: `(subst '(fruit apples pears) '(fruit apples`
`oranges) a)`

Practice: Using the last example, substitute **cashews** for **almonds**.

entmod is a special AutoLISP function that is called after an entity is changed with **subst**. **entmod** simply tells AutoLISP that you've modified a particular entity. You'll see how this is used to modify the drawing database later.

Here's a quick example that will show you graphically how AutoLISP can modify the database. First, draw a line in AutoCAD from **0,0** to **0,40**:

Type: `LINE <RETURN> 0,0 <RETURN> 0,40`
`<RETURN><RETURN>`

Response: `A vertical line is drawn.`

Be sure you're ZOOMed out enough so you can see the whole line, and watch the line as you press **< RETURN >**:

Type: `(entmod (subst (subst 20 40 (assoc 11`
`(entget (entlast)))) (assoc 11`
`(entget (entlast))) (entget (entlast))))`

Response: `((-1 . <Entity name: 60000208>) (0 . "LINE")`
`(8 . 0)(10 0.0 0.0 0.0)`
`(11 0.0 20.0 0.0))`[*]

Did you notice how the line was instantly halved in length? Now you have the power to do practically anything you want with your drawing database.

Because this is a book about linking AutoCAD drawing files to outside databases, all the examples concentrate on that result. But, as you've seen in the previous example, it's easy to manipulate the graphic elements, too.

GUIDELINES FOR MODIFYING DATABASES

Before you get involved in modifying your drawings with AutoLISP, you should know about certain limitations:

- You can add an entity record to the database *only* at the end of the list, *only* by using the *command function.*

- You *can't* change an entity record's type (i.e., you can't change **LINE** to **POLYLINE**). You have to delete the desired entity record with **entdel** and then add a new entity to the drawing with the **command** function.[**]

- You *can't* change an entity record's **TEXT STYLE**, **LINETYPE**, **SHAPE** or **BLOCK NAME**, unless the definitions you're changing them to exist in the tables section of your drawing. An exception to this rule is the **LAYER NAME**. A desired **LAYER NAME** *does not* have to exist in the tables section to be used.

---

[*]   The modified entity association list.

[**] This new entity then, of course, will be at the end of the drawing database.

- **entdel** *will not* delete an **ATTRIB** subentity record linked to an **INSERT** record, nor will it delete a **VERTEX** subentity record linked to a **POLYLINE** record. One technique for removing **VERTEX**es from a **POLYLINE** involves stepping through the desired **POLYLINE** record and adding the coordinates of all the vertices bound to a list using cons; deleting the undesired **VERTEX** coordinates from the coordinate list; deleting the old **POLYLINE** record with **entdel** and then creating a new **POLYLINE** with the desired vertices with the **command** function.

- You *can't* **ADD** an **ATTRIB** subentity record to an **INSERT** entity record nor can you **ADD** a new **VERTEX** to a **POLYLINE** entity record.

- You *can't* change the **ATTRIBUTE TAG** in an **ATTRIB** subentity record, since that tag is a reference to an **ATTDEF** entity in the blocks section of the drawing database.

- You *can't* add a field to an entity record if that field *does not* already exist. For example, if an entity did not have an **ELEVATION** assigned to it (Group Code 38) when it was created, then the Group Code won't even show up as a field in the database—thus you could not change it with **subst**. You could, however, add an **ELEVATION** by using the **CHANGE** command with the following form: (**COMMAND** "CHANGE" <entity name> "" "P" "E" <desired elevation goes here> ""). This is also true for **THICKNESS**, **LINETYPE**, **BYLAYER** and **COLOR BYLAYER**.

MODIFYING YOUR DRAWING WITH AN OUTSIDE DATABASE

INTRODUCTION

Throughout the rest of this chapter, you'll go step by step through a programming project which illustrates some of the techniques for developing an AutoLISP program to find and modify specific drawing entities from the drawing database.

You're encouraged to carry out the examples on your own computer. Don't just believe that these functions work — try them out for yourself. You're also encouraged to experiment with the examples. Try different values. How does the illustrated function work on different list structures? Maybe you can rewrite the illustrations to suit your own purposes or to solve your own problems.

THE PROBLEM

A large corporation occupies a huge office building. Because this is a growing corporation, employees are moved around within the building frequently. This isn't done to keep the personnel and facility planning departments busy, but to accommodate the company's growth. New departments spring up overnight; existing divisions are decimated wholesale to staff new endeavors. Employees are drafted from the ranks of the competition. This is a company driven by great hopes to accomplish even greater deeds. Within the walls of this seemingly ordinary corporate headquarters lies the legendary *Raiders of the Lost Market Share.*

The head of the Facilities Department of this large and still unnamed corporation has a real problem on his hands. He has a difficult time keeping track of all the people (not to mention the furniture) in this office building. All of the employee location information is kept and maintained in a regular alphanumeric database. But since the people in the Facilities Department are visually oriented, they need a visual way of keeping track of their people (and furniture).

So they decide that the solution to their dilemma is to create an AutoCAD drawing of the building floorplan and **INSERT** blocks containing the Employee Information Attributes into the floorplan drawing.

This works for a while, but turns out to not be the ideal solution. Just as soon as the Facilities Department finishes a floorplan and inserts all of the employees' names into the right workstations, the powers-that-be decide that a new department needs to be formed or an old division needs to have new life-blood injected into it.

It doesn't seem fair. As soon as they have the right names in the right places on the drawing, the corporation decides to move people around to different locations, and the Facilities Department has to spend a lot of time updating drawings.

Figure 1: The ROOMTAG Block

The problem is this: when the floorplans were first done in AutoCAD, it was decided to label all private offices and open plan workstations with a unique location number and the name of the employee currently using that space. Here's how they did it.

First, they made up a block, similar to Figure 1, with two visible attributes. The block was called **ROOMTAG** and the attribute tags were called **ROOMNO** and **EMPNAME**. Next, they inserted the **ROOMTAG** block at every private office and work station, entering at the prompts, the room (or workstation) number and employee's name.

Sometimes the information was extracted from the drawing file using the **ATTEXT (Attribute Extract)** command and that data was used in other databases.

It was very difficult to keep the employee location information up to date and accurate in the drawing database, and it was not easy to update employee location information in the drawing.

When employee moves were decided upon, they were usually worked out in advance on a regular database program. Here was one place where all of the employee locations were accurately maintained.

The problem was, that although alpha-numeric database information could be extracted from an AutoCAD drawing file, there was no easy way to put that database information into an AutoCAD drawing.

THE PROBLEM SUMMARY

The question: Is it possible to take outside database information and use it to update an already existing drawing without having to manually enter every piece of data? The answer: Yes. Here's how it's done:

THE SOLUTION

First, you need a little preparation. Take the sample drawing file you made at the beginning of this chapter, and insert the **ROOMTAG** block five times using room numbers **100, 110, 120, 130, 140** and **150**. Save the drawing file.

Next, using a text editor in non-document mode, type the following lines exactly as shown (with two spaces between the number and the name):

```
100   JONES
110   SMITH
120   BROWN
130   GREEN
140   MUSTARD
150   SCARLETT
```

Finally, save this file under the filename **TEST.SDF**. That's the sample data file you'll be using to update the roomtags. The file is in a standard **S**pace **D**elimited **F**ile format that can be output by most database and spreadsheet programs.

READING THE DATA FILE

First you need to write a function that will read this data file and format the **SDF** format into an association list. That function might look like this:

```
(defun extfile ()
;Creates an empty list called FILELIST.
  (setq filelist ())
;Opens the test file in the read mode.
  (setq file (open "TEST.SDF" "r"))
;Reads the first line in the file.
  (setq record (read-line file))
;Starts a loop that will continue until the whole file is read.
```

```
(while record
```
;Sets the value of **ROOMNO** to the first 3 characters in the line.
```
    (setq roomno (substr record 1 3))
```
;Sets the value of **EMPNAME** to the rest of the line.
```
    (setq empname (substr record 6))
```
;Sets the value of **RECLIST** to a list of **ROOMNO** and **EMPNAME**.
```
    (setq reclist (list roomno empname))
```
;Adds the list **RECLIST** to the list **FILELIST**.
```
    (setq filelist (cons reclist filelist))
```
;Reads the next line of the file and
```
    (setq record (read-line file))
```
;begins again if there are more lines in the file
```
  )
```
;Closes the database file.
```
  (close file)
)
```

The result of running that function would be an association list that looks like this:

Type: `!filelist`

Response:
```
(("150" "SCARLETT") ("140" "MUSTARD")
    ("130" "GREEN") ("120" "BROWN")
    ("110" "SMITH") ("100" "JONES"))
```

FINDING THE RIGHT BLOCKS

Next, you need to search through the drawing database to find all instances of inserted blocks with attributes and then check to see if any of the attributes match the attributes that you are interested in changing.

The following function, **findatt**, will search through the drawing database for any block insertions with attributes attached to them, and then it will call the function **bldprop**. The function **bldprop** will determine if the block found is a valid one, and then it will build an association list of attributes using the attribute value of **ROOMNO** as the key. Here is the commented code for **findatt**.

```
(defun findatt ()
;defines an empty list
  (setq proplist ())
  (setq e (entnext))
;begins a search loop through the drawing database
  (while e
;reads the current entity type
    (setq enttyp (cdr (assoc 0 (entget e))))
;if current entity is an INSERT then it reads the block name.  If the current
;entity is not a block then blknm will be set to nil.
    (setq blknm (cdr (assoc 2 (entget e))))
    (if
      (and
;if current entity is of type "INSERT"
        (equal enttyp "INSERT")
;and it contains an attribute
        (equal (cdr (assoc 66 (entget e))) 1)
      )
;then call the function bldprop to build a list of the attribute values
      (bldprop e)
      )
;otherwise go to the next entity in the drawing database
    (setq e (entnext e))
  )
)
```

The function **bldprop** will create a property list for each valid block insertion found and then it will add that property list to the front of the list called **proplist**. When the drawing database has been completely searched, **proplist** will contain a list of every instance of the block **ROOMTAG** and the values of its attributes. A property list in this application is simply an association list of the properties of a particular instance of the block **ROOMTAG**.

What is a property? Visualize this: the block **ROOMTAG** is a label that describes certain things about an object in the drawing that we call a room. In our simple example, the only things that we are describing about this "room" is the room number and the name of the current occupant of that room. The room number and the occupant name are the properties of that room that are unique to that room. In a more complex example, we could have included the size of the room, the job title of the occupant or even the color of the paint on the walls — and these would all be properties that could be associated with that particular room.

Here is the code for the function **bldprop**:

```
(defun bldprop (e)
;Creates an empty list called dblist.
  (setq dblist ())
;Begin a search loop through all entities from INSERT to
;SEQEND*
  (while (not (equal (cdr (assoc 0
      (entget e))) "SEQEND"))
    (cond
;If attributes follow flag is set, then this entity is INSERT and
      ((cdr (assoc 66 (entget e)))
;reset dblist and recordlist
        (setq dblist ())
        (setq recordlist ())
;add the entity name for this INSERT to recordlist
        (setq recordlist (cons (cdr
          (assoc -1 (entget e))) recordlist))
;add the BLOCK name to the front of recordlist**
        (setq recordlist (cons (cdr
          (assoc 2 (entget e))) recordlist))
;add recordlist to dblist***
        (setq dblist (cons recordlist dblist))
      )
;If the entity is an ATTRIB
      ((equal (cdr (assoc 0 (entget e)))
        "ATTRIB")
;reset recordlist
        (setq recordlist ())
;add this attribute value to recordlist
```

---

* These entities, by their location, will be ATTRIBs.

** recordlist now looks like this: ("ROOMTAG" entity name: 600000014)

***dblist now looks like this: (("ROOMTAG" entity name: 600000014))

```
        (setq recordlist (cons (cdr (assoc 1
            (entget e))) recordlist))
```
;add this attribute tag (EMPNAME) to the front of ;recordlist
```
        (setq recordlist (cons (cdr (assoc 2
            (entget e))) recordlist))
```
;add recordlist to the front of dblist *
```
        (setq dblist (cons recordlist dblist))
```
;If this attribute tag is ROOMNO
```
        (if (equal (cdr (assoc 2 (entget e)))
            "ROOMNO")
```
;then set the value of KEY to the attribute value of this
;entity.
```
            (setq key (cdr (assoc 1 (entget e))))
          )
        )
      )
```
;Looks for the next entity in the database
```
    (setq e (entnext e))
```
;and if the next entity is not a SEQEND to go through this
;loop again.
```
    )
```
;After all the attributes for this block have been found:
;Reverse the order of dblist so that it will be in the
;order that we want it **
```
  (setq dblist (reverse dblist))
```
;Add the value of KEY to the front of dblist ***
```
  (setq dblist (cons key dblist))
```
;Finally, add dblist to the front of proplist
```
  (setq proplist (cons dblist proplist))
)
```

---

*   dblist now looks like this: (("EMPNAME" "John Jones") ("ROOMTAG"
     Entity name: 600000014))

**   dblist now looks like this:(("ROOMTAG" Entity name: 600000014)
     ("EMPNAME" "John Jones") ("ROOMNO" "100"))

***dblist now looks like this:("100" ("ROOMTAG" Entity name:
     600000014) ("EMPNAME" "John Jones") ("ROOMNO" "100"))

All this function does is look through the drawing database for **ATTRIBUTE** records every time a block with attributes is found by the function **findatt**. It then creates a property list, which is essentially an association list of association lists. When this function is called from within your test drawing, the list it produces will look something like this:

```
(
("150"
("ROOMTAG" <Entity name: 600001B8>)
("EMPNAME" "vacant")
("ROOMNO" "150")
)
("140"
("ROOMTAG" <Entity name: 60000168>)
("EMPNAME" "vacant")
("ROOMNO" "150")
)
etcetera
)
```

This looks similar to the drawing database you examined in the last chapter. It's actually an abbreviated version of that list that contains only the essential information you need. The **proplist** becomes an index of every occurrence of a **ROOMTAG** block in the drawing database indexed by the **ROOMNO**. So, instead of searching through the entire database for a specific **ROOMNO**, you now can just look up the **ROOMNO** value in **proplist** and find the entity name of the block insertion that contains the searched-for attribute value.

Now you have two lists: the list of room numbers and names that we created from the database file, and the list of blocks and attributes from the drawing database. You still need a function that will look at a room number on the **filelist** and check **proplist** to see if there is a **ROOMTAG** with a room number that matches. If it does find a match, then it will use **subst** and **entmod** to change the value of the attribute **EMPNAME** to the new value found in **filelist**. Here's how that function should look:

```
(defun chgname ()
```
;Sets a working list inlist to be the value of FILELIST
```
  (setq inlist filelist)
```
;As long as there are items left in inlist, do this loop
```
  (while inlist
```
;Sets looklist to be the first sublist in INLIST
```
    (setq looklist (car inlist))
```
;Resets inlist to be inlist less the first sublist
```
    (setq inlist (cdr inlist))
```
;Sets ROOMNO to be the first item in looklist and
;EMPNM to be the last item.
```
    (setq roomnum (car looklist))
    (setq empnm (last looklist))
    (cond
```
;If ROOMNO from the outside data file is found in proplist
```
      ((assoc roomnum proplist)
```
;then set the value of chgattlist to the sublist in
;proplist that contains that key.
```
        (setq chgattlist (assoc roomnum
            proplist))
```
;Set CE to the value of the entity name of the INSERT
;entity from the chosen sublist.
```
        (setq ce (last (cadr chgattlist)))
```
;Start a loop that looks at entities in the drawing database
;beginning at the chosen INSERT entity and continuing until
;it reaches SEQEND.
```
        (while (not (equal (cdr (assoc 0
            (entget ce)))"SEQEND"))
```
;Sets ATTAG to whatever is found for Group Code 2 for
;this entity.
```
          (setq attag (cdr (assoc 2
              (entget ce))))
          (cond
```
;Checks to see if the attribute tag for this entity is
;EMPNAME.
```
            ((equal attag "EMPNAME")
```
;If it is, then it changes the attribute value of that attribute
;to the name from the outside database.
```
              (entmod (subst (CONS '1 empnm)
                  (assoc 1 (entget ce))
                  (entget ce)))
```
;Updates the entity that has just been changed with subst.

```
            (entupd ce)
          )
        )
        (setq ce (entnext ce))
      )
    )
  )
 )
)
```

Finally, you need to write a short function that will call all of these other functions. Let's put the whole thing together, and see how it works. The calling function is the main function that calls the other functions:

```
(defun c:update ()
 (extfile)
 (findatt)
 (chgname)
)
```

THE FINAL PROGRAM

Here's the whole program, again, without the comments. Presenting it like this should make it easier for you to see its overall structure.

update starts the program running and calls the other functions:

```
(defun c:update ()
 (extfile)
 (findatt)
 (chgname)
)
```

extfile reads the outside database:

```
(defun extfile ()
 (setq filelist ())
 (setq file (open "TEST.SDF" "r"))
 (setq record (read-line file))
 (while record
   (setq roomno (substr record 1 3))
```

```
      (setq empname (substr record 6))
      (setq reclist (list roomno empname))
      (setq filelist (cons reclist filelist))
      (setq record (read-line file))
    )
    (close file)
)
```

findatt does the loop through the whole drawing database, and stops and calls **bldprop** when it finds a block with attributes:

```
(defun findatt ()
  (setq proplist ())
  (setq e (entnext))
  (while e
    (setq enttyp (cdr (assoc 0 (entget e))))
    (setq blknm (cdr (assoc 2 (entget e))))
    (if
      (and
        (equal enttyp "INSERT")
        (equal (cdr (assoc 66 (entget e))) 1)
      )
      (bldprop e)
    )
    (setq e (entnext e))
  )
)
```

bldprop builds the property list from the drawing database:

```
(defun bldprop (e)
  (setq dblist ())
  (while (not (equal (cdr (assoc 0 (entget e))) "SEQEND"))
    (cond
      ((cdr (assoc 66 (entget e)))
        (setq dblist ())
        (setq recordlist ())
        (setq recordlist (cons (cdr
            (assoc -1 (entget e))) recordlist))
        (setq recordlist (cons (cdr (assoc 2
            (entget e))) recordlist))
        (setq dblist (cons recordlist dblist))
```

```
    )
    ((equal (cdr (assoc 0 (entget e)))
        "ATTRIB")
      (setq recordlist ())
      (setq recordlist (cons (cdr
          (assoc 1 (entget e))) recordlist))
      (setq recordlist (cons (cdr
          (assoc 2 (entget e))) recordlist))
      (setq dblist (cons recordlist dblist))
      (if (equal (cdr (assoc 2 (entget e))) "ROOMNO")
        (setq key (cdr (assoc 1 (entget e)))))
      )
    )
  )
  (setq e (entnext e))
 )
 (setq dblist (reverse dblist))
 (setq dblist (cons key dblist))
 (setq proplist (cons dblist proplist))
)
```

chgname is the function that actually updates the drawing database with new employee names for the roomtags.

```
(defun chgname ()
 (setq inlist filelist)
 (while inlist
   (setq looklist (car inlist))
   (setq inlist (cdr inlist))
   (setq roomnum (car looklist))
   (setq empnm (last looklist))
   (cond
     ((assoc roomnum proplist)
       (setq chgattlist (assoc roomnum
           proplist))
       (setq ce (last (cadr chgattlist)))
       (while (not (equal (cdr
           (assoc 0 (entget ce)))"SEQEND"))
         (setq attag (cdr (assoc 2
             (entget ce))))
         (cond
           ((equal attag "EMPNAME")
```

```
             (entmod (subst (CONS '1 empnm)
                 (assoc 1 (entget ce))
                 (entget ce)))
             (entupd ce)
          )
        )
        (setq ce (entnext ce))
      )
     )
    )
   )
  )
```

Save this file under the name **UPDATE.LSP** and run it in your sample drawing:*

Type: (load "update") <RETURN>

Response: CHGNAME

Type: update <RETURN>

Response: Watch the names change on your drawing.**

We have attempted to keep these functions general in nature so you can use them with minor modifications in your own applications, similar to the way that we based some of the new functions on **entlst** . At this point, you've just barely scratched the surface of what you can do with AutoLISP in the linking of AutoCAD drawings and other types of databases. But now that

---

*   If you find that this routine doesn't work the first time, exit AutoCAD, rename **ACAD.LSP** and try it again. That will make more memory available for this routine.

** On large drawings with several hundred block insertions to be linked into a property list, AutoLISP may run out of memory. If you run into that problem, the solution can be found on *The AutoCAD Database Diskette*. This shouldn't be a problem with extended AutoLISP.

you've learned how to establish a two-way link between AutoCAD and other types of databases, you can begin to get some idea of the power and possibilities of AutoLISP.

SUMMARY

This chapter has presented some state-of-the-art information and techniques about AutoLISP applications. In it you've learned to actually modify the data within the drawing database and to update the information in an AutoCAD drawing from an outside database.

In Chapter 9, you'll examine the drawing database from the entirely different perspective of the **DXF** file format. You'll also learn how to modify the AutoCAD **DXF** file with BASIC programs.

UNDERSTANDING AND USING DXF FILES

chapter 9

In the last four chapters, you learned how to use AutoLISP to directly access and manipulate the AutoCAD drawing database. However, AutoLISP is only one of two important ways to read and change the drawing database. Another method is to read and write **DXF** (**D**rawing e**X**change **F**ormat) files. The **DXF** file of a drawing contains all the information in the drawing database for that drawing, formatted to be easily read by you or a computer.

In this chapter, you'll learn about **DXF** files, their many important uses, and how to read and understand them. Finally, you'll learn how to write useful programs in BASIC that will write, read and modify **DXF** files.

DXF OVERVIEW

DXF files were developed to allow users flexibility in managing data and translating AutoCAD drawings into file formats that could be read and used by other CAD systems. **DXF** has become the de facto standard of interchanging CAD drawing files for almost all microcomputer (and many larger) CAD systems. Almost every CAD system we're aware of has some sort of facility for reading and writing **DXF** files.

The **DXF** file standard has become ubiquitous — you can actually use the format without ever using AutoCAD! For example, we've translated many drawing files from CADvance directly to VersaCAD, using **DXF** files, without touching AutoCAD.

We've also used **DXF** files to import AutoCAD and VersaCAD drawings as illustrations in Ventura Publisher documents. The layout and page formatting of this book was done with Ventura Publisher, and all the AutoCAD drawings were inserted into these pages by using **DXF** files.

DXF BINARY FORMAT

AutoCAD Release 10 now offers a new, additional **DXF** file format called **DXF BINARY**. The data in the **DXF** binary file is exactly the same as in the standard **DXF** format, but all the data is in binary form rather than ASCII.

Binary format has three advantages. It's more compact — as much as 33 percent smaller; AutoCAD can read and write the binary **DXF** file much faster; and the binary file carries the numeric precision to 16 decimal places.

At this time, there are no other programs that will read or write the **DXF** binary format, but that should change when programmers become familiar with the format.

WHAT YOU SEE IS NOT ALWAYS WHAT YOU GET WITH DXF

You should know that **DXF** file conversion from one CAD system to another is not 100 percent perfect. Other CAD systems don't always have the same entity types as AutoCAD, or the entity type differs enough so that the translation doesn't always work as you would expect.

For example, AutoCAD is the only CAD system we know that lets you *name* layers (in most other CAD systems, the layers are numbered). So when you export an AutoCAD drawing to another CAD system via a **DXF** file, the AutoCAD layer name gets translated into a seemingly arbitrary layer number in another system.

Even if you assign numbers to AutoCAD drawing layers before you translate the drawing, those layer numbers may not appear as the same layer numbers in the other CAD system. Conversely, when you import a **DXF** file from another CAD system into AutoCAD, the layer numbers in the AutoCAD drawing may not be the same numbers as in the original AutoCAD drawing.

Another area of translation inaccuracy has to do with entity definitions. Most of the time, the drawing that was translated from another CAD system will *look* the same as the original when viewed on the display screen, but there will be many differences in the entity definitions that may make the resultant drawing file difficult or impossible to use. That's caused by different CAD systems having different drawing primitives and different ways of describing those graphic primitives in their drawing database.

For example, VersaCAD has a primitive called a **RECTANGLE**; AutoCAD does not. When a VersaCAD drawing is translated to AutoCAD, any instances of **RECTANGLE** primitives appear in AutoCAD as a block called **UNITSQUARE** (a 1" x 1" square scaled to the size of the original **RECTANGLE** primitive). However, because a rectangle is an unequally scaled square, the block **UNITSQUARE** will always have different **X** and **Y** scales. Because the **X** and **Y** scales of the **UNITSQUARE** block are different, you won't be able to **EXPLODE** that rectangle for editing.

That could be a major problem if you were planning to edit the drawing. One solution to this particular problem would be to **EXPLODE** all the **RECTANGLE** primitives in VersaCAD before making the translation.

Blocks from AutoCAD will only translate to their individual component parts in VersaCAD. Symbols in VersaCAD will show up as individual entities in AutoCAD. Symbols from CADvance, however, will show up as blocks in AutoCAD and vice versa.

POLYLINES don't exist in VersaCAD, so they'll show up in VersaCAD as individual lines. **POLYLINE CURVES** and **ELLIPSES** from AutoCAD will show up as straight **LINE** segments in VersaCAD.

LINES in CADvance look like **POLYLINES** to AutoCAD, so all lines in a CADvance drawing show up in AutoCAD as **POLYLINES**. Unfortunately, the **POLYLINE** structures from CADvance won't be properly **CLOSED** (the starting vertex and ending vertex of a CADvance **POLYLINE** square, for example, will have the same coordinates).

POLYLINE ARCS and CURVES won't be translated properly into Ventura Publisher. A POLYLINE ARC will show up as a straight LINE, and a CURVE will show up as LINE segments.

Most CAD systems' DXF translators make a stab at translating everything they find in a DXF file, but some don't even try. Unless you know that in advance, the results can be disastrous. For example, one translator (used for translating DXF files to a CALMA system) will only translate POLYLINES and ignore everything else. In that case, a preprocessor program must be written to convert every entity in an AutoCAD drawing into a POLYLINE before the file can be translated to the CALMA format.

Those are just a few examples of some problems you may encounter in making DXF file translations. But by the time you read this book, many of the problems might be fixed. Currently, several software houses are aware of the problems with their translators, and they are taking steps to fix them. Remember that microcomputer-based CAD is less than ten years old, and universal standards aren't created overnight. You can expect DXF to become a much more powerful and accurate tool in the future.

WHAT YOU CAN DO WITH A DXF FILE

You now know what DXF files were designed for, and how they can and can't be used. Now you'll learn how to write and modify DXF files.

Why, you may ask, would you want to know how to read and write a DXF file? A fair question. One of the examples in this chapter is a BASIC program that will create a DXF file from a text file. That file then can be loaded into the AutoCAD drawing editor to give you a drawing that consists of the text file converted to AutoCAD text. Now, you have a block of text in your drawing that was easier to put in than by typing directly into the drawing file.

Here are a few other ideas for programs to read and write DXF files:

Keep Track of Different Items in a Drawing — You
could write a program that can read a DXF file and count instances of certain types of entities that you specify. As an example of this, you could keep track of the number of nuts and bolts in an assembly drawing.

Changing Entities in a Drawing — Since a DXF file is a
complete file of the drawing, you could write a program to change any of the properties of such entities as LAYER, LINETYPE or COLOR.

Performing Calculations — A structural drawing of a
building could be translated to a DXF file, and then read by a program that would perform stress calculations on the elements of that drawing. The results of the calculations could then be used to create a new DXF file to be read by AutoCAD for a visual evaluation of the results.

Generating Charts in AutoCAD — A program can be
written to generate graphs of certain mathematical functions. The results of those functions could be used to produce a DXF file and to be loaded into AutoCAD to view or plot the results.

NC and Tool Path Generation — Computer controlled
machine tools use a special computer language called NC, or numeric control — which instructs the machine tool to follow a particular path when cutting a part. The part is based on a geometric description of the drawing. For example, in NC code, a line from 0,0 to 2,5 is represented by the following code:

```
G00X2.0Y5.0
```

An AutoCAD drawing contains all the essential information for creating a tool path; the DXF file which contains this geometric information can be translated into NC code. Each entity in the DXF file is translated into the corresponding entity in NC code.

While this mammoth subject is outside the scope of this book, third-party DXF file translators and AutoLISP-based products are available which perform NC translation and tool path tasks.

Altering Drawings from the Database — Sophisti-
cated programs like Synthesis can read a user-created master drawing, then create a **DXF** file from that drawing. Modifications are then made to drawing entities and dimensions according to your specifications. For example, if you need 50 versions of a window, programs like Synthesis allow you to manipulate entities to create those 50 windows from one basic drawing. This kind of programming is quite complex, and falls outside the range of *The AutoCAD Database Book*. However, the material presented in this and previous chapters should give you enough information to determine whether your money would be well spent on third-party parametric programming software.

WHY USE DXF?

Many of these applications can be accomplished using AutoLISP. So why go to all the trouble of producing a **DXF** file, operating on it with another program, then reading **DXF** back into another drawing file? There are at least three basic reasons for operating on a **DXF** file with an outside program, instead of using AutoLISP:

Speed — If you're searching through a large drawing database to count or modify entities, you'll find that AutoLISP can be quite slow. Here's a BASIC version of **blkcnt**[*] that, when compiled, will run at least five times faster than the AutoLISP version.

```
10 CNT=0
20 INPUT "ENTER THE NAME OF THE DXF FILE TO READ"INFILE$
30 INFILE$=INFILE$+".DXF"
40 OPEN "I",1,INFILE$
50 WHILE IN$<>"EOF"
60     LINE INPUT #1,IN$   'read line from DXF
70     'If block INSERT then count it.
80     IF IN$="INSERT" THEN CNT=CNT+1
```

---

[*] The **blkcnt** routine appears in Chapter 6.

```
90      IF IN$="EOF" THEN CLOSE  'close file at end
100 WEND
110 PRINT "THERE ARE" CNT "BLOCKS IN THIS DRAWING"
120 END
```

Memory Size — With AutoLISP, you're limited (unless you're using extended AutoLISP) to 45K of memory for both the AutoLISP program and any memory necessary to hold intermediate data and results. This isn't a lot of memory, and if your data manipulations are at all complex, you'll find that you'll quickly run out of memory (*node space* in AutoLISP).

Complete Database Access — With AutoLISP, you are limited to access and modify only the data in the Entities Section of the drawing database. With AutoCAD Version 2.6 and later, you now can look at other sections of the drawing database, such as BLOCKS and **TABLES**, but you won't be able to modify anything in those sections. With a **DXF** file, you have access to the entire drawing database and the freedom to make any changes necessary for your application.

One of the programming examples in this chapter is a BASIC program that adds a new entity to the beginning of the Entities Section of the **DXF** file. That would be impossible to do with AutoLISP, because you wouldn't be able to change the order of the entities in the database.

LOOKING AT A DXF FILE

So far, we've discussed what can be done with a **DXF** file. But what does it look like? Let's find out.

Because the complete **DXF** file for even the simplest drawing (one entity) is at least eight pages long (and would make this book look padded), we're not going to reproduce one here. Instead, you can make your own:

Start a new AutoCAD drawing and call it **TEST**. Draw a **LINE** from **0,0** to **9,9**. Then,

Type: DXFOUT<RETURN>

Response: File name:<TEST>

Type: `<RETURN>` (The file will be named TEST.DXF)

Response: `Enter decimal places of accuracy (0 to 16)/`
`entities/binary <6>`

Type: `<RETURN>`

When the **DXF** file has been completed, **END** the drawing and exit AutoCAD. At this point, you can either load **TEST.DXF** into a text editor to look at, or you can print it out for a reference copy. To print this file, be sure your printer is turned on (otherwise your program may crash) and have at least eight pages of continuous paper in your printer. Now, at the DOS prompt:

Type: `COPY TEST.DXF PRN <RETURN>`

Pretty long, isn't it—especially for just one line. Let's take a closer look.

The first six pages down to the first **ENDSEC** are called the header section, which describes the AutoCAD drawing environment that existed when the **DXF** file was created. Very little of this information is necessary for your immediate purposes, and you can find an adequate explanation of these variables in Appendix C of the *AutoCAD Reference Manual*.

The next section is called the tables section, which contains information about linetypes (**LTYPE**), layers, text styles and views that you may have defined in your drawing. Because this is a simple drawing, only the defaults, **CONTINUOUS** linetype, **LAYER 0** and **STANDARD** text have been defined in the table. If an entity were to have a hidden linetype and be drawn on a layer called **FLOOR**, then **HIDDEN** linetype and layer **FLOOR** would have to be defined in this section.

The third section is the blocks section, where the entity description for each block in the drawing resides. That section is discussed in greater detail later. Because there were no blocks in the **TEST** drawing, nothing is in the blocks section.

The section of most concern at this point is the Entities Section, which should look like this (without the comments):

0	Indicates the start of a file separator
SECTION	Start of a file section
2	Indicates name will be on the next line
ENTITIES	Name of the section
0	Start of an entity—type follows
LINE	The type of entity
8	Indicates **LAYER** name follows
0	Name of layer that this entity resides
10	Next line will be starting X coord.
0.0	Starting X coord.
20	Next line will be starting Y coord
0.0	Starting Y coord.
11	Next line will be ending X coord.
9.0	Ending X coord.
21	Next line will be ending Y coord.
9.0	Ending Y coord.
0	Next line will be a file separator
ENDSEC	The end of the Entities Section
0	Next line will be a file separator
EOF	Indicates the end of the **DXF** file

If you changed the format of this entity record to a more conventional data format, it might look like this:

0	8	10	20	11	21
LINE	0	0.0	0.0	9.0	9.0

or:

TYPE	LAYER	START X	START Y	END X	END Y
LINE	0	0.0	0.0	9.0	9.0

Now the entity data start to look like a more conventional database format. If you had continued your lines to draw a diamond, the database would look like this:

TYPE	LAYER	START X	START Y	END X	END Y
LINE	0	0.0	0.0	9.0	9.0
LINE	0	9.0	9.0	18.0	0.0
LINE	0	18.0	0.0	9.0	-9.0
LINE	0	9.0	-9.0	0.0	0.0

You may have noticed that everything in the entities section appears in groups of two—a number, followed by a description. Those two items are, in fact, called *groups*. The first item is the Group Code, which indicates both the type of value the group contains and the general use of the group (a Group Code of **0** to **9** indicates that the value of that group will be a string; a Group Code of **10** to **59** indicates that the value will be a real number; and a Group Code of **60** to **79** indicates an integer value for the group).[*]

Appendix C of the *AutoCAD Reference Manual* includes descriptions of all of the Group Codes. Appendix B of this book provides commented **DXF** listings for all AutoCAD drawing entities.

REVISING DXF FILES

Now that you've seen how readable a **DXF** file can be, let's modify the **TEST.DXF** file. Start by loading the **DXF** file into a text editor and add the following lines *just before* the **0** in front of **ENDSEC** (before EOF). (Be sure to add the leading spaces where indicated.):

```
0
LINE
    8
0
  10
9.0
20
9.0
11
18.0
```

---

[*]   Two coordinates are output to a **DXF** file only if they are non-zero.

```
 21
0.0
  0
LINE
  8
0
10
18.0
20
0.0
 11
9.0
 21
-9.0
  0
LINE
  8
0
10
9.0
 20
-9.0
 11
0.0
 21
0.0
```

Now, save your new **DXF** file, enter AutoCAD, and start a new drawing called **TEST2**:

Type: DXFIN <RETURN>

Response: File Name <TEST2>

Type: TEST <RETURN>

Your new **DXF** file will now be loaded. If all goes well and there are no typos in your file, AutoCAD will accept your **DXF** file and then you can see what you've done. If it's a diamond, congratulations! You've just written your first **DXF** file, and you've done an

AutoCAD drawing without using AutoCAD. Think of all the money you can save by not having to spend $2850 on AutoCAD to make drawings!

Of course, it's very tedious to write a **DXF** file by hand. This exercise demonstrates how simple the **DXF** file structure really is. If you want more practical experience with **DXF** files, go to Appendix B, pick out a few entity types, add them to your **DXF** file and see what happens when you load that file into AutoCAD.

Let's try another experiment. There's nothing special about the current AutoCAD environment, so let's see if you can eliminate a good percentage of your **DXF** file. First, make a back-up copy of your **TEST.DXF** file, load your **DXF** file into your text editor again and do a **BLOCK DELETE** of the Header Section of your file — all the way down through **ENDSEC**. Save the **DXF** file, and now load it into a **NEW** AutoCAD drawing.

It still works, doesn't it? That's because the Header Section mostly determines how the drafting environment variables are set. Because all the variables in a drawing file have default values to begin with, the Header Section only changes those variables that are different from the default values in the **DXF** file. Since you didn't change any of the drafting variables in your **TEST** drawing, all header file variables were default variables anyway.

The only known Header Section that's valuable to keep track of in some cases is the variable called **$INSBASE**. That variable is the coordinate for the insertion point of a drawing that's used as a block inserted into other drawings. You'll use the $INSBASE variable in one of the examples.

Let's try something a little more radical. Take your back-up **DXF** file and delete every variable group in the Header Section *except* the **$INSBASE** part. Your Header Section should look like this:

```
0
SECTION
  2
HEADER
  9
$INSBASE
10
0.0
  20
```

```
0.0
 0
ENDSEC
```

Now, go into your AutoCAD drawing editor and do a **DXFIN** for this file. It still works! That means the only information you really need in your Header Section is variables that aren't set to default values.

Let's do something even more radical. Take your **DXF** file, and delete everything *except* the Entities Section. Your **DXF** file should look something like this:

```
0
SECTION
  2
ENTITIES
. . . . .        (listing of line entities)
. . . . .
  0
ENDSEC
  0
EOF
```

Now load the **DXF** file into your AutoCAD editor and see what happens. Even that works. You've now reduced your **DXF** file size from 3441 bytes to 291 bytes. So what's the purpose of all the information we've just eliminated?

Header Section — The Header Section, mentioned earlier, contains all the drawing variables that were current when the **DXF** file was created. That can be useful when you're using the **DXF** file for file translations. However, when reading and creating **DXF** files with a program other than another CAD program, you don't really care what the current layer or snap resolution is.

Tables Section — Any **LINETYPE**, **LAYER** or **TEXT** Style referenced in either the Entities Section or the Blocks Section must first be defined here. If AutoCAD finds a reference to a **LAYER** name, **LINETYPE** or **TEXT** style in either the Entities

Section or the Blocks Section that hasn't been defined in the Tables Section, it will reject the whole **DXF** file.[*] The format for the Tables Section is explained in Appendix B.

Blocks Section — The Blocks Section contains all the Block Definitions used in the drawing. It's similar in structure to the Entities Section. Each Block Definition starts with the name **BLOCK** followed by a list of all entities that make up that block (including **INSERT** references to other blocks that may be nested within that block) and ending with the name **ENDBLK**.

Programs that write **DXF** files usually won't write Block Definitions because they would tend to add unnecessary complexity to the program. On the other hand, programs designed to read **DXF** files must be capable of properly interpreting the Block Section. The Block Section format, including the Attribute Definition Structure, is addressed in Appendix B.

With this chapter and Appendix B as a guide, you should be well on your way to mastering the structure of **DXF** files. Now, let's concentrate on how to write programs in BASIC to read and write **DXF** files.

A FEW WORDS ABOUT USING BASIC

After much discussion, we decided to use BASIC to present the concepts and programs in this chapter. BASIC wasn't our first choice, but because everyone reading this book probably has at least a nodding acquaintance with BASIC, and because everyone has BASIC (it usually comes with your computer), it's the most accessible computer language to use.

---

[*]   Since Release 9, AutoCAD has become more forgiving and will accept undefined layer names in the blocks and entities sections.

HOW TO USE THE PROGRAM EXAMPLES IN THIS CHAPTER

The programs in this section have been debugged and tested, and are simple versions meant to be illustrative, as well as useful. They were designed so that you could try them out and modify them for your own purposes when you understand how they operate. Each was written to solve a real problem for a client. The actual program listings were merged into this chapter from the program files to minimize the possibility of typographical errors.

This isn't a tutorial on how to use BASIC — we assume that you either have some familiarity with it, or can read one of the 15,000 books about BASIC already available.

TYPING IN THE PROGRAMS

If you've never had the opportunity or inclination to try BASIC, here's a quick tutorial to get you started. If you don't already know how to load the BASIC editor that came with your computer, the following instructions will guide you through that procedure.

If you have an IBM PC:

Type: BASICA <RETURN>

Response: Ok

If you have an IBM PC compatible or a "Clone":

Type: GWBASIC <RETURN>

Response: Ok

Now you're in the BASIC Program Editor.

Type: AUTO 10 <RETURN>

Response: 10

Now you've started the Automatic Line numbering feature, and you can type in each line of the BASIC program (minus the line number).

After you've typed in the whole program:

Type: `SAVE "[the program name]" <RETURN>`

Response: `Ok`

Type: `RUN`

And, if you haven't made any typographical errors, your program will run.

MODIFYING A DXF FILE WITH BASIC

Below is a simple program that illustrates methods of reading, modifying and writing a **DXF** file with a BASIC program. The program also demonstrates something you can't do with AutoLISP — namely add to or change the order of the drawing entities in the drawing database.

THE PROBLEM

We were involved in a project that involved translating many drawing symbols from AutoCAD to VersaCAD via **DXF**. With AutoCAD, you can put the Insertion Base Point of a block anywhere you want, and that coordinate will show up in a Header Record called **$INSBASE**. VersaCAD, on the other hand, wants to use the first point in its drawing database as the **Handle (Insertion Base) Point**. Of course, none of the Insertion Bases on the AutoCAD drawings was the first drawing entities.

THE SOLUTION

We wrote a simple program (shown below) that would take a **DXF** file from AutoCAD, find the coordinates of the Insertion Base Point (**$INSBASE**), then add a Point Entity with the same coordinates as the Insertion Base Point to the beginning of the Entities Section of the **DXF** file.

That program (called **DXFFIX**) reads a **DXF** file, line by line, then writes each line out to a temporary file.

When it reaches the variable **$INSBASE** (Line 210), it goes to a subroutine that stores the coordinates of that record to variables.

When it reaches the beginning of the Entities Section (Line 240), it goes to another subroutine that writes a Point Entity at the beginning of the Entities Section with coordinates that match those of **$INSBASE**. **DXFFIX** then reads the rest of the **DXF** file and writes it to the temporary file. After the complete file is read, the program erases the old **DXF** file and renames the temporary file to the name of the old **DXF** file.

```
10  '
20  'This section reads the DXF file that the
30  'user names and then opens that file to read.
40  'It then opens a temporary output file called
50  'TEMP.TMP hold the new DXF file as it is written.
60  INPUT "FILE TO READ";INFILE$
70  INFILE$=INFILE$+".DXF"
80  OUTFILE$="TEMP.TMP"
90  OPEN "I",1,INFILE$
100 OPEN "O",2,OUTFILE$
110 '
120 'This section is a While Loop that reads
130 'each line of the DXF file and then writes
140 'that line out to the temporary file.
150 'If the line is of interest, it is sent
160 'to a subroutine.
170 WHILE IN$<>"EOF"
180     LINE INPUT #1,IN$ 'read line from DXF
190 'If Start of $INSBASE section is found
200 'go to subroutine that gets coordinates
210     IF IN$="$INSBASE" THEN GOSUB 390
220 'If Entities Section is reached, go to
230 'subroutine that inserts the point in the list
240     IF IN$="ENTITIES" THEN GOSUB 560
250     PRINT#2,IN$ 'Write line to temp file
260     PRINT IN$ 'Write line to screen
```

```
270     IF IN$="EOF" THEN CLOSE  'close file at end
280 WEND
290 'Kill old DXF file and rename temp file to
300 'name of old DXF file.
310 KILL INFILE$
320 NAME OUTFILE$ AS INFILE$
330 END
340 '
350 'This subroutine reads the Insertion Base
360 'coordinates and puts them into variables
370 'BASE3$ and BASE5$. Notice that the DXF
380 'values are strings and not numbers.
390 BASE1$=IN$
400 LINE INPUT #1,BASE2$
410 LINE INPUT #1,BASE3$      'X Coordinate
420 LINE INPUT #1,BASE4$
430 LINE INPUT #1,BASE5$      'Y Coordinate
440 LINE INPUT #1,BASE6$
450 PRINT#2,BASE1$
460 PRINT#2,BASE2$
470 PRINT#2,BASE3$
480 PRINT#2,BASE4$
490 PRINT#2,BASE5$
500 IN$=BASE6$
510 RETURN
520 '
530 'When the Entities Section is reached,
540 'this subroutine will add a POINT Entity
550 'to the beginning of the Entities Section.
560 PRINT#2,IN$
570 PRINT#2,0
580 PRINT#2,"POINT"
590 PRINT#2,8
600 PRINT#2,"0"
610 PRINT#2,10
620 PRINT#2,BASE3$   '$INSBASE X Coordinate
630 PRINT#2,20
640 PRINT#2,BASE5$   '$INSBASE Y Coordinate
650 LINE INPUT #1,IN$
660 RETURN
```

This program illustrates the basic methods of **DXF** file reading and writing. To utilize this program, you can substitute other types of entities to add to the new **DXF** file.

CREATING A DXF FILE FROM OTHER SOURCES

This program takes a text file produced on a text editor and formats the text into a **DXF** file. You have absolute control over the size of the text and the width of the columns with this program. You can specify the height of the text in either inches or points. You can even specify that the text be formatted into multiple columns.

HOW THE PROGRAM WORKS

When you format text with a word processor, all the characters are the same width. So, when you request right justification on a document, the word processor simply adds extra spaces to a line until that line flushes out to the right margin.

With proportional type and AutoCAD text fonts, that process is a little more involved. Each character in a type font takes up as much space as is necessary for that character—an **M** or a **W** takes up more space on a line than an **I** or a **P**. If you were to take a formatted word processor file and insert it into a drawing file with a proportional type font, it's likely you would end up with lines too short or too long for the column width you thought you had specified. For example, a line with 40 upper case letters would be more than twice as long as a line with 40 lower case characters.

This program reads a text file one character at a time. It then takes that character and gets the width of that letter from a shape width file **.SWD** (a shape width file for Simplex appears in Appendix D).[*] It then places that character in a line of text in a **DXF** file and adds the width of that letter to a variable. It continues adding characters from the text file to that line until the line is almost full. At that point, when the program reaches a space (indicating the end of a word), it starts a new line of text in the **DXF** file.

This program is a little more sophisticated than most AutoCAD text formatting programs because it takes into account the fact that each letter is a different width. The program gives you control of the line width independent of the line width in the text file. Here's the listing for this program with comments:

```
10  ON ERROR GOTO 3120
20  CCOUNT=0:ROT$="0":W$="":Y$="":L$=""
30  VCOUNT=0:WVCOUNT=0:XLOC=0:YLOC=0:LS$=""
40  CDEPTH=0:COLDIST=0:CWP=0:CWI=0:PSIZE=0:HGT=0
50  SCREC$="Y"
60  CLS:KEY OFF
70  DIM CWARRAY(256)
80  DIM INARRAY$(82)
90  DIM OUTARRAY$(200)
100 GOSUB 1640
110 IF CDEPTH>0 AND COLDIST=0 THEN GOTO 3200
120 IF SCREC$="Y" OR SCREC$="y" THEN CLS
130 '
140 'LOAD CHARACTER WIDTH ARRAY
150 'This routine loads an array with all of the
160 'character width information from the .SWD file
170 'Each cell number is the ASCII code of a character,
180 'and the contents are the width of that character in
```

---

[*] Each letter in an AutoCAD font file is created on a grid. Each individual unit of measurement in this grid is called a vector. Vectors have no inherent length, except in relationship to a scale applied to the font. The letter **M**, for example, may be 25 vectors high by 25 vectors wide or the letter I may be 25 vectors high by 6 vectors wide. An **SWD** file is merely a file that contains the ASCII code and the vector width for each character for a particular font. Because the character width varies from font to font, each font needs its own **SWD** file.

```
190  'vectors
200  OPEN "I",1,FILE1$
210  WHILE EOF(1) <> -1
220      INPUT#1,P,CW
230      CWARRAY(P)=CW
240  WEND
250  CLOSE
260  GOSUB 360   'to calculate vector length
270  OPEN "I",2,FILE2$  'open text file
280  OPEN "O",3,FILE3$  'open DXF file
290  GOSUB 2060   'to write Table Section of DXF
300  GOSUB 550   'to main subroutine
310  PRINT "TEXT FILE TRANSLATION
     COMPLETE...Press any key to continue"
320  A$=INKEY$: IF A$="" GOTO 320
330  CLS
340  END
350  '
360  'CALCULATE VECTOR LENGTH
370  'This routine calculates the actual vector
380  'length based on the text height and information
390  'in the SWD file (CWARRAY).
400  IF PSIZE >0 THEN HT=PSIZE*.0138
     *(CWARRAY(0)/CWARRAY(10))
410  VLEN=HGT/CWARRAY(0)
420  'Calculates column width in inches if column width
430  'was expressed as picas.
440  IF CWP>0 THEN CWI=CWP*.1656
450  'Calculates the number of vectors in a line
460  IF CWI>0 THEN TVEC=INT(CWI/VLEN)
470  'Calculates the height of the letters if
480  'the height was expressed in points.
490  HGT=INT(HGT*1000):HGT=HGT/1000
500  HGT$=STR$(HGT):HGT$=MID$(HGT$,2,5)
510  'Calculates the distance between each line of text
520  LFLEN=VLEN*CWARRAY(10)
530  RETURN
540  '
550  'INPUT CHARACTERS
560  'This subroutine reads the data file
570  'one character at a time and then sends
580  'them to a subroutine that checks its
```

```
590   'length and adds it to a string
600   WHILE EOF(2) <> -1
610      AR$=INPUT$(1,#2)
620         GOSUB 670  'to character sort routine
630   WEND
640   GOSUB 1510  'to print the last line routine
650   RETURN
660   '
```

This section takes each character and decides what to do with it.

```
670   'CHARACTER SORT ROUTINE
680   'This routine looks at each character and figures
690   'out what to do with it.
700   '
710   'If letter is a vertical bar, then do the end
720   'of paragraph routine.  Get next letter.
730   IF AR$=CHR$(124) THEN GOSUB 1150:GOTO 1020
740   'If letter is a space and it's the beginning of
750   'a line, then ignore it and get the next letter.
760   IF AR$=CHR$(32) AND VCOUNT=0 THEN GOTO 1020
770   'If letter is a period and it's the beginning of
780   'a line, then next letter will be a control character.
790    'Set the FLAG and get the next letter.
800    IF AR$=CHR$(46) AND VCOUNT=0 THEN
       FLAG=1:GOTO 1020
810    'If letter is UC M then put an "EM QUAD" space in
820    'the line of text.  Reset flag.  Get the next letter.
830    IF AR$=CHR$(77) AND FLAG=1 THEN
       L$=CHR$(228):GOSUB 1040:FLAG=0:GOTO 1020
840    'If letter is not a space and not a line feed and
850    'not a vertical bar and not a carriage return and not
860    'a tab, then add the letter to the word being formed.
870    'Get the next letter.
880    IF AR$<>CHR$(32) AND AR$<>CHR$(10) AND
       AR$<>CHR$(124) AND AR$<>CHR$(13) AND
       AR$<>CHR$(9) THEN L$=AR$:GOSUB 1040:GOTO
       1020
890    'If letter is a space and it is not at the beginning
900    'of a line, then add it to the end of the word being
910    'formed, add that word to the line of text, start a
```

```
920    ' new word and get the next letter.
930    IF AR$=CHR$(32) AND VCOUNT>0 THEN
       L$=AR$:GOSUB 1040:GOSUB 1260:GOTO 1020
940    ' If letter is a carriage return and it is not at the
950    ' beginning of a line, then add a space to the end of
960    ' the word being formed, add the word to the line of
970    ' text, start a new word and get the next letter .
980    '
990    IF AR$=CHR$(13) AND WVCOUNT>0 THEN
       L$=CHR$(32):GOSUB 1040:GOSUB
       1260:GOTO 1020
1000   IF AR$=CHR$(13) THEN GOTO 1020
1010   IF AR$=CHR$(10) THEN GOTO 1020
1020   RETURN
1030   '
```

The following routines format each character into a word, and then each word into a line until the line has been filled; it then starts a new line.

```
1040   ' LETTERS INTO WORDS
1050   ' This subroutine sets each valid letter into a
1060   ' word and keeps track of the vector length of
1070   ' that word.
1080   W$=W$+L$
1090   VCOUNT=VCOUNT+CWARRAY(ASC(L$))
1100   WVCOUNT=WVCOUNT+CWARRAY(ASC(L$))
1110   L2$=L$
1120   L$=" "
1130   RETURN
1140   '
1150   ' SHORT LINE PROCESS
1160   ' If the end of a paragraph is reached before the
1170   ' line is filled, then this routine is invoked
1180   IF WVCOUNT+TVCOUNT=>TVEC THEN GOSUB 1350
1190   TVCOUNT=TVCOUNT+WVCOUNT
1200   Y$=Y$+W$
1210   WVCOUNT=0
1220   IF TVCOUNT<TVEC THEN GOSUB 1350
1230   W$=" "
1240   RETURN
1250   '
```

```
1260  'WORDS INTO LINES
1270  'Adds a completed word to the line of text
1280  IF WVCOUNT+TVCOUNT=>TVEC THEN GOSUB1350
1290  TVCOUNT=TVCOUNT+WVCOUNT  'adds word vector to
      line vector
1300  Y$=Y$+W$  'adds word to line
1310  W$=""  'resets word variable
1320  WVCOUNT=0  'resets word vector count
1330  RETURN
1340  '
1350  'PRINT LINE
1360  'This subroutine prints the formatted line
1370  'to the DXF file
1380  '
1390  'Strips any spaces from beginning of line.
1400  IF LEFT$(Y$,1)=CHR$(32) THEN
      Y$=RIGHT$(Y$,(LEN(Y$)-1))
1410  IF LS$<>"" AND LEFT$(Y$,1)=LS$ THEN
      Y$=RIGHT$(Y$,(LEN(Y$)-1))
1420  GOSUB 2650  'write start of DXF text line
1430  PRINT #3,Y$  'write the text line to the DXF file
1440  GOSUB 2950    'write the end of DXF text line
1450  IF SCREC$="y" OR SCREC$="Y" THEN PRINT Y$
1460  TVCOUNT=0  'reset line vector count
1470  Y$=""  'reset line variable
1480  VCOUNT=0  'reset vector count
1490  RETURN
1500  '
1510  'Print last line
1520  'This subroutine prints the last line in
1530  'the file.
1540  IF LEFT$(Y$,1)=CHR$(32) THEN
      Y$=RIGHT$(Y$,(LEN(Y$)-1))
1550  IF LS$<>"" AND LEFT$(Y$,1)=LS$ THEN
      Y$=RIGHT$(Y$,(LEN(Y$)-1))
1560  GOSUB 2650  'write start of DXF text line
1570  PRINT #3,Y$  'write the text to DXF file
1580  GOSUB 2950  'write the end of the DXF text line
1590  GOSUB 3020    'write the end of the DXF file
1600  IF SCREC$="y" OR SCREC$="Y" THEN PRINT Y$
1610  CLOSE
1620  RETURN
```

The following section of the program produces data entry screens so that you can enter the information about text height, column width, column depth, etc.

```
1630 '
1640 'DATA ENTRY ROUTINE
1650 CLS
1660 TYP$="":CWI=0:HGT=0:MCOL$="":STL$="":
     FILE1$="":FILE2$=""
1670 FILE3$="":FILE4$="":CWP=0:PSIZE=0
1680 INPUT "Text Height to be specified in
     <I>nches or <P>icas: ";TYP$
1690 IF TYP$="I" OR TYP$="i" THEN GOSUB 1720
     ELSE GOSUB 1800
1700 RETURN
1710 '
1720 REM DATA ENTRY ROUTINE (for height in inches)
1730 CLS
1740 INPUT "Enter Column Width in inches:
                     ";CWI
1750 INPUT "Enter Text Height in decimal
     inches:          ";HGT
1760 INPUT "Do you wish multiple columns
     (Y or N):        ";MCOL$
1770 IF MCOL$="y" OR MCOL$="Y" THEN GOSUB
     1880 ELSE GOSUB 1940
1780 RETURN
1790 '
1800 REM DATA ENTRY ROUTINE (for height in points)
1810 CLS
1820 INPUT "Enter Column Width in Picas
     (1/6 inch):      ";CWP
1830 INPUT "Enter Type Size in Points
     (1/72 inch):        ";PSIZE
1840 INPUT "Do you wish multiple columns
     (Y or N):        ";MCOL$
1850 IF MCOL$="y" OR MCOL$="Y" THEN
     GOSUB 1880 ELSE GOSUB 1940
1860 RETURN
1870 '
1880 'MULTIPLE COLUMN INPUT
```

```
1890 INPUT "Enter Column depth in
     inches:                "; CDEPTH
1900 INPUT "Enter Gutter distance between
     Columns:        ";COLDIST
1910 GOSUB 1940
1920 RETURN
1930 '
1940 'REST OF INPUT ROUTINE
1950 INPUT "Enter the name of the text
     STYLE:            ";STL$
1960 INPUT "Enter the name of the FONT
     file:             ";FILE1$
1970 FILE4$=FILE1$
1980 FILE1$=FILE1$+".SWD"
1990 INPUT "Enter the name of the Text
     file to translate:";FILE2$
2000 INPUT "Enter the name for the .DXF
     file:             ";FILE3$
2010 FILE3$=FILE3$+".DXF"
2020 INPUT "IS THE ABOVE INFORMATION
     CORRECT? (Y or N)";CRCT$
2030 IF CRCT$="n" OR CRCT$="N" THEN GOTO 1640
2040 RETURN
```

This next section looks very long, but all it does is write the Tables Section of the **DXF** file to a disk file according to how the text is to be formatted.

```
2050 '
2060 'DXF TABLE SECTION WRITING ROUTINE
2070 'This routine writes the table section
2080 'of the DXF file.
2090 PRINT #3,0
2100 PRINT #3,"SECTION"
2110 PRINT #3,2
2120 PRINT #3,"TABLES"
2130 PRINT #3,0
2140 PRINT #3,"TABLE"
2150 PRINT #3,2
2160 PRINT #3,"LAYER"
2170 PRINT #3,70
2180 PRINT #3,2
```

```
2190 PRINT #3,0
2200 PRINT #3,"LAYER"
2210 PRINT #3,2
2220 PRINT #3,"TEXT"        ' LAYER NAME
2230 PRINT #3,70
2240 PRINT #3,0
2250 PRINT #3,62
2260 PRINT #3,7
2270 PRINT #3,6
2280 PRINT #3,"CONTINUOUS"       ' LINETYPE NAME
2290 PRINT #3,0
2300 PRINT #3,"ENDTAB"
2310 PRINT #3,0
2320 PRINT #3,"TABLE"
2330 PRINT #3,2
2340 PRINT #3,"STYLE"
2350 PRINT #3,70
2360 PRINT #3,2
2370 PRINT #3,0
2380 PRINT #3,"STYLE"
2390 PRINT #3,2
2400 PRINT #3,STL$   ' the name of the text style chosen
2410 PRINT #3,70
2420 PRINT #3,0
2430 PRINT #3,40
2440 PRINT #3,"0.0"
2450 PRINT #3,41
2460 PRINT #3,1
2470 PRINT #3,50
2480 PRINT #3,0
2490 PRINT #3,71
2500 PRINT #3,0
2510 PRINT #3,42
2520 PRINT #3,1
2530 PRINT #3,3
2540 PRINT #3,FILE4$     ' name of SHX file for text
2550 PRINT #3,0
2560 PRINT #3,"ENDTAB"
2570 PRINT #3,0
2580 PRINT #3,"ENDSEC"
2590 PRINT #3,0
2600 PRINT #3,"SECTION"
```

```
2610 PRINT #3,2
2620 PRINT #3,"ENTITIES"
2630 RETURN
```

These subroutines will write the **DXF** entry for each line of text formatted to the disk file.

```
2640 '
2650 'DXF LINE START HEADER ROUTINE
2660 'This subroutine writes the lines
2670 'before the text string in the DXF file.
2680 '
2690 'If multicolumn option has been chosen,
2700 'the program goes to this subroutine and checks to see if
2710 'the column depth has been exceeded.
2720 IF CDEPTH >0 THEN GOSUB 2870
2730 PRINT #3,0
2740 PRINT #3,"TEXT"      'TEXT ENTITY
2750 PRINT #3,8
2760 PRINT #3,"TEXT"        'LAYER NAME
2770 PRINT #3,10
2780 PRINT #3,XLOC     'X Start of text
2790 PRINT #3,20
2800 PRINT #3,YLOC     'Y Start of text
2810 YLOC=YLOC-LFLEN   'move to next line
2820 PRINT #3,40
2830 PRINT #3,HGT$
2840 PRINT #3,1
2850 RETURN
2860 '
2870 'MULTICOLUMN SWITCH
2880 'If a column depth is specified, then
2890 'this subroutine will be called.
2900 NCDEPTH=0-CDEPTH
2910 IF YLOC<=NCDEPTH THEN XLOC=XLOC+COLDIST+CWI
2920 IF YLOC<=NCDEPTH THEN YLOC=0
2930 RETURN
2940 '
2950 'DXF LINE END HEADER ROUTINE
2960 'This subroutine writes the 2 lines
2970 'after the text string in the DXF file.
2980 PRINT #3,7
```

```
2990 PRINT #3,STL$
3000 RETURN
3010 '
3020 'DXF FILE END ROUTINE
3030 'When the whole text file has been translated,
3040 'this routine writes the closing lines of the
3050 'DXF file.
3060 PRINT #3,0
3070 PRINT #3,"ENDSEC"
3080 PRINT #3,0
3090 PRINT #3,"EOF"
3100 RETURN
```

These are simply error-trapping routines. They are included so that the program won't crash if you type in a wrong file name or input invalid data.

```
3110 '
3120 'FILE NOT FOUND ERROR TRAP
3130 CLS
3140 IF ERR=53 OR ERR=64 THEN PRINT "FILE
     SPECIFIED NOT FOUND...PLEASE TRY AGAIN"
3150 PRINT
3160 PRINT
3170 PRINT "     Press any key to continue"
3180 A$=INKEY$: IF A$="" THEN 3180
3190 GOTO 100
3200 'DATA ENTRY ERROR TRAP
3210 CLS
3220 PRINT "INVALID DATA...PLEASE TRY AGAIN"
3230 PRINT
3240 PRINT
3250 PRINT "        Press any key to continue"
3260 A$=INKEY$: IF A$="" THEN 3260
3270 GOTO 100
```

HOW TO USE THIS PROGRAM

Because different text editors use different methods for ending a paragraph, you must add a *vertical bar* to the end of each paragraph and for each blank line in your text file (the vertical bar usually is found on the backslash key). That lets the program know the end of a paragraph is reached when it finds a vertical bar in the text file (see line 730).

You must have an **SWD** file available for the font you specify when you run this program. An **SWD** file for Simplex appears in Appendix D (with instructions on how to create it), and **SWD** files for Simplex, Complex and Italic are on *The AutoCAD Database Diskette*.

Now you can go into your BASIC Interpreter and run this program, answer the prompts and the program will produce a **DXF** file with the text formatted exactly to your specifications. At this point, you can start a new drawing in AutoCAD and, after typing **DXFIN <RETURN>** you can load your **DXF** text file and view the results.

CREATING A DXF FILE FROM OTHER SOURCES

This program takes a text file produced on a text editor and formats the text into a DXF file. You have absolute control over the size of the text and the width of the columns with this program. You can specify the height of the text to be either in inches or points. You can even specify that the text be formatted into multiple columns.

HOW IT WORKS

When you format text with a word processor, all of the characters are the same width, so when you request right justification on a document, the word processor simply adds extra spaces to a line until that line flushes out to the right margin. With proportional type and AutoCAD text fonts this process is a little more involved. Each character in a type font takes up exactly as much space as

is necessary for that character—an M or a W takes up more space on a line than an I or a P. If you were to take a formatted word processor file and insert it into a drawing file with a proportional type font, it is very likely that you would end up with lines that are too short and lines that are too long for the column width that you thought that you had specified. For example, a line with 40 upper case letters would be more than twice as long as a line with 40 lower case characters.

This program reads a text file one character at a time. It then takes that character and gets the width of that letter from a shape width file .SWD (a shape width file for Simplex appears in the appendix). It then places that character in a line of text in a DXF file and adds the width of that letter to a variable. It continues adding characters from the text file to that line until the line is almost full. At that point, when the

Figure 1: Sample of formatted text output.

SUMMARY

In this chapter, you've discovered what a **DXF** file is and what it looks like. You've also learned some of the pitfalls of using the **DXF** file format to translate files from one CAD system to another. You've received some hands-on experience on how to modify and create **DXF** files.

Finally, you've explored some programming techniques in BASIC used in developing programs to modify and create **DXF** files. Appendix B provides detailed information on **DXF** file structure, which will aid you in creating and modifying your own files and programs.

APPENDICES

Appendix A: The AutoCAD Database Revealed and Commented

Appendix B: DXF Database: Commented Listing

Appendix C: The DXB File Format

Appendix D: How To Create Your Own SWD Files

Appendix E: Using a Text Editor
Inside AutoCAD

For Further Reading

appendix A

THE AUTOCAD DATABASE REVEALED AND COMMENTED

To understand and manipulate the AutoCAD drawing database, you must have a complete knowledge of the database structure. The drawing database is complex, and available information on database structure is terse at best. Although we've spent almost two years writing programs to manipulate the AutoCAD drawing database, there are still times when we feel we haven't mastered all its fine points.

The next two appendices contain a complete annotated listing of all AutoCAD drawing entities with variations that can be found in the AutoCAD drawing database. This appendix contains the association list format of the database that's accessed and manipulated with AutoLISP. Appendix B contains the **DXF** file format of the same database. The drawing from which we generated these databases is shown in Figure 3.

We've found these listings to be extremely valuable for our own use. Now, instead of looking up the Group Codes in the *AutoCAD Reference Manual* (which has been greatly improved for Release 10) and trying to figure out what they mean, you can look up the actual data structure for the entity type that interests you and immediately see what the exact structure looks like for that record type.[*]

AutoCAD versions since Version 2.6 give users the ability to access and read (only) the Tables Section of the drawing database (Blocks, Linetypes, Layers, Views and Viewports — in Release 10) in addition to providing three new entity types. We're including this new information at the end of each appendix so it won't be confused with the information about the earlier versions of AutoCAD.

THE 3D DATABASE

Life was much simpler before AutoCAD Release 10's new 3D drawing database structure. Fortunately, the AutoCAD drawing database was designed so that it could be expanded into 3D without having to start over again. It's obvious from examining the Release 10 database that this is the direction in which AutoCAD has been going for the past three years.

Autodesk, Inc., says that Release 10 contains a true 3D database. In our examination of the database structure, we would have to say that it's only a 2.95D database, since Release 10 still can't handle a few things in 3D such as certain intersecting surfaces. But this is quibbling — it'll probably take at least a year for anyone to explore the limits of Release 10. And then there will be Release 11 to talk about.

Basically, all entities in AutoCAD are divided into two categories: 3D entities and planar entities. 3D entities can be positioned at any point in 3D space, such as LINES and 3DFACES. Planar entities, on the other hand, are entities that by their nature must be described on a 2D plane. CIRCLES and TEXT are examples of planar entities. What follows are some of the properties that both define and describe 3D entities and planar entities.

---

[*]   Since this book was first published, we've found the information in the appendix so useful for our own purposes that we refer to it constantly whenever we write AutoLISP code.

3D ENTITIES

3D entities can be described by any series of coordinates in 3D space. (See Figure 1 for an illustration of the various 3D entities in 3D space.)

- A LINE can be described by two 3D coordinates for the starting and ending points.

- A POINT can be described by one coordinate.

- A 3DFACE can be defined by the three or four coordinates that describe its vertices in space.

- A 3D POLYLINE is a special case of the POLYLINE entity that's generated internally by AutoCAD with one of the 3D surface (or mesh) commands, such as **TABSURF** or **EDGESURF**. The Coons Surface in Figure 1 is an example of a 3D polyline. Each of the vertices, or intersections, in this figure (there are 169) is described in the drawing database with a VERTEX record as a 3D coordinate.

With the exception of LINES and POINTS, none of the 3D entities can be extruded into the Z axis.

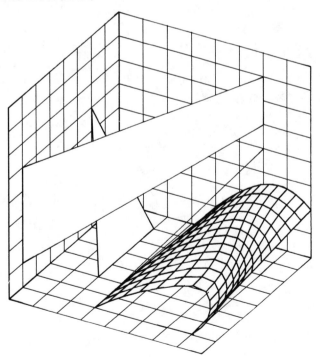

Figure 1

PLANAR ENTITIES

Planar entities are normally considered to be two dimensional, and are usually constructed on a plane. CIRCLES, ARCS, SOLIDS and TEXT are examples of planar entities. All planar entities can be extruded into the Z axis.

You're probably already familiar with planar entities if you've been using AutoCAD for any length of time. The only two drawing entities that weren't planar before Release 10 were 3DFACE and 3DLINE. In the past, however, you were limited to placing these entities on the base X Y plane. Now, you can create a plane anywhere in space with the User Coordinate System and place these entities on that plane; this lets you create more realistic 3D representations of objects. Figure 2 shows several planar entities placed on three different planes in space.

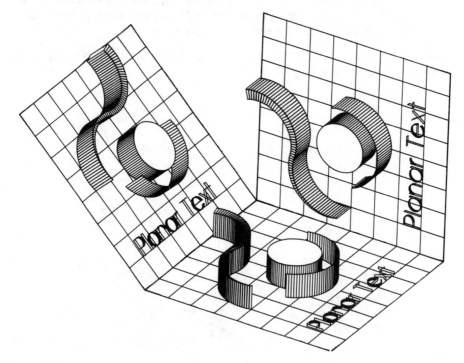

Figure 2

HOW THIS APPENDIX IS STRUCTURED

This appendix is divided into three sections. The first section describes all of the two-dimensional or planar entities. The second section is devoted to three-dimensional entities. The last part of this appendix describes the data structure of the TABLES section of the drawing database and how to access block information.

There is a general discussion of each entity type at the beginning of each section, and each entity description begins with some specific background information about that entity.

ASSOCIATION LIST FORMAT

This appendix is the drawing database format you'll see when using AutoLISP. The association lists have been reformatted slightly so that the structure of each record becomes clear. The actual record appears in the left column and the appropriate comments for each field appear next to that field in the right column. Here's how the first LINE association list would actually look if you used AutoLISP code to retrieve the list:

```
((-1 . <Entity name: 60000018>) (0 . "LINE") (8 .
"0") (10 1.0 1.0 0.0) (11 9.0 1.0 0.0))
```

These records were actually generated from an AutoCAD drawing (Figure 3) by modifying our sample function **entlst** to write the association lists to a disk file. Then, we simply placed each field on a separate line and added our comments.

TWO-DIMENSIONAL ENTITIES

The following listings were generated from the drawing file shown in Figure 3. This is the same drawing file that we used in previous editions, except that we used Release 10 to generate the listing so that it would reflect any changes found in the new database structure.

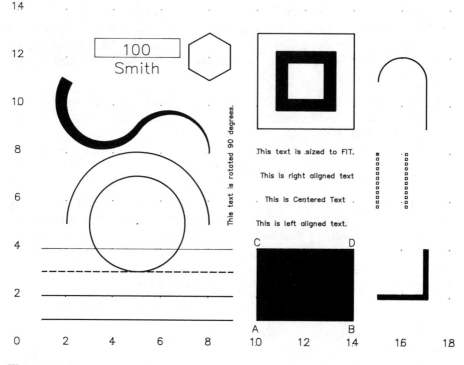

Figure 3

There are three differences between the data structures of Release 10 and any version before Release 10. Two differences are very important and one is of mild interest. Let's take the easy one first.

If the **X** coordinate of a point is 1.0, then AutoCAD will report it as 1.0 instead of 1.000000. This definitely makes for a more compact database, and as a bonus makes it a little more readable.

The next most important difference is that now all coordinates in each record are in a 3D format—that is, there are now **X**, **Y** *and* **Z** components for each coordinate point *even if the Z is always 0*[*]. This is particularly important information for those of you who use the **last** function to extract the

---

[*]   If the system variable FLATLAND has been set to 1, then AutoLisp will report only the **X** and **Y** part of the coordinate.

Y element of a coordinate list. Always use **car** to extract the **X**, **cadr** to extract the **Y** and **caddr** to extract the **Z** element of the coordinate list.

THE USER COORDINATE SYSTEM

The most important difference in the 2D entity data structure is that if the entity is placed on a User Coordinate plane, then that fact will be reported with the presence of a **210** group in the record. A Group 210 list might look like this:

```
(210 1 0 0)
```

Group 210 is a coordinate point that represents the extrusion into the Z axis from the User Coordinate plane relative to the World Coordinate System. This is a difficult concept to grasp, and we will take it in easy steps.

There are now two coordinate systems in AutoCAD. The first of these is called the World Coordinate System and it's the original Cartesian three-coordinate (X, Y and Z) system with coordinate 0,0,0 in the lower left-hand corner — this is always the constant base coordinate system in AutoCAD, everything else is ultimately measured relative to its coordinates.

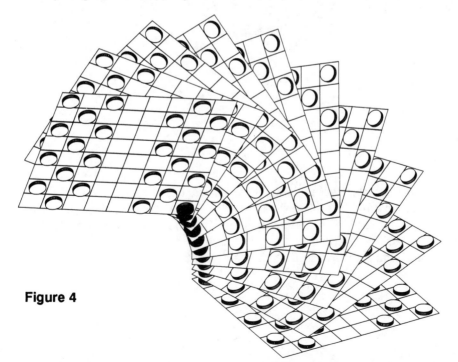

Figure 4

You can define the User Coordinate System to be any plane in space. Figure 4 is an illustration of ten checkerboards. The first board lies on the World Coordinate plane, and the others lie on nine different User Coordinate planes that have been defined as being rotated out from the World Coordinate plane.

Each entity on one of these "construction planes" is described by coordinates that are relative to that specific plane (the square with the black checker is 0,0,0 in the local User Coordinate System for that plane). When Group 210 appears in an entity record, it means that particular entity was drawn on a User Coordinate plane; the coordinate value of Group 210 represents the offset of that particular User Coordinate plane and the World Coordinate plane.

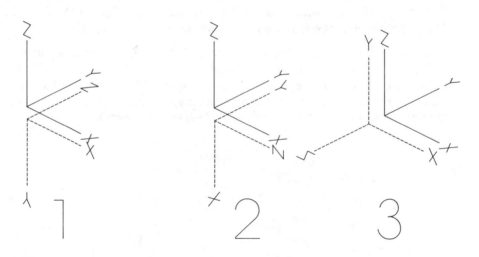

Figure 5

Figure 5 illustrates the relationship between the World Coordinate plane and three different User Coordinate planes. The **X Y Z** solid lines in Figure 5 represent the World Coordinate System. The line that represents the **Z** axis starts at 0,0,0 and ends at 0,0,1 — this is the normal direction of extrusion into the **Z** axis in the World Coordinate System.

If you rotated the **Z** axis clockwise 90 degrees around the **X** axis, then you would have created a User Coordinate plane that lies on the **X Z** axis of the World Coordinate plane as in Figure 5-1. The **Z** axis would then be represented by a line from 0,0,0 to 0,1,0 relative to the World Coordinate System. The coordinate 0,1,0 would then show up in the Group 210 field of any entity that is constructed on that plane*.

Figure 5-2 shows the construction plane rotated counterclockwise 90 degrees around the **Y** axis, producing a UCS that's on the **Y Z** axis of the WCS. Group 210 would be 1,0,0 since the **Z** axis is extruded into the **X** plane of the WCS. Finally, Figure 5-3 illustrates the UCS when it's rotated counterclockwise along the **X** axis, producing a **Z** extrusion offset of 0,-1,0 relative to the WCS.

LINE

The first LINE listing is for a simple LINE entity. A line can sometimes be considered a 2D entity, because if it has been drawn on a UCS plane its record will contain a Group **210**.

`(`	
`(-1 . <Entity name: 60000018>)`	Entity name (record index).
`(0 . "LINE")`	Entity type.
`(8 . "0")`	Layer name for this entity.
`(210 0.0 1.0 0.0)`	Offset **Z** extrusion **X Y Z** coordinates from the WCS — this line was constructed on a plane rotated 90 degrees counterclockwise around the **X** axis of the WCS.
`(10 1.0 1.0 0.0)`	Starting **X Y Z** coordinates.
`(11 9.0 1.0 0.0)`	Ending **X Y Z** coordinates.
`)`	

---

*   Including any 3D entities that were constructed when that UCS was active.

EXTRUDED LINE

This LINE listing is for a line that has a **Z** coordinate thickness and elevation. Notice that in this entity listing there are two new groups — Group **38** and Group **39**. These groups are valid groups for all entity types, but will appear *only* in an entity that's been assigned an elevation and/or thickness that's non-zero. The example below illustrates how and where they'll show up in an entity association list. You can check any entity for a non-zero elevation value by this AutoLISP form:

```
(COND ((CDR (ASSOC 38 (ENTGET E))) (<do if
       condition is true>)))
```

```
(
(-1 . <Entity name: 60000030>)      Entity name (record index).

(0 . "LINE")                        Entity type.

(8 . "0")                           Layer name for this entity.

(38 . 2.0)                          If Group 38 exists in the en-
                                    tity list, then this entity has a
                                    Z elevation that is not zero,
                                    and the second element of
                                    this list is the elevation.

(39 . 4.0)                          If Group 39 appears in the
                                    list, then this entity has a Z
                                    thickness greater than zero.
                                    The second element in this
                                    list is the thickness extruded
                                    in the local Z axis.

(10 1.0 2.0 0.0)                    Starting X Y Z coordinates.

(11 9.0 2.0 0.0)                    Ending X Y Z coordinates.
)
```

LINE BY LINETYPE

This next LINE listing is for a line that has a linetype different than the one set for the layer on which this entity resides.

`(`	
`(-1 . <Entity name: 60000048>)`	Entity name (record index).
`(0 . "LINE")`	Entity type.
`(8 . "0")`	Layer name for this entity.
`(6 . "HIDDEN")`	If Group Code **6** appears, the linetype for this entity isn't the same linetype set for the layer for this entity.
`(10 1.0 3.0 0.0)`	Starting **X Y Z** coordinates.
`(11 9.0 3.0 0.0)`	Ending **X Y Z** coordinates.
`)`	

LINE "BYCOLOR" WITH ENTITY HANDLE

This last LINE listing has a different color than the one assigned to that entity's layer. This listing also shows an example of what the entity handle field (Group **5**) looks like when it's used in a drawing database. See Chapter 3 for information about entity handles and Chapter 7 for some examples of accessing entities in the drawing database by their entity handles.

`(`	
`(-1 . <Entity name: 60000060>)`	Entity name (record index).
`(0 . "LINE")`	Entity type.
`(8 . "0")`	Layer name for this entity.
`(62 . 1)`	If Group Code **62** appears, then the color for this entity is different than the entity's layer color. Color number 1 is RED. This number is always an integer with a range from 1 to 256.
`(10 1.0 4.0 0.0)`	Starting **X Y Z** coordinates.
`(11 9.0 4.0)`	Ending **X Y Z** coordinates.

```
(5 . "1F")
```

This is the entity handle. Entity handles are automatically assigned to each entity in a drawing after the HANDLES ON command is invoked. The entity handle is a sequentially assigned, four-byte long integer expressed as a string with any leading zeros removed. This ID number is permanently assigned to an entity and is very useful for linking individual entities to records in a database outside of AutoCAD. This example is just a simulation, because once you turn entity handles on you won't be able to turn it off again; all subsequent records will contain the entity handle field.

```
)
```

CIRCLE

CIRCLE has only two defining measurements: the **X Y Z** coordinates for the center, and the **radius**.

```
(
(-1 . <Entity name: 60000090>)    Entity name (record index).
(0 . "CIRCLE")                    Entity type.
(8 . "0")                         Layer name for this entity.
(10 5.0 5.0 0.0)                  Center X Y Z coordinates.
(40 . 2.0)                        Radius.
)
```

ARC

ARC is described with a center, a radius, a starting angle and an ending angle. The arc is *always drawn counterclockwise* from the starting angle to the ending angle. You can find the actual coordinates for the starting or ending points of the arc by using the **POLAR** function like this:

```
(setq start-point (polar center start-angle
     radius))
```

or:

```
(setq start-point (polar (cdr (assoc 10
     (entget e))) (cdr (assoc 50 (entget e)))
     (cdr (assoc 40 (entget e)))))
```

(	
(-1 . <Entity name: 600000a8>)	Entity name (record index).
(0 . "ARC")	Entity type.
(8 . "0")	Layer name for this entity.
(10 5.0 5.0 0.0)	Center-point **X Y Z** coordinates.
(40 . 3.0)	Arc radius.
(50 . 0.0)	Starting angle in radians. All angles in the AutoCAD drawing database are expressed in radians. There are two times PI radians (or 6.283185307, etc.) in a full 360-degree circle.
(51 . 3.14159)	Ending angle in radians.
)	

SOLID

A SOLID is a filled three- or four-sided figure, uniquely described by two opposing pairs of points rather than by four points around the perimeter (as a normal rectilinear shape would be described).

In Figure 3, the solid is properly defined by the first pair of points **A** and **B** (the base) and then by the second pair of points **C** and **D** (the top). If this were a square figure, rather than a solid, it would be correctly described by the following sequence of points: **A**, **C**, **D**, **B** and **A**. If the solid were to be triangular in form, it would be described with the first two points as the base (**10** and **11**), and the third point for the apex (**12**).

`(`	
`(-1 . <Entity name: 600000c0>)`	Entity name (record index).
`(0 . "SOLID")`	Entity type.
`(8 . "0")`	Layer name for this entity.
`(10 10.0 1.0 0.0)`	First **X Y Z** coordinate point for base.
`(11 14.0 1.0 0.0)`	Second **X Y Z** coordinate point for base.
`(12 10.0 4.0 0.0)`	First **X Y Z** coordinate point for top.
`(13 14.0 4.0 0.0)`	Second **X Y Z** coordinate point for top. If this solid were triangular in form, this group would not appear in the listing.
`)`	

TEXT AND SHAPE

The next several listings will deal with various types of TEXT and SHAPE entities.

Obviously, text is a 2D entity, although it can be extruded in the **Z** axis just like any other planar entity. One quality that we've never liked about the text entity is that when you do a hidden line removal on a drawing, any text that lies behind a solid will show through that solid. There's a solution to that problem though: Simply extrude the text slightly into the Z axis (as little as .001 inches will do) and it will no longer show through the solids.

There's only one TEXT entity, but there are a number of variations of that entity based on how the text has been formatted in the drawing editor. These formatting variations of the TEXT entity can be very confusing, so we'll illustrate most of them by example listings.

In all the TEXT entity listings below, the text is the same height and style. Only the format is different (i.e., CENTER, RIGHT, FIT, etc.).

SHAPE entities look exactly like TEXT entities, except that no text formatting information is contained in the record description. The .SHX format for text FONTS and SHAPES are identical. The only difference between the two files is that the FONT.SHX file contains letter forms, numbered to conform to the ASCII code for those letters, and a SHAPE.SHX file contains forms other than letters, numbered arbitrarily. FONT files and SHAPE files can even be used interchangeably in a drawing for certain purposes (usually not a good practice).

It might be helpful at this point to explain just how text and shapes are handled in AutoCAD's drawing database. The actual information on how each letter of text or each shape is to be formed isn't in the drawing database, but is contained in a separate SHAPE file that has the extension .SHX. You can get an idea of how a SHAPE file looks and how it's constructed by looking in Appendix B of the *AutoCAD Reference Manual*.

The TEXT and SHAPE entities in the drawing database contain only information about sizing, scaling and formatting text and shapes. When AutoCAD finds a TEXT or SHAPE entity in the drawing database, it looks for the .SHX file named in the entity record on your hard disk. It then extracts all appropriate data from that file and uses that information to actually construct the forms of the letters or shapes. Finally, that information is sent to your screen or plotter.

If the .SHX files referenced in your drawing aren't on your hard disk when you load your drawing into the drawing editor, and no alternate .SHX file is named, none of the text defined by that .SHX file will appear in your drawing.

The description of TEXT and SHAPE entities will become more apparent when you study the annotated listings below. The first text listing will be addressed in greater detail than the subsequent records. For the remaining text listings, we'll comment at length only on the variations.

LEFT TEXT

The first listing is for standard left-justified text, the kind you get when you just pick a starting point in response to the TEXT command.

```
(
(-1 . <Entity name: 600000d8>)     Entity name (record index).
(0 . "TEXT")                       Entity type.
(8 . "0")                          Layer name for this entity.
(10 10.0 5.0 0.0)
```
The insertion point's **X Y Z** coordinate for this line of text. This is the actual starting point of the line of text. This point is always at the *beginning* of the text string.

```
(40 . 0.2)
```
The body height of the uppercase letters for this line of text.

```
(1 . "This is left
    aligned text.")
```
The actual text string for this entity. These characters will appear on your screen. This text string can have a maximum length of 255 characters.

```
(50 . 0.0)
```
The rotation angle for this line of text in radians. The pivot point for this angle is always at the insertion point (Group **10**) which may be different from the starting point of the text, depending on the text format.

```
(41 . 1.0)
```
Relative **X** scale, or width factor. Most of the time this will be **1.0**. If, when you define your text style with

the STYLE command,[*] you use a width factor other than 1, it will show up here.

(51 . 0.0)

The obliquing angle of the text in radians. If you define this text style to have slant-ing letters, the angle of that slant would be in this group. If the characters aren't slanted, this number will be **0.0**.

(7 . "NORMAL")

The name assigned to the STYLE definition for this text style. In this example, the text style was named NOR-MAL. This is NOT the name of the font file, which ap-pears in the STYLE table in the Tables section of the drawing database where the complete definition for the NORMAL text style is found (the name of the font file for NORMAL is SIMPLEX).

(71 . 0)

Text generation flag. This is a bit-coded flag with the second (**2**) and third (**4**) bits capable of being set. If both bits are **0**, then text will ap-pear normal. If the second bit is set (**2**), then the text will appear mirrored in the **X** axis (left to right). If the third bit (**4**) is set, the text will ap-pear upside down. Only one bit will be set at a time. See

---

[*]   See Section 4.10.1 of the *AutoCAD Reference Manual.*

(72 . 0)

Text justification type flag. This is *not* a bit-coded flag. The value of this number determines how the text is justified. In this example, **0** means the text will be left justified. We'll explain what other numbers mean in the other TEXT entity descriptions.

(11 0.0 0.0 0.0)

Alignment point. This is the **X Y Z** coordinate point where the text was inserted. Because this TEXT entity is left justified, the point where the text was inserted and the insertion point are the same. This coordinate is **0,0,0**. See the other TEXT entity descriptions for more information.

)

CENTERED TEXT

The only difference between this TEXT entity listing and the preceding one is that this text is **centered** on an **alignment point** (Group **11**). Text always has a base point at the *beginning* of the TEXT entity (in this example, just before the **T** in "This"). If you specify **Center** alignment when inserting your line of text into the drawing, AutoCAD will calculate a point to the left of the center point half the length of your text string. This point is the actual insertion point for the TEXT entity.

(

(-1 . ⟨Entity name: 600000f0⟩)   Entity name (record index).

(0 . "TEXT")   Entity type.

(8 . "0")   Layer name for this entity.

```
(10 10.3571 6.0 0.0)
```
Insertion point **X Y Z** coordinate for this line of text. This is the actual starting point of the line of text. Compare this coordinate with the one in Group 11. The difference is 1.6429— half the width of the text on the screen.

```
(40 . 0.2)
```
This is the body height of the uppercase letters for this line of text.

```
(1 . "This is Centered Text")
```
The actual text string for this entity.

```
(50 . 0.0)
```
The rotation angle for this line of text in radians.

```
(41 . 1.0)
```
Relative **X** scale, or width factor.

```
(51 . 0.0)
```
The obliquing angle of the text in radians.

```
(7 . "NORMAL")
```
Text STYLE for this entity.

```
(71 . 0)
```
Text generation flag.

```
(72 . 1)
```
Text justification type flag. The value of this number determines how the text is justified. In this example, **1** means that the text will be centered.

```
(11 12.0 6.0 0.0)
```
The actual **centered** Insertion **X Y Z** coordinate of this text string. This is the point picked for inserting the text after the center option was picked in the TEXT command.

```
)
```

RIGHT-ALIGNED TEXT

If right-aligned text were specified, then the actual TEXT entity insertion point would be a point to the left of the alignment point *equal in distance to the total width* of the TEXT entity.

```
(
(-1 . <Entity name: 60000108>)
```
Entity name (record index).

```
(0 . "TEXT")
```
Entity type.

```
(8 . "0")
```
Layer name for this entity.

```
(10 10.1619 7.0 0.0)
```
Insertion point **X Y Z** coordinate for this line of text. This is the actual starting point of the line of text.

```
(40 . 0.2)
```
The body height of the uppercase letters for this line of text.

```
(1 . "This is right
    aligned text")
```
The actual text string for this entity.

```
(50 . 0.0)
```
The rotation angle for this line of text in radians.

```
(41 . 1.0)
```
Relative **X** scale, or width factor.

```
(51 . 0.0)
```
The obliquing angle of the text characters in radians.

```
(7 . "NORMAL")
```
Text STYLE for this entity.

```
(71 . 0)
```
Text generation flag.

```
(72 . 2)
```
Text justification type flag. The value of this number determines how the text is justified. In this example, **2** means the text will be RIGHT ALIGNED.

`(11 14.0 7.0 0.0)`	The actual *right* insertion **X Y Z** coordinate of this text string. This is the point picked for inserting the text after the right option was picked in the **TEXT** command.
`)`	

TEXT TO "FIT"

The difference between this TEXT entity listing and a standard TEXT entity is that this text is fitted between a starting and ending point. After you pick the points, AutoCAD will adjust the **Relative X Scale Factor** (Group **41**) for this TEXT entity so that it will fit between the specified starting and ending points. An **alignment point** (Group **11**), halfway between the starting and ending points, is also calculated. Again, text always has a base point at the *beginning* of the TEXT entity (in this example, just before the T in "This"), or at the starting point for **fitted text**. This point is the actual insertion point for the TEXT entity.

`(`	
`(-1 . <Entity name: 60000120>)`	Entity name (record index).
`(0 . "TEXT")`	Entity type.
`(8 . "0")`	Layer name for this entity.
`(10 10.0 8.0 0.0)`	Insertion point **X Y Z** coordinate for this line of text. This is the actual starting point of the line of text.
`(40 . 0.2)`	The body height of the uppercase letters for this line of text. The height will remain the same, no matter how much the text is "squeezed" to fit.
`(1 . "This text is` `    sized to FIT.")`	The actual text string for this entity.

(50 . 0.0)	The rotation angle for this line of text in radians.
(41 . 1.04218)	Relative **X** scale, or width factor. This is the factor that changes when a TEXT entity is "stretched" or "squeezed" to fit between two points. In this example, the text had to be stretched slightly to fit, because the factor is slightly greater than 1.
(51 . 0.0)	The obliquing angle of the text in radians.
(7 . "NORMAL")	Text style for this entity.
(71 . 0)	Text-generation flag.
(72 . 5)	Text-justification type flag. The value of this number determines how the text is justified. In this example, **5** means that the text will be sized to fit.
(11 14.0 8.0 0.0)	The actual **centered** insertion **X Y Z** coordinate of this text string. This is the point calculated by AutoCAD to be halfway between the starting and ending points picked for inserting the text after the **FIT** option was picked in the TEXT command.

)

ROTATED TEXT

This example is simply left-justified text, rotated 90 degrees counterclockwise.

(

(-1 . <Entity name: 60000138>)	Entity name (record index).

`(0 . "TEXT")`	Entity type.
`(8 . "0")`	Layer name for this entity.
`(10 9.0 5.0 0.0)`	Insertion point **X Y Z** coordinate for this line of text. This is the actual starting point of the line of text.
`(40 . 0.2)`	The body height of the uppercase letters for this line of text.
`(1 . "This text is rotated` `   90 degrees.")`	The actual text string for this entity.
`(50 . 1.5708)`	The rotation angle for this line of text in radians. In this case, the text was rotated **90** degrees or **PI/2**.
`(41 . 1.0)`	Relative **X** scale, or width factor.
`(51 . 0.0)`	The obliquing angle of the text in radians.
`(7 . "NORMAL")`	Text STYLE for this entity.
`(71 . 0)`	Text generation flag.
`(72 . 0)`	Text justification type flag.
`(11 0.0 0.0 0.0)`	Alignment point. This is the **X Y Z** coordinate point where the text was inserted. Because this TEXT entity is left justified, the point where the text was inserted and the insertion point are the same, and that coordinate is **0,0,0**.
`)`	

Two remaining text justification types that we haven't illustrated are **ALIGNED** and **MIDDLE**.

Aligned — is similar to FIT, except the text height (Group **40**) is adjusted to fit instead of the relative **X** scale factor (Group **41**). The text justification type (Group **72**) for ALIGNED is **3**.

Middle — is similar to CENTER, except that the text is centered with the alignment point (Group **11**) in both the **X** and the **Y** axis. The text justification type (Group **72**) for MIDDLE is **4**.

BLOCK INSERTION, ATTRIBUTE AND SEQEND

Although a block may contain nothing but 3D entities and be fully rounded in all respects, the actual INSERT record that controls the placement, rotation and scale of the block is still a 2D entity and must be placed within the constraints of a construction plane. For all practical purposes, you can rotate the axes of your 3D block to any angle by rotating the UCS to the desired angle before inserting the block.

The following four entity association lists represent a block insertion that contains two attributes. The only difference between this block insertion record and that of a block that doesn't contain attributes is that in the latter, Group **66** is set to **0**.

The actual list of entities that makes up any given block or attribute can be found in the block section of the drawing database. Since Version 2.6, we now have access, via AutoLISP, to the information contained in the block section. Later, in the third section of this appendix, we'll examine the block section of this drawing and you'll learn how to extract information about block entities.

3D NOTE: If you have inserted a block using a **Z** coordinate or snapped the insertion point of the block to a point in the drawing that had a **Z** coordinate of other than 0 in the current UCS, then Group **38** will show up in this record with the elevation of the block insertion point.

BLOCK INSERTION

```
(
  (-1 . <Entity name: 60000150>)    Entity name (record index).
  (0 . "INSERT")                    Entity type.
  (8 . "0")                         Layer name for this entity.
```

`(66 . 1)`	"Attributes Follow" flag. If this number is **1**, all the records that follow this record will be attributes attached to this block until a SEQEND entity type is reached. If this number is **0**, then no attributes are attached to this block.
`(2 . "ROOMTAG")`	The name of this block. If an INSERT record is found with a block name that starts with an asterisk (*), then that block is "anonymous," created by an internal AutoCAD operation. Hatch patterns and arrowheads are examples of anonymous blocks.
`(10 5.0 12.0 0.0)`	The **X Y Z** coordinate of the insertion point for this instance of the block.
`(41 . 0.05)`	The **X** scale for this insertion of this block.
`(42 . 0.05)`	The **Y** scale for this insertion of this block.
`(50 . 0.0)`	The rotation angle in radians for this BLOCK insertion.
`(43 . 0.05)`	The **Z** scale for this insertion of this BLOCK.
`(70 . 0)`	Column count for MINSERT. If this or any of the next three groups has a value other than **0**, then this INSERT was done with the MINSERT command, and this record represents multi-

	ple occurrences of the referenced BLOCK in the drawing file.[*]
`(71 . 0)`	Row count for MINSERT.
`(44 . 0.0)`	Column spacing for MINSERT.
`(45 . 0.0)`	Row spacing for MINSERT.
`)`	

ATTRIBUTES

The next two listings are for the two attributes linked to the block insertion above. Notice the similarity to the TEXT entity listing. Because the attribute entity is primarily a carrier of textual data, it could be considered a specialized type of TEXT entity. All text formatting features available with the TEXT command are available with attributes. The actual attribute prompts that appear when this block is inserted are stored in the block section of the drawing database in an entity called ATTDEF.

`(`	
`(-1 . <Entity name: 60000168>)`	Entity name (record index).
`(0 . "ATTRIB")`	Entity type.
`(8 . "0")`	Layer name for this entity.
`(10 4.08571 11.3286 0.0)`	Insertion point **X Y Z** coordinate for this attribute. This is the actual starting point of the text of this attribute.
`(40 . 0.45)`	The body height of the uppercase letters for this attribute. The original height of this text, when this attribute was defined, was 9". When we inserted the block attached to this attribute into the drawing, we scaled the

---

[*]   See Section 9.1.6 in the *AutoCAD Reference Manual* for more information about MINSERT.

block to .05X scale. AutoCAD automatically recalculated all the sizes of the attributes associated with that block to be the same relative size.[*]

`(1 . "Smith")`

The attribute value given this particular insertion of this attribute. This value is linked to the attribute tag "EMPNAME."

`(2 . "EMPNAME")`

The attribute tag, the key searched for when attributes are extracted using the AT-TEXT command. The attribute tag remains the same for all instances of this attribute, while each instance can have different values linked to it. Think of the attribute tag as a field name and the attribute value as the value contained in that field in a database record.

`(70 . 0)`

The attribute flag. It's a bit-coded flag with the first (**1**), second (**2**) third (**4**) and fourth (**8**) bits capable of being set. If no bits are set in this group (**0**), then the attribute will be visible. If the first (**1**) bit is set, it means that the attribute will be invisible. If the second (**2**) bit is set, then the attribute value will be a constant. If the third (**4**) bit is set, then verification will be required

---

[*]   For a comparison, see this same block with attributes listed in Chapter 7.

on input of any value for this attribute. If the fourth **(8)** bit is set, then this is a preset attribute. See the beginning of Appendix B for more information about bit-coded flags.

(73 . 0)

The field length. This group code is still not being used.

(50 . 0.0)

The rotation angle for this attribute text in radians.

(41 . 1.0)

Relative **X** scale, or width factor.

(51 . 0.0)

The obliquing angle of the attribute text in radians.

(7 . "STAND")

Text style for this attribute entity.

(71 . 0)

Text-generation flag. This group works the same way as Group **71** in the TEXT entity record.

(72 . 1)

Text justification type flag. The attribute text in this example is centered. This group has the same values as the TEXT entity Group **72**.

(11 4.975 11.3286 0.0)

The actual **centered** insertion **X Y Z** coordinate of this attribute text string. This point was picked for inserting the attribute text after the CENTER option was picked in the ATTDEF command when this attribute was defined.

)

The following ATTRIB listing is almost identical to the one above. We wanted to show you an example of how two (or more) attributes could be linked with the same Block INSERT record. We'll comment only on those fields that are different from the preceding ATTRIB record.

```
(
(-1 . <Entity name: 60000180>)
(0 . "ATTRIB")
(8 . "0")
(10 4.43929 12.1 0.0)
(40 . 0.45)
(1 . "100")
```

The attribute value for the attribute tag ROOMNO. Notice that all numbers are carried as strings.

```
(2 . "ROOMNO")
```

The attribute tag to which the value "100" is linked.

```
(70 . 0)
(73 . 0)
(50 . 0.0)
(41 . 1.0)
(51 . 0.0)
(7 . "STAND")
(71 . 0)
(72 . 1)
(11 4.975 12.1 0.0)
)
```

The next entity, SEQEND, appears only at the end of a series of attribute records (or, as we'll see later, at the end of a series of polyline vertexes). SEQEND serves two purposes: 1) It marks the end of a series of attributes linked to a block insertion, and 2) It contains the entity name (or record number) of the block insertion to which it's linked.

There are two strategies for using SEQEND in searching for occurrences of block insertions with attributes.

Strategy one: Knowing that every record between INSERT and SEQEND will be an ATTRIB record linked to the INSERT record, we can step through the database until we find an INSERT record and check it to see if Group **66** is set to 1 (Attributes Follow Flag). Now we can examine every record after this INSERT record for specific attribute values until we reach the SEQEND record.

Strategy two: This involves looking for pairs of INSERT SEQEND records. When a pair of this type has been found, you can look at the Group **2** of SEQEND for the entity name of the INSERT record and use that entity name to go back to the beginning of the attribute list.

```
(
 (-1 . <Entity name: 60000198>)     Entity name (record index).

 (0 . "SEQEND")                     Entity type.

 (8 . "0")                          Layer name for this entity.

 (-2 . <Entity name: 60000150>)     Entity name (record index)
                                    of the INSERT entity to
                                    which this SEQEND is
                                    linked.

)
```

TWO-DIMENSIONAL (2D) POLYLINES

The **POLYLINE** entity in Release 10 can now be either a 2D polyline or a 3D polyline, depending on the value of certain groups within the POLYLINE and the VERTEX record. 3D polylines will be extensively discussed in the 3D entity section of this appendix. Here we will touch on the differences between a 2D polyline and a 3D polyline.

A **2D polyline** looks like a series of line and arc segments connected to form one continuous entity. 2D polylines have many properties not available for other entities:

- They can have a specified width, which can be varied from one end of a segment to the other to form a taper.

- Polyarcs or polyline arcs are polyline segments with "Bulge Factor" information added.*

- Vertexes can be moved, added to or subtracted from polylines.

- Curve-fitting information can be added to any polyline.

- Ellipses and polygons are actually polyline structures.**

2D polylines may look like a series of connected lines and arcs on the screen, but their database description is completely different from that of lines and arcs. A polyline actually consists of a series of coordinate points, and each coordinate point is called a *vertex*. AutoCAD takes the coordinate information for each vertex and draws lines between each vertex point (these aren't LINE entities).

Try to visualize the polyline data structure as a "connect-the-dot" picture, with AutoCAD drawing in the lines between the dots when it displays a polyline on the screen. If you were to draw a square using lines, that square would consist of four LINE entities describing eight coordinate points (the starting point of each line would be identical to the ending point of the preceding line). If you draw the same square using polylines, you would have one polyline entity that consisted of four vertex sub-entities, with each vertex describing one corner of that square.

There are two types of **3D polylines**. The first type is generated by the 3DPOLY command and will construct a 0-width, non-extruded polyline in 3D space. The second type is referred to as a **3D POLYGON MESH**, and although it's described by the POLYLINE entity record in the drawing database, it's generated internally by the AutoCAD commands 3DMESH, RULESURF, TABSURF, REVSURF and EDGESURF. The most important information to know at this point is how to tell the difference between a 2D polyline and a 3D polyline when your AutoLISP program runs into a POLYLINE entity in the drawing database. That's simple: IF THE VALUE OF GROUP 70 IN THE POLYLINE ENTITY RECORD IS GREATER THAN 7 THEN THAT POLYLINE, AND THE VERTEX RECORDS THAT FOLLOW, DESCRIBE A 3D POLYLINE.

---

*   See the section on tapered polyarcs for information on how the bulge factor is
       calculated.
**   See the *AutoCAD Reference Manual* for more information about POLYLINES.

POLYLINE DATA FORMAT

The polyline data format consists of three parts. The first part is the Header Record entity, called polyline. The POLYLINE record signals the start of the polyline data structure and contains some general information about the polyline. The structure of this record is quite similar to the INSERT record followed by ATTRIB. The second part of the polyline data structure is a series of entity records called VERTEX. VERTEX contains the coordinates and other information about each vertex or point in the polyline. Finally, the SEQEND entity appears as the last record in the polyline data structure to signal the end of that structure.

POLYLINE HEADER

```
(
(-1 . <Entity name: 600001b0>)      Entity name (record index).
(0 . "POLYLINE")                    Entity type.
(8 . "0")                           Layer name for this entity.
(66 . 1)                            Vertex follows flag. Since
                                    the polyline header record
                                    cannot exist unless at least
                                    two vertex entities follow it,
                                    this flag would seem redun-
                                    dant. It does, however, fol-
                                    low a consistent data struc-
                                    ture.

(70 . 1)                            Polyline flag. This is a bit-
                                    coded flag. If the bit is not set
                                    (0), then the polyline is open; if
                                    the bit is set (1), as in this ex-
                                    ample, the polyline is closed.
                                    When a polyline is closed, it
                                    will appear on the screen with
                                    a line connecting the last ver-
                                    tex in the polyline with the first
                                    vertex. You close a polyline
                                    by using the C option in the
                                    PLINE command. If the flag
                                    were set to 0, then the polyline
                                    would be U-shaped instead of
```

square. The following applies
to Release 9 or later: If bit 2
(**2**) is set, then the polyline has
been curve fitted and if bit 3
(**4**) has been set then the
polyline has been spline fitted.
The following bit flags are
used in Release 10 and later
to indicate whether you have
a 3D polyline or a 3D polygon
mesh: If the fourth (**8**) bit is
set, then it is a 3D polyline. If
the fifth bit (**16**) is set, then it is
a 3D polygon mesh. These bit
flags will be described in more
detail in the 3D section of this
appendix.

```
(40 . 0.0)
```

Default starting width. The
only time that Group **40** is
not **0** is either in the polyline
record or at the specific vertex record, where the starting width is changed. The
starting polyline width is assumed to be always the
same until it is changed.

```
(41 . 0.0)
```

Default ending width. The
only time that Group **41** is
not **0** is either in the polyline
record or at the specific vertex record where the ending
width is changed. The en-
ding polyline width is assumed to be always the
same until it's changed. The
ending width of the current
vertex becomes the starting
width of the next vertex.

`(71 . 0)`	Polygon mesh **M** vertex count. This is non-zero only if this polyline is a 3D polygon mesh.
`(72 . 0)`	Polygon mesh **N** vertex count. This is non-zero only if this polyline is a 3D polygon mesh.
`(73 . 0)`	Polygon mesh smooth surface **M** density. This is non-zero only if this polyline is a 3D polygon mesh.
`(74 . 0)`	Polygon mesh smooth surface **N** density. This is non-zero only if this polyline is a 3D polygon mesh.
`(75 . 0)`	Smooth surface type (see 3D section for more information).
`)`	

VERTEXES

The following four vertex records describe a 2D polyline square with the polylines having zero width:

`(`

`(-1 . name: 600001c8)`	Entity name (record index).
`(0 . "VERTEX")`	Entity type.
`(8 . "0")`	Layer name for this entity. Theoretically, you could place each vertex of a polyline on a separate layer, but this doesn't seem to have any practical use.
`(10 10.0 13.0 0.0)`	**X Y Z** coordinate for this vertex.

(40 . 0.0)

Starting polyline width. This is always **0**, unless the starting width is changed at this vertex.

(41 . 0.0)

Ending polyline width. This is always **0**, unless the ending width is changed at this vertex.

(42 . 0.0)

Polyline bulge factor. This group is always **0**, unless it is describing a polyarc.

(70 . 0)

Vertex flag. This is a bit-coded flag where only the first (**1**) and second (**2**) bits are set. If the first bit (**1**) is set, then the next vertex record was an extra, added by AutoCAD to create a smoother curve. If the second bit (**2**) is set, it means that a curve-fitted tangent has been defined, and that tangent information will appear in Group Code **50** below. The following applies to Release 9 or later: If the fourth bit (**8**) is set, then this is an extra vertex created by spline fitting. If the fifth bit (**16**) is set, then this vertex is a spline-frame control point and is not actually part of the visible polyline. 3D polyline vertex flags will be discussed in the 3D section (sixth and seventh bit).

`(50 . 0.0)`	Curve-fitted tangent direction, in radians. This is always **0**, unless "Fit Curve" has been used on this polyline and the second bit **(2)** flag in Group Code **70** above has been set.*
`)`	

We'll comment only briefly on the following vertex records unless they're different from the preceding vertex record. These records are included to show how a complete polyline data structure would look.

`(`	
`(-1 . <Entity name: 60000le0>)`	Entity name (record index).
`(`	
`(0 . VERTEX)`	Entity type.
`(8 . "0")`	Layer name for this entity.
`(10 14.0 13.0 0.0)`	**X Y Z** coordinate for this vertex.
`(40 . 0.0)`	Starting polyline width.
`(41 . 0.0)`	Ending polyline width.
`(42 . 0.0)`	Polyline bulge factor.
`(70 . 0)`	Vertex flag.
`(50 . 0.0)`	Curve-fitted tangent direction in radians.
`)`	
`(`	
`(-1 . <Entity name: 60000lf8>)`	Entity name (record index).
`(0 . "VERTEX")`	Entity type.
`(8 . "0")`	Layer name for this entity.

---

*   See Section 5.4.1.1 in the *AutoCAD Reference Manual* for more information about curve fitting.

`(10 14.0 9.0 0.0)`	**X Y Z** coordinate for this vertex.
`(40 . 0.0)`	Starting polyline width.
`(41 . 0.0)`	Ending polyline width.
`(42 . 0.0)`	Polyline bulge factor.
`(70 . 0)`	Vertex flag.
`(50 . 0.0)`	Curve-fitted tangent direction in radians.
`)`	
`(`	
`(-1 . <Entity name: 60000210>)`	Entity name (record index).
`(0 . "VERTEX")`	Entity type.
`(8 . "0")`	Layer name for this entity.
`(10 10.0 9.0 0.0)`	**X Y Z** coordinate for this vertex.
`(40 . 0.0)`	Starting polyline width.
`(41 . 0.0)`	Ending polyline width.
`(42 . 0.0)`	Polyline bulge factor.
`(70 . 0)`	Vertex flag.
`(50 . 0.0)`	Curve-fitted tangent direction in radians.
`)`	

POLYLINE SEQEND

This SEQEND record is exactly the same record found at the end of a list of ATTRIB records. It marks the end of the list of vertex records that define a polyline.

`(`	
`(-1 . <Entity name: 60000228>)`	Entity name (record index).
`(0 . "SEQEND")`	Entity type.

```
(8 . "0")
(-2 . <Entity name: 600001b0>)
```
Entity name (record index) of the polyline entity to which this SEQEND is linked.

```
)
```

WIDE POLYLINE

This next polyline record describes a closed, 2D polyline box in which the polyline has a width of .5". Note that the starting and ending widths of .5" (Groups **40** and **41**) appear only in the polyline record and not in any subsequent vertex records. The only time these fields would *not* be **0** in a polyline or a vertex record is when the starting or ending widths are changed *in that record*. Those values are kept until changed in another record. Therefore, if you wish to change the width of a polyline with an AutoLISP routine using **subst**, you would have to change Group **40** and **41** records *only* at the vertex in which you want to change the width.

```
(
(-1 . <Entity name: 60000240>)
```
Entity name (record index).

```
(0 . "POLYLINE")
```
Entity type.

```
(8 . "0")
```
Layer name for this entity.

```
(66 . 1)
```
Vertex follows flag.

```
(70 . 1)
```
Polyline flag.

```
(40 . 0.5)
```
Default starting polyline width. This is where the polyline starting width is defined.

```
(41 . 0.5)
```
Default ending polyline width. This is where the polyline ending width is defined.

```
(71 . 0)
```
Polygon mesh **M** vertex count.

```
(72 . 0)
```
Polygon mesh **N** vertex count.

`(73 . 0)`	Polygon mesh smooth surface **M** density.
`(74 . 0)`	Polygon mesh smooth surface **N** density.
`(75 . 0)`	Smooth surface type.
`)`	
`(`	
`(-1 . <Entity name: 60000258>)`	Entity name (record index).
`(0 . "VERTEX")`	Entity type.
`(8 . "0")`	Layer name for this entity.
`(10 11.0 10.0 0.0)`	**X Y Z** coordinate for this vertex.
`(40 . 0.)`	Starting polyline width. This field returns to **0**, even though the starting width remains at **.5**.
`(41 . 0.0)`	Ending polyline width. This field returns to **0**, even though the ending width remains at **.5**.
`(42 . 0.0)`	Polyline bulge factor.
`(70 . 0)`	Vertex flag.
`(50 . 0.0)`	Curve-fitted tangent direction in radians.
`)`	
`(`	
`(-1 . <Entity name: 60000270>)`	Entity name (record index).
`(0 . "VERTEX")`	Entity type.
`(8 . "0")`	Layer name for this entity.
`(10 11.0 12.0 0.0)`	**X Y Z** coordinate for this vertex.
`(40 . 0.0)`	Starting polyline width.

`(41 . 0.0)`	Ending polyline width.
`(42 . 0.0)`	Polyline bulge factor.
`(70 . 0)`	Vertex flag.
`(50 . 0.0)`	Curve-fitted tangent direction in radians.
`)`	
`(`	
`(-1 . <Entity name: 60000288>)`	Entity name (record index).
`(0 . "VERTEX")`	Entity type.
`(8 . "0")`	Layer name for this entity.
`(10 13.0 12.0 0.0)`	**X Y Z** coordinate for this vertex.
`(40 . 0.0)`	Starting polyline width.
`(41 . 0.0)`	Ending polyline width.
`(42 . 0.0)`	Polyline bulge factor.
`(70 . 0)`	Vertex flag.
`(50 . 0.0)`	Curve-fitted tangent direction in radians.
`)`	
`(`	
`(-1 . <Entity name: 600002a0>)`	Entity name (record index).
`(0 . "VERTEX")`	Entity type.
`(8 . "0")`	Layer name for this entity.
`(10 13.0 10.0 0.0)`	**X Y Z** coordinate for this vertex.
`(40 . 0.0)`	Starting polyline width.
`(41 . 0.0)`	Ending polyline width.
`(42 . 0.0)`	Polyline bulge factor.
`(70 . 0)`	Vertex flag.

`(50 . 0.0)`	Curve-fitted tangent direction in radians.
`)`	
`(`	
`(-1 . <Entity name: 600002b8>)`	Entity name (record index).
`(0 . "SEQEND")`	Entity type.
`(8 . "0")`	Layer name for this entity.
`(-2 . <Entity name: 60000240>)`	Entity name (record index) of the polyline entity to which SEQEND is linked.
`)`	

SIMPLE 2D POLYLINE WITH A POLYARC

This polyline structure is one straight line followed by a semicircle (180-degree half circle, the largest arc that can be created with a single polyarc). The only difference between the first vertex record and the second (other then the coordinates) is that the second vertex contains a **polyline bulge factor** of **1.** The bulge factor is 1/4 of the tangent of the included angle of the arc. If the bulge factor is **0**, then the polyline segment that extends from that vertex will be straight. If the bulge factor is **1**, as in this case, then the polyline segment will appear as a semicircle. Later on, in the Tapered Polyarc section, we will explain how to derive the arc information from the bulge factor.

`(`	
`(-1 . <Entity name: 600002d0>)`	Entity name (record index).
`(0 . "POLYLINE")`	Entity type.
`(8 . "0")`	
`(66 . 1)`	Vertex follows flag.
`(70 . 0)`	Polyline flag.
`(40 . 0.0)`	Default starting polyline width.

`(41 . 0.0)`	Default ending polyline width.
`(71 . 0)`	Polygon mesh **M** vertex count.
`(72 . 0)`	Polygon mesh **N** vertex count.
`(73 . 0)`	Polygon mesh smooth surface **M** density.
`(74 . 0)`	Polygon mesh smooth surface **N** density.
`(75 . 0)`	Smooth surface type.
`)`	
`(`	
`(-1 . <Entity name: 600002e8>)`	Entity name (record index).
`(0 . "VERTEX")`	Entity type.
`(8 . "0")`	Layer name for this entity.
`(10 17.0 9.0 0.0)`	**X Y Z** coordinate for this vertex.
`(40 . 0.0)`	Starting polyline width.
`(41 . 0.0)`	Ending polyline width.
`(42 . 0.0)`	Polyline bulge factor.
`(70 . 0)`	Vertex flag.
`(50 . 0.0)`	Curve-fitted tangent direction in radians.
`)`	
`(`	
`(-1 . <Entity name: 60000300>)`	Entity name (record index).
`(0 . "VERTEX")`	Entity type.
`(8 . "0")`	Layer name for this entity.
`(10 17.0 11.0 0.0)`	**X Y Z** coordinate for this vertex.

`(40 . 0.0)`	Starting polyline width.
`(41 . 0.0)`	Ending polyline width.
`(42 . 1.0)`	Polyline bulge factor. A bulge factor of **1** means that this polyline segment will be a semicircle.
`(70 . 0)`	Vertex flag.
`(50 . 0.0)`	Curve-fitted tangent direction in radians.
`)`	
`(`	
`(-1 . <Entity name: 60000318>)`	Entity name (record index).
`(0 . "VERTEX")`	Entity type.
`(8 . "0")`	Layer name for this entity.
`(10 15.0 11.0 0.0)`	**X Y Z** coordinate for this vertex.
`(40 . 0.0)`	Starting polyline width.
`(41 . 0.0)`	Ending polyline width.
`(42 . 1.0)`	Polyline bulge factor. The bulge factor if the preceding polyarc were continued back to the starting point of the polyarc (a full circle).
`(70 . 0)`	Vertex flag.
`(50 . 0.0)`	Curve-fitted tangent direction, in radians.
`)`	
`(`	
`(-1 . <Entity name: 60000330>)`	Entity name (record index).
`(0 . "SEQEND")`	Entity type.
`(8 . "0")`	Layer name for this entity.

```
(-2 . <Entity name: 600002d0>)
```
Entity name (record index) of the polyline entity to which SEQEND is linked.

```
)
```

TAPERED POLYARCS

This entry describes two different types of polyline structures: tapered polylines and polyarcs. Figure 6, later in this chapter, is a detailed illustration of this polyline structure. The first thing to notice is that, although the illustration shows only two arcs and three vertexes, there are actually four vertex sub-records in this polyline record — the coordinates for the first two vertex records are identical. That's because there are actually three polyarcs, the first of which was forced to have the same starting and ending point.* At the end of this record listing, we'll explain how to extract the arc description information from the bulge factor.

```
(
(-1 . <Entity name: 60000348>)
```
Entity name (record index).

```
(0 . "POLYLINE")
```
Entity type.

```
(8 . "0")
```
Layer name for this entity.

```
(66 . 1)
```
Vertex follows flag.

```
(70 . 0)
```
Polyline flag.

```
(40 . 0.0)
```
Default starting polyline width.

```
(41 . 0.0)
```
Default ending polyline width.

```
(71 . 0)
```
Polygon mesh **M** vertex count.

```
(72 . 0)
```
Polygon mesh **N** vertex count.

```
(73 . 0)
```
Polygon mesh smooth surface **M** density.

---

*   You have to use this technique if you're starting a polyline with a polyarc of less than 180 degrees.

`(74 . 0)`	Polygon mesh smooth surface **N** density.
`(75 . 0)`	Smooth surface type.
`)`	
`(`	
`(-1 . <Entity name: 60000360>)`	Entity name (record index).
`(0 . "VERTEX")`	Entity type.
`(8 . "0")`	Layer name for this entity.
`(10 8.0 8.0 0.0)`	**X Y Z** coordinate for this vertex.
`(40 . 0.0)`	Starting polyline width.
`(41 . 0.0)`	Ending polyline width.
`(42 . 1.0)`	Polyline bulge factor. This is the first polyarc forced to the same starting and ending point — in this circumstance, the bulge factor is always **1**.
`(70 . 0)`	Vertex flag.
`(50 . 0.0)`	Curve-fitted tangent direction, in radians.
`)`	
`(`	
`(-1 . <Entity name: 60000378>)`	Entity name (record index).
`(0 . "VERTEX")`	Entity type.
`(8 . "0")`	Layer name for this entity.
`(10 8.0 8. 0.00)`	**X Y Z** coordinate for this vertex.
`(40 . 0.0)`	Starting polyline width.
`(41 . 0.25)`	Ending polyline width. The first visible polyarc of this structure starts at **0** width, and ends with a width of **.25**.

`(42 . 0.72075)`	Polyline bulge factor. How to calculate this bulge factor is explained at the end of this polyline listing.
`(70 . 0)`	Vertex flag.
`(50 . 0.0)`	Curve-fitted tangent direction, in radians.
`)`	
`(`	
`(-1 . <Entity name: 60000390>)`	Entity name (record index).
`(0 . "VERTEX")`	Entity type.
`(8 . "0")`	Layer name for this entity.
`(10 5.0 9.0 0.0)`	**X Y Z** coordinate for this vertex.
`(40 . 0.25)`	Starting polyline width. This is the same width as the ending polyline width of the previous vertex, but because it's different than the *starting width* of the previous vertex, then the starting width has changed; this must show up here.*
`(41 . 0.5)`	Ending polyline width.
`(42 . -0.94598)`	Polyline bulge factor. If the bulge factor is a negative number, it means the polyarc was generated clockwise from its starting point.
`(70 . 0)`	Vertex flag.
`(50 . 0.0)`	Curve-fitted tangent direction, in radians.

---

*   The starting and ending width fields always remain at 0 unless there's a change in width from the previous vertex record

```
)
(
(-1 . <Entity name: 600003a8>)
```
Entity name (record index).

```
(0 . "VERTEX")
```
Entity type.

```
(8 . "0")
```
Layer name for this entity.

```
(10 2.0 11.0 0.0)
```
X Y Z coordinate for this vertex.

```
(40 . 0.5)
```
Starting polyline width. This width is, of course, different than the starting width of the last vertex — the starting width of the *next* polyline segment (if there were one).

```
(41 . 0.5)
```
Ending polyline width.

```
(42 . -0.57142)
```
Polyline bulge factor. This is the bulge factor of a proposed polyarc of the same radius as the last polyarc and if it were continued until it intersected with the right angle of a right triangle constructed so that the hypotenuse was congruent with the chord of the last polyarc (see Figure 6).

```
(70 . 0)
```
Vertex flag.

```
(50 . 0.0)
```
Curve-fitted tangent direction in radians.

```
)
(
(-1 . <Entity name: 600003c0>)
```
Entity name (record index).

```
(0 . "SEQEND")
```
Entity type.

```
(8 . "0")
```
Layer name for this entity.

```
(-2 . <Entity name: 60000348>)
```
Entity name (record index) of the polyline entity to which SEQEND is linked.

```
)
```

BULGE FACTOR CALCULATIONS

A polyarc isn't constructed from a center point reference like ARCS and CIRCLES. A polyarc is described as having a start point (the current vertex), an end point (the next vertex), and a bulge factor. Sometimes it's important to derive the center point and radius for a polyarc—here is how to do it using the first polyarc in Figure 6 as an example.

First, find the included angle from the bulge factor. The bulge factor is 1/4 the tangent of the included angle of the arc, so you can apply this AutoLISP form to the second vertex in the preceding listing:

```
(setq incang (* 4 (atan 0.72075)))
```

This returns the included angle of 2.498091 radians.

Now, find the length of the chord from the current vertex to the next vertex with this AutoLISP form:

```
(setq chord (distance (list 8 8) (list 5 9)))
```

The chord length is 3.162278.

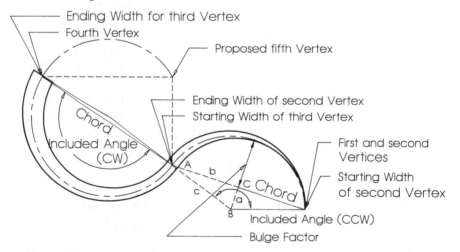

Figure 6: The bulge factor.

Next, find the radius of the polyarc by using a little trigonometry. Look at Figure 6. Using half the included angle and half of the chord length, you can find the length of hypotenuse **c** in the right triangle **A B C**–this is the radius of the polyarc. But before you can do that, you have to find angle **A** with this AutoLISP form:

```
(setq anga (- (/ pi 2) (/ incang 2)))
```

Find the radius with this form:

```
(setq rad (/ (/ chord 2) (cos anga)))
```

The radius for this polyarc is 1.666667.

To find the center point, first find the angle of the chord of the polyarc from the current vertex to the next vertex with this form:

```
(setq chordang (angle (list 8 8) (list 5 9)))
```

Then add angle **A** to **chordang** if the bulge factor is positive, or subtract angle **A** from **chordang** if the bulge factor is negative. The answer is easy, in this case: 0 radians.

Finally, use the **polar** function to find the center point:

```
(setq center (polar <coordinate of current vertex>
<angle from start to center> rad))
```

From this information, it's simple to derive the starting and ending angles for this polyarc.

POLYGONS

Polygons are not separate entity types, but are simply closed 2D polylines generated by AutoCAD according to your specifications when you use the POLYGON command. There's no obvious way to set a polyline width when creating a polygon, but you can always give the polygon a line width with the PEDIT command. Below is the association list data record for a hexagon, generated with the POLYGON command:

```
(
(-1 . <Entity name: 600003d8>)      Entity name (record index).
(0 . "POLYLINE")                    Entity type.
(8 . "0")                           Layer name for this entity.
(66 . 1)                            Vertex follows flag.
```

`(70 . 1)`	Vertex flag.
`(40 . 0.0)`	Default starting polyline width.
`(41 . 0.0)`	Default ending polyline width.
`(71 . 0)`	Polygon mesh **M** vertex count.
`(72 . 0)`	Polygon mesh **N** vertex count.
`(73 . 0)`	Polygon mesh smooth surface **M** density.
`(74 . 0)`	Polygon mesh smooth surface **N** density.
`(75 . 0)`	Smooth surface type.
`)`	
`(`	
`(-1 . <Entity name: 600003f0>)`	Entity name (record index).
`(0 . "VERTEX")`	Entity type.
`(8 . "0")`	Layer name for this entity.
`(10 8.0 11.0 0.0)`	**X Y Z** coordinate for this vertex.
`(40 . 0.0)`	Starting polyline width.
`(41 . 0.0)`	Ending polyline width.
`(42 . 0.0)`	Polyline bulge factor.
`(70 . 0)`	Vertex flag.
`(50 . 0.0)`	Curve-fitted tangent direction, in radians.
`)`	
`(`	
`(-1 . <Entity name: 60000408>)`	Entity name (record index).
`(0 . "VERTEX")`	Entity type.

`(8 . "0")`	Layer name for this entity.
`(10 8.86603 11.5 0.0)`	**X Y Z** coordinate for this vertex.
`(40 . 0.0)`	Starting polyline width.
`(41 . 0.0)`	Ending polyline width.
`(42 . 0.0)`	Polyline bulge factor.
`(70 . 0)`	Vertex flag.
`(50 . 0.0)`	Curve-fitted tangent direction, in radians.
`)`	
`(`	
`(-1 . <Entity name: 60000420>)`	Entity name (record index).
`(0 . "VERTEX")`	Entity type.
`(8 . "0")`	Layer name for this entity.
`(10 8.86603 12.5 0.0)`	**X Y Z** coordinate for this vertex.
`(40 . 0.0)`	Starting polyline width.
`(41 . 0.0)`	Ending polyline width.
`(42 . 0.0)`	Polyline bulge factor.
`(70 . 0)`	Vertex flag.
`(50 . 0.0)`	Curve-fitted tangent direction, in radians.
`)`	
`(`	
`(-1 . <Entity name: 60000438>)`	Entity name (record index).
`(0 . "VERTEX")`	Entity type.
`(8 . "0")`	Layer name for this entity.
`(10 8.0 13.0 0.0)`	**X Y Z** coordinate for this vertex.
`(40 . 0.0)`	Starting polyline width.

```
(41 . 0.0)                              Ending polyline width.
(42 . 0.0)                              Polyline bulge factor.
(70 . 0)                                Vertex flag.
(50 . 0.0)                              Curve-fitted tangent direc-
                                        tion, in radians.
)
(
(-1 . <Entity name: 60000450>)          Entity name (record index).
(0 . "VERTEX")                          Entity type.
(8 . "0")                               Layer name for this entity.
(10 7.13397 12.5 0.0)                   X Y Z coordinate for this ver-
                                        tex.
(40 . 0.0)                              Starting polyline width.
(41 . 0.0)                              Ending polyline width.
(42 . 0.0)                              Polyline bulge factor.
(70 . 0)                                Vertex flag.
(50 . 0.0)                              Curve-fitted tangent direc-
                                        tion, in radians.
)
(
(-1 . <Entity name: 60000468>)          Entity name (record index).
(0 . "VERTEX")                          Entity type.
(8 . "0")                               Layer name for this entity.
(10 7.13397 11.5 0.0)                   X Y Z coordinate for this ver-
                                        tex.
(40 . 0.0)                              Starting polyline width.
(41 . 0.0)                              Ending polyline width.
(42 . 0.0)                              Polyline bulge factor.
(70 . 0)                                Vertex flag.
```

`(50 . 0.0)`	Curve-fitted tangent direction, in radians.
`)`	
`(`	
`(-1 . <Entity name: 60000480>)`	Entity name (record index).
`(0 . "SEQEND")`	Entity type.
`(8 . "0")`	Layer name for this entity.
`(-2 . <Entity name: 600003d8>)`	Entity name (record index) of the polyline entity to which SEQEND is linked.
`)`	

TRACE

A trace looks something like a 2D polyline on the screen. But if you examine the data structure, you'll find it similar to a solid. Generally, traces have been superseded by polylines.

`(`	
`(-1 . <Entity name: 60000498>)`	Entity name (record index).
`(0 . "TRACE")`	Entity type.
`(8 . "0")`	Layer name for this entity.
`(10 15.0 2.1 0.0)`	X Y Z coordinate of the first corner of the starting side.
`(11 15.0 1.9 0.0)`	X Y Z coordinate of the second corner of the starting side.
`(12 16.9 2.1 0.0)`	X Y Z coordinate of the first corner of the ending side. This is a mitered corner, and it shares the same coordinate as the first corner of the starting side in the next trace.

`(13 17.1 1.9 0.0)`	**X Y Z** coordinate of the second corner of the ending side. This is a mitered corner, and it shares the same coordinate as the second corner of the starting side in the next trace.
`)`	
`(`	
`(-1 . <Entity name: 600004b0>)`	Entity name (record index).
`(0 . "TRACE")`	Entity type.
`(8 . "0")`	Layer name for this entity.
`(10 16.9 2.1 0.0)`	**X Y Z** coordinate of the first corner of the starting side. This is a mitered corner, and it shares the same coordinate as the first corner of the ending side in the previous trace.
`(11 17.1 1.9 0.0)`	**X Y Z** coordinate of the second corner of the starting side. This is a mitered corner, and it shares the same coordinate as the second corner of the ending side in the previous trace.
`(12 16.9 4.0 0.0)`	**X Y Z** coordinate of the first corner of the ending side.
`(13 17.1 4.0 0.0)`	**X Y Z** coordinate of the second corner of the ending side.
`)`	

ASSOCIATIVE DIMENSION BLOCK ENTITY

Ordinarily, when you dimension a drawing with the DIM commands, the various parts of the dimension structure, such as extension lines, dimension lines and text are made up of LINE and TEXT entities and aren't inherently distinguishable as dimensions in the drawing database.*

The ASSOCIATIVE DIMENSION entity represents a unique type of entity. On the one hand, it is like a BLOCK entity in that its actual data description is in the blocks section and the whole dimension structure of text, extension lines, dimension lines and arrowheads is treated as a single entity in the drawing. On the other hand, when you operate on this entity with the STRETCH, SCALE or ROTATE commands, AutoCAD will update the dimension text to reflect its new size or orientation. Every time you add a dimension, AutoCAD creates an unique block definition for that dimension in the blocks section, and then references that block with a DIMENSION record in the entities section.** We think it would be wise to use ASSOCIATIVE DIMENSION sparingly, because it seems to take up almost twice the space in the drawing database as an ordinary dimension does. This tends to create larger drawing files than necessary.

The ASSOCIATIVE DIMENSION entity will be created any time you add a dimension to a drawing when the system variable, **DIMASO**, is set to ON. When an ASSOCIATIVE DIMENSION entity is created, a number of special points are inserted into your drawing at strategic locations. Those points are called defining points, and their coordinates are found in Group Codes **10** through **16**.

Defining points are always inserted on a special layer AutoCAD creates, called DEFPOINTS. For example, if you were to dimension a line, then DEFPOINTS would be placed at the beginning and end of the line, at the end point of the dimension line and at the center of the dimension text. If you later lengthened this line with the STRETCH command, the DEFPOINT for

---

*   The only unique entity that shows up in this type of dimension is the arrowhead, which, strictly speaking, is an "anonymous" block.

**   If you delete a DIMENSION entity in your drawing, the block reference for that entity will remain in the blocks section.

the endpoint of the line would have a new coordinate location and AutoCAD would recalculate the dimension* and display that new dimension as the dimension text.

Below is a database listing for a simple horizontal dimension.**

```
(
(-1 . <Entity name: 600004c8>)      Entity name (record index).
(0 . "DIMENSION")                    Entity type.
(8 . "0")                            Layer name for this entity.
(2 . "*D3")                          Block name. The asterisk at
                                     the beginning of the block
                                     name indicates that it's an
                                     "anonymous" block created
                                     by AutoCAD. D indicates
                                     that this is an ASSOCIATIVE
                                     DIMENSION block and 3 is
                                     the unique block number for
                                     this particular dimension en-
                                     tity.
(10 -6.66384 6.20647 0.0)            The dimension line defining
                                     point. This point is the ac-
                                     tual end point of the dimen-
                                     sion line. The distance be-
                                     tween this DEFPOINT and
                                     the Group Code 13 DEF-
                                     POINT below determines the
                                     distance between the dimen-
                                     sioned object and the
                                     dimension line (and also the
                                     length of the extension line).
(11 -7.41384 6.20648 0.0)            Middle-of-text defining point,
                                     usually midway along the
                                     dimension line. This point is
                                     recalculated to remain at the
```

---

*   And possibly the dimension text location, to keep the dimension text centered.
**   Also see the block definition listing for this entity in Appendix B.

	midpoint of the dimension line if any other DEFPOINTS are moved.
`(12 0.0 0.0 0.0)`	Insertion points for CLONES of a dimension. This would be the insertion point (Group Code **10**) of the *next* AS-SOCIATIVE DIMENSION entity if you use the BASELINE or CONTINUE options to do a string of dimensions in one direction.
`(70 . 0)`	Dimension type flag. This is a bit-coded flag with the first (**1**), second (**2**) and third (**4**) bits capable of being set. If no bits are set (**0**) then this dimension is a horizontal, vertical or rotated dimension. Other flag codes: **1**=aligned, **2**=angular, **3**=diameter and **4**=radius.
`(1 . "")`	Explicit dimension text string. When you create a dimension, you're prompted for the dimension text. You can press **<RETURN>** to accept the actual measured dimension, or you can type in your own text. If you type in your own text for the dimension, then that text will show up here, and it will not be updated if you stretch the dimension later. The null string (two quotation marks) in this case means the dimension text will be up-dated. The actual dimension is calculated from the dis-

	tance between the coordinates in Group Codes **13** and **14**.
(13 -8.16384 5.93543 0.0)	Extension DEFINING POINT for the starting point of the Dimension entity. This point also corresponds to the starting point of the line being dimensioned in this example.
(14 -6.66384 5.93543 0.0)	Extension DEFINING POINT for the ending point of the Dimension entity. This point also corresponds to the ending point of the line being dimensioned in this example.
(15 0.0 0.0 0.0)	Extension DEFINING POINT for diameter, radius and angular dimensions. If this dimension isn't a diameter, radius or angular dimension, then these coordinates will be **0,0,0**.
(16 0.0 0.0 0.0)	Extension DEFINING POINT for the dimension arc in angular dimensions. This would be analogous to Group Code **10** for other dimension types. If this dimension isn't an angular dimension, then these coordinates will be **0,0,0**.
(40 . 0.0)	Leader length for radius and diameter dimensions.
(50 . 0.0)	Angle of rotation for linear dimensions, specifically: HORIZONTAL, VERTICAL or ROTATED dimensions.
)	

3D ENTITIES

This section will explore the association list data structure of 3D entities. There are five types of 3D entities: LINE, POINT, 3DFACE, 3D POLYLINE and 3D POLYGON MESH. 3D polyline and 3D polygon mesh are actually variations of the standard polyline structure and they differ from 2D polylines only by the way the Group **70** polyline flags are set.

We have extracted the 3D entity data from Figure 7 to use as examples of the data record listing.

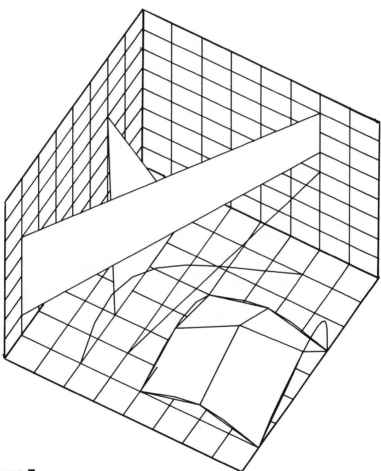

Figure 7

LINE

This is a listing for a LINE entity that was drawn in 3D space. The only major difference between this listing and the LINE listing in the 2D section is that the **Z** coordinate of the end point is not **0**.

One other interesting thing about the line is that you can extrude it into the **Z** axis—even if it's drawn in 3D space. If you extrude the line, it will be extruded into the **Z** axis of the current UCS plane and the end points will be perpendicular to the current **Z** axis. If the line has been extruded into a UCS that's different from the WCS, then the entity record will contain a Group **210** field.

```
(
(-1 . <Entity  name: 60000450>)    Entity name (record index).
(0 . "LINE")                       Entity type.
(8 . "0")                          Layer name for this entity.
(10 2.0 5.0 0.0)                   Starting X Y Z coordinates.
(11 8.0 2.0 4.0)                   Ending X Y Z coordinates.
)
```

3DFACE

The 3DFACE entity is similar in structure to a SOLID entity. Unlike the SOLID entity, however, 3DFACE is constructed by picking the corners in a circular fashion, rather than by describing two points for the base and either one or two points for the top of the surface. 3DFACE always has three coordinates given for each corner and can have either three or four vertexes or corners. When you use the HIDE command, 3DFACE will appear opaque when the view has its hidden lines removed.

3DFACEs don't make up a true 3D solid. You are actually describing a 3D figure by assembling a bunch of 2D surfaces* together in a 3D environment. If you were to reproduce the tetrahedron (a completely closed solid) in the "real world," you would cut four triangles out of a piece of paper (2D) and glue or tape them together to form the tetrahedron (3D).

In order to have a proper 3D surface,** each adjacent pair of corners must have one coordinate (either **X, Y** or **Z**) in common.***

To create a 3D solid from 3DFACEs, the appropriate edges of adjacent 3DFACEs must be *congruent*.****

One new feature has been added to 3DFACES in Release 10 — the ability to specify one or more edges of a 3DFACE to be invisible. This is a particularly useful feature for using 3DFACES to construct an irregularly shaped seamless surface.

This first 3DFACE is triangular, so the first corner and the fourth corner are the same.

(	
(-1 . <Entity name: 60000468>)	Entity name (record index).
(0 . "3DFACE")	Entity type.
(8 . "0")	Layer name for this entity.
(10 3.0 6.0 0.0)	**X Y Z** coordinates of the starting corner.
(11 7.0 6.0 0.0)	**X Y Z** coordinates of the second corner.
(12 6.0 8.0 5.0)	**X Y Z** coordinates of the third corner.
(13 3.0 6.0 0.0)	**X Y Z** coordinates of the last corner. Since this face is triangular, then these coordinates will be the same as the first corner.

---

*   In computer graphics, these 2D surfaces are called patches.
**   ie., a flat surface.
*** In other words, each edge of a 3D surface must lie on the same plane.
**** What constitutes an appropriate edge will vary, depending on the solid.

```
(70 . 0)
```
Invisible edge, bit-coded flag. If bit one (1) is set, then the first edge will be invisible. If bit two (2) is set, then the second edge will be invisible. Bit three (4) and bit four (8) control the visibility of the third and fourth edges, respectively. All four bits can be set to make all of the edges of a 3DFACE invisible.

```
)
```

This is a four-sided 3DFACE.

```
(
(-1 . <Entity name: 60000480>)    Entity name (record index).
(0 . "3DFACE")                    Entity type.
(8 . "0")                         Layer name for this entity.
(10 1.0 8.0 1.0)                  X Y Z coordinates of the first corner.
(11 1.0 8.0 5.0)                  X Y Z coordinates of the second corner.
(12 8.0 2.0 7.0)                  X Y Z coordinates of the third corner.
(13 8.0 2.0 5.0)                  X Y Z coordinates of the last corner.
(70 . 0)                          Invisible edge bit-coded flag.
)
```

3D POINT

A point is defined by its **X Y Z** coordinates in 3D space. A point can also be extruded into the **Z** axis from the current UCS plane.

```
(
(-1 . <Entity name: 60000498>)    Entity name (record index).
```

`(0 . "POINT")`	Entity type.
`(8 . "0")`	Layer name for this entity.
`(10 5.0 3.0 7.0)`	**X Y Z** coordinates of the point.
`(50 . 0.0)`	The angle of the **X** axis of the UCS, relative to the WCS, that was current when this point was created. This information is used by Point Display Mode (PDMODE) to know how to display the alternate point graphic symbols (see Section 4.2 of the *AutoCAD Reference Manual* for information about PDMODE.).
`)`	

3D POLYLINE

This next data listing describes a 3D polyline that was created by constructing four vertices in space and then SMOOTHING it with PEDIT into a 3D spline curve. This 3D polyline is shown in Figure 7.

The problem with spline fitting a polyline with PEDIT is that it adds many more vertices to the figure, which makes it extremely confusing to work with through AutoLISP. The best way to deal with curve-fitted polylines (of any type) is to modify only vertexes that don't have the first and eighth bits set in the Group **70** Vertex Flags field, and then to use PEDIT on the modified polyline to regenerate the curve.

For example, in the following polyline listing there are 13 vertices, but only four of them (the first and the last three vertexes) actually control the shape of the curve—they are called the *control points.* The other nine vertices are added to the polyline by AutoCAD to smooth the curve.

`(`	
`(-1 . <Entity name: 60002310>)`	Entity name (record index).
`(0 . "POLYLINE")`	Entity type.
`(8 . "0")`	Layer name for this entity.

(66 . 1)	Vertex follows flag.
(10 0.0 0.0 0.0)	
(40 . 0.0)	Default starting width. Since this is a 3D polyline that can't have a width at this time, this field isn't used.
(41 . 0.0)	Default ending width. Since this is a 3D polyline, this field isn't used.
(70 . 12)	Polyline flag. This is a bit-coded flag. If the bit is not set (0) then this is an open polyline; if the bit is set (1), it's a closed polyline. If bit 2 (2) is set, then this polyline has been curve-fitted and if bit 3 (4) has been set, then this polyline has been spline-fitted. If the fourth (8) bit is set, then this is a 3D polyline. If the fifth bit (16) is set, then this is a 3D polygon mesh. The sixth bit (32) is set only to indicate that this structure is a polygon mesh and it is closed in the **N** direction. Since the value of this group is **12**, it means that the third bit and fourth bits have been set (4 + 8 = 12); that tells us that this is a 3D polyline that has been spline-fitted.
(71 . 0)	Polygon mesh **M** vertex count.
(72 . 0)	Polygon mesh **N** vertex count.

`(73 . 0)`	Polygon mesh smooth-surface **M** density.
`(74 . 0)`	Polygon mesh smooth-surface **N** density.
`(75 . 6)`	Smooth curve type flag. This is *not* a bit-coded flag. Since this is a 3D polyline and not a 3D polygon mesh, this field indicates the type of curve fitting applied; the type depends on the value set in the system variable SPLINESEGS, specifiying either a quadratic B-spline (**5**) or a cubic B-spline curve (**6**). Don't confuse the SPLINESEGS variable with the SURFTYPE variable, which controls the surface fitting of 3D meshes—they're independent of one another. A **0** value means that this polyline has not been curve fitted. A **5** means that this is a quadratic B-spline curve. A **6** defines the polyline as a cubic B-spline curve.These are the only valid values for a polyline that's not a polygon mesh.

`)`

This first vertex is the starting point for this polyline, and it's also used as a control point. This is one of only four vertexes (out of 13) that was used to define this 3D polyline before it was curve fitted. Usually the only spline frame control points that actually lie on the fitted curve are the first and last vertexes of a polyline.

`(`

`(-1 . <Entity name: 60002328>)`	Entity name (record index).
`(0 . "VERTEX")`	Entity type.

`(8 . "0")`	Layer name for this entity.
`(10 1.0 6.0 0.0)`	**X Y Z** coordinates for this vertex.
`(40 . 0.0)`	Polyline starting width.
`(41 . 0.0)`	Polyline ending width.
`(42 . 0.0)`	Polyline bulge factor. Since this is a 3D polyline and there are no 3D polyarcs at present, this field isn't used.
`(70 . 48)`	Vertex flag. This is a bit-coded flag. If the first bit (**1**) is set, then the next vertex record was added by AutoCAD as an extra vertex to create a smoother curve. If the second bit (**2**) is set, a curve-fitted tangent has been defined, and that tangent information will appear in Group Code **50** below. If the fourth bit (**8**) is set, then this is an extra vertex created by spline fitting. If the fifth bit (**16**) is set, then this vertex is a spline frame control point and is not actually part of the visible polyline. If the sixth bit is set (**32**), then this is a 3D polyline vertex. The seventh bit (**64**) indicates a 3D polygon mesh vertex. Since the value of this flag is 48 (16+32=48), then this vertex is a spline frame control point of a 3D polyline.

```
(50 . 0.0)
```
Curve-fitted tangent direction, in radians. This is always **0**, unless "Fit Curve" has been used on this polyline; the system variable SPLINESEGS has been set to **5** (quadratic B-spline); and the second bit (**2**) flag in Group Code **70** above has been set.*

```
)
```

The next nine vertex records were generated internally by AutoCAD with the spline curve option of the PEDIT command to generate a smooth curve based on the location of the original four vertexes (that are now control points). If you want to modify the shape of this curve, move the control point vertexes only and then use PEDIT to resmooth the curve.

```
(
(-1 . <Entity name: 600023d0>)
```
Entity name (record index).

```
(0 . "VERTEX")
```
Entity type.

```
(8 . "0")
```
Layer name for this entity.

```
(10 1.0 6.0 0.0)
```
X Y Z coordinates for this vertex.

```
(40 . 0.0)
```
Polyline starting width.

```
(41 . 0.0)
```
Polyline ending width.

```
(42 . 0.0)
```
Polyline bulge factor.

```
(70 . 40)
```
Vertex flag. This is a bit-coded flag. Since the value of this flag is 40 ($32 + 8 = 40$), this is a spline vertex created by spline fitting (**8**) and this is also a 3D polyline vertex (**32**).

---

*   See Section 5.4.1.1 in the *AutoCAD Reference Manual* for more information about curve fitting.

```
(50 . 0.0)                           Curve-fitted tangent direc-
                                     tion, in radians.

)
```

The next eight vertex records are identical in function to the previous vertex record, so they will be commented on only briefly.

```
(

(-1 . <Entity name: 600023e8>)       Entity name (record index).

(0 . "VERTEX")                       Entity type.

(8 . "0")                            Layer name for this entity.

(10 1.66797 5.91016 1.3125)          X Y Z coordinates.

(40 . 0.0)                           Polyline starting width.

(41 . 0.0)                           Polyline ending width.

(42 . 0.0)                           Polyline bulge factor.

(70 . 40)                            Vertex flag.

(50 . 0.0)                           Curve-fitted tangent direction.

)

(

(-1 . <Entity name: 60002400>)       Entity name (record index).

(0 . "VERTEX")                       Entity type.

(8 . "0")                            Layer name for this entity.

(10 2.21875 5.65625 2.25)            X Y Z coordinates.

(40 . 0.0)                           Polyline starting width.

(41 . 0.0)                           Polyline ending width.

(42 . 0.0)                           Polyline bulge factor.

(70 . 40)                            Vertex flag.

(50 . 0.0)                           Curve-fitted tangent direction.

)

(

(-1 . <Entity name: 60002418>)       Entity name (record index).
```

```
(0 . "VERTEX")                              Entity type.
(8 . "0")                                   Layer name for this entity.
(10 2.72266 5.26172 2.8125)                 X Y Z coordinates.
(40 . 0.0)                                  Polyline starting width.
(41 . 0.0)                                  Polyline ending width.
(42 . 0.0)                                  Polyline bulge factor.
(70 . 40)                                   Vertex flag.
(50 . 0.0)                                  Curve-fitted tangent direction.
)
(
(-1 . <Entity name: 60002430>)             Entity name (record index).
(0 . "VERTEX")                              Entity type.
(8 . "0")                                   Layer name for this entity.
(10 3.25 4.75 3.0)                          X Y Z coordinates.
(40 . 0.0)                                  Polyline starting width.
(41 . 0.0)                                  Polyline ending width.
(42 . 0.0)                                  Polyline bulge factor.
(70 . 40)                                   Vertex flag.
(50 . 0.0)                                  Curve-fitted tangent direction.
)
(
(-1 . <Entity name: 60002448>)             Entity name (record index).
(0 . "VERTEX")                              Entity type.
(8 . "0")                                   Layer name for this entity.
(10 3.87109 4.14453 2.8125)                 X Y Z coordinates.
(40 . 0.0)                                  Polyline starting width.
(41 . 0.0)                                  Polyline ending width.
(42 . 0.0)                                  Polyline bulge factor.
```

```
(70 . 40)                               Vertex flag.
(50 . 0.0)                              Curve-fitted tangent direction.
)
(
(-1 . <Entity name: 60002460>)         Entity name (record index).
(0 . "VERTEX")                         Entity type.
(8 . "0")                              Layer name for this entity.
(10 4.65625 3.46875 2.25)              X Y Z coordinates.
(40 . 0.0)                             Polyline starting width.
(41 . 0.0)                             Polyline ending width.
(42 . 0.0)                             Polyline bulge factor.
(70 . 40)                              Vertex flag.
(50 . 0.0)                             Curve-fitted tangent direction.
)
(
(-1 . <Entity name: 60002478>)         Entity name (record index).
(0 . "VERTEX")                         Entity type.
(8 . "0")                              Layer name for this entity.
(10 5.67578 2.74609 1.3125)            X Y Z coordinates.
(40 . 0.0)                             Polyline starting width.
(41 . 0.0)                             Polyline ending width.
(42 . 0.0)                             Polyline bulge factor.
(70 . 40)                              Vertex flag.
(50 . 0.0)                             Curve-fitted tangent direction.
)
(
(-1 . <Entity name: 60002490>)         Entity name (record index).
```

`(0 . "VERTEX")`	Entity type.
`(8 . "0")`	Layer name for this entity.
`(10 7.0 2.0 0.0)`	**X Y Z** coordinates.
`(40 . 0.0)`	Polyline starting width.
`(41 . 0.0)`	Polyline ending width.
`(42 . 0.0)`	Polyline bulge factor.
`(70 . 40)`	Vertex flag.
`(50 . 0.0)`	Curve-fitted tangent direction.
`)`	
`(`	

The last three vertex records are spline frame control points. None of the control points are actually part of the curve, but they control how the curve should look. You can tell that these are control points because the third bit **(8)** is set in Group **70**.

`(-1 . <Entity name: 60002340>)`	Entity name (record index).
`(0 . "VERTEX")`	Entity type.
`(8 . "0")`	Layer name for this entity.
`(10 3.0 6.0 4.0)`	**X Y Z** coordinates.
`(40 . 0.0)`	Polyline starting width.
`(41 . 0.0)`	Polyline ending width.
`(42 . 0.0)`	Polyline bulge factor.
`(70 . 48)`	Vertex flag.
`(50 . 0.0)`	Curve-fitted tangent direction.
`)`	
`(`	
`(-1 . <Entity name: 60002358>)`	Entity name (record index)
`(0 . "VERTEX")`	Entity type.
`(8 . "0")`	Layer name for this entity.
`(10 3.0 4.0 4.0)`	**X Y Z** coordinates.

(40 . 0.0)	Polyline starting width.
(41 . 0.0)	Polyline ending width.
(42 . 0.0)	Polyline bulge factor.
(70 . 48)	Vertex flag.
(50 . 0.0)	Curve-fitted tangent direction.
)	
(	
(-1 . <Entity name: 60002370>)	Entity name (record index).
(0 . "VERTEX")	Entity type.
(8 . "0")	Layer name for this entity.
(10 7.0 2.0 0.0)	**X Y Z** coordinates.
(40 . 0.0)	Polyline starting width.
(41 . 0.0)	Polyline ending width.
(42 . 0.0)	Polyline bulge factor.
(70 . 48)	Vertex flag.
(50 . 0.0)	Curve-fitted tangent direction.
)	
(	
(-1 . <Entity name: 60002388>)	Entity name (record index).

The SEQEND record always comes at the end of a series of polyline vertexes.

(0 . "SEQEND")	Entity type.
(8 . "0")	Layer name for this entity.
(-2 . <Entity name: 60002310>)	Entity name (record index) of the polyline entity to which SEQEND is linked.
)	

3D POLYGON MESH

3D polygon meshes are used to describe complex curved surfaces in 3D space. They are generated by the 3DMESH, RULESURF, TABSURF, REV-SURF and EDGESURF commands in AutoCAD Release 10. These commands will generate a polyline record in the drawing database, with one VERTEX record for each vertex that shows up in the drawn 3D surface.

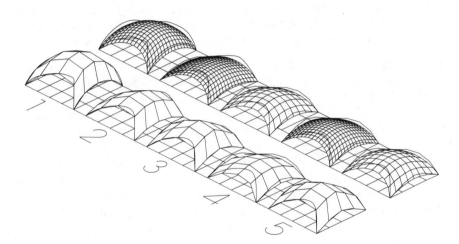

Figure 8

You can set a number of different system variables to determine how many vertices will be generated for a given 3D polygon mesh. They are SURFTAB1, SURFTAB2, SURFTYPE, SURFU and SURFV. Figure 8 shows 10 different polygon meshes that are based on the same basic shape, but different system variables have been set to generate each surface. All of the surfaces were generated with the EDGESURF command, using four smoothed polylines as the defining edges. The system variables SURFTAB1 and SURFTAB2 were set to 4.*

---

*   SURFTAB1 and SURFTAB2 determine how many segments are generated in the M and N directions for each surface.

Figure 8-1 was generated as a quadratic B-spline surface. Figure 8-2 was generated the same way, except the surface was spline fitted with PEDIT. Figure 8-3 was generated as a cubic B-spline surface. Figure 8-4 is a cubic B-spline surface that was smoothed with PEDIT. Figure 8-5 is a Bezier surface.

The second set of five surfaces is identical to the first, except that they have been smoothed with the PEDIT command where the SURFU and SURFV system variables have been set to either 8 or 16. SURFU and SURFV determine how many mesh segments to use in smoothing a given surface.

The 3D surface commands produce some very interesting shapes and it's a lot of fun playing with them, but they can take up a lot of space in the drawing database, and if you use them frequently in a drawing, it can really slow things down. This large vertex structure also makes it difficult for us to show how the database is structured without printing hundreds of pages.

After generating a lot of 3D surfaces and studying the results, we have reached some interesting conclusions. What mainly determines the shape of these 3D surfaces is not the internal data structure of the polygon mesh (i.e., where individual vertices are located), but such things as the defining edges that are picked when the surface is generated, and the system variables that are used to generate the surface. Most of the information that determines where the individual vertices lie is contained in either the POLYLINE record or in the defining edge records (that are not part of the mesh). So you don't have to change the coordinates of individual vertices in the polygon mesh—you can simply change the way that the surface is defined by changing the defining edges and the way the surface is generated.

3D POLYGON MESH DATA STRUCTURE

The following 3D polygon mesh data structure represents the simplest 3D surface that can be generated by the EDGESURF command. This 3D surface is the one with four sides in Figure 7. If you look closely at Figure 7, you can see the four curved polylines that were used to define the edges of this surface. The curved polyline on the right is particularly evident. As you can imagine, the greater the number of surfaces defined, the smoother the curved surface will be and the more closely its edges will follow the defining polyline edges. To illustrate this, look at Figure 8-1-2—this surface was generated exactly the same way as the example in Figure 7, except it was smoothed with PEDIT to a surface mesh of 16x16 (which contains 289 vertices).

```
(
(-1 . <Entity name: 60002a00>)
(0 . "POLYLINE")
(8 . "0")
(66 . 1)
(10 0.0 0.0 0.0)
(70 . 16)




(40 . 0.0)


(41 . 0.0)
```

	Entity name (record index).
	Entity type.
	Layer name for this entity.
	Vertex follows flag.
	Polyline flag. This is a bit-coded flag. If the bit is not set (0), then this is an open polyline; if the bit is set (1), it's a closed polyline. If bit 2 (2) is set, then this polyline has been curve fitted and if bit 3 (4) has been set, then this polyline has been spline-fitted. If the fourth (8) bit is set, then this is a 3D polyline. If the fifth bit (16) is set, then this is a 3D polygon mesh. The sixth bit (32) is set only to indicate that this structure is a polygon mesh and that it is closed in the **N** direction. Since the value of this group is **16**, it means that the fourth bit has been set; this tells us that this is a 3D polygon mesh.
	Default starting width. Since this is a 3D polygon mesh, and it can't have a width at this time, this field isn't used.
	Default ending width. Since this is a 3D polygon mesh, this field isn't used.

(71 . 3)   Polygon mesh **M** vertex
                                            count. This is the number of
                                            vertices in the **M** direction of
                                            this surface as defined by the
                                            value of SURFTAB1 +1.*

(72 . 3)   Polygon mesh **N** vertex
                                            count. This is the number of
                                            vertices in the **N** direction of
                                            this surface as defined by
                                            SURFTAB2 + 1.

(73 . 0)   Polygon mesh smooth-sur-
                                            face **M** density. If PEDIT
                                            was used to smooth this sur-
                                            face, the value found in the
                                            system variable SURFU
                                            would be found here.

(74 . 0)   Polygon mesh smooth-sur-
                                            face **N** density. If PEDIT was
                                            used to smooth this surface,
                                            the value found in the sys-
                                            tem variable SURFV would
                                            be found here.

(75 . 0)   Smooth-surface type flag.
                                            This is *not* a bit-coded flag.
                                            Since this is a 3D polygon
                                            mesh, this field indicates the
                                            type of surface fitting applied;
                                            the type depends on the
                                            value set in the system vari-
                                            able SURFTYPE specifiying
                                            either a quadratic B-spline
                                            surface (**5**), a cubic B-spline
                                            surface (**6**) or a Bezier surface
                                            (**8**). Don't confuse the
                                            SURFTYPE variable with the
                                            SPLINESEGS variable, which

---

*   See Section 4.9 in the *AutoCAD Reference Manual* for more information about **M**
      and **N** directions.

controls the curve fitting of polylines — they're independent of one another. A **0** value means that this 3D polygon mesh has not been curve fitted.

)

One way of determining the number of VERTEX records that follow the POLYLINE record is to multiply the values found in Group **71** and **72** and then add that value to the product of multiplying the values of Group **73** and **74**. In this example, it's (3x3) + (0x0) = 9.

3D POLYGON MESH VERTEX

The following listing is the first VERTEX record of this 3D polygon mesh. 3D polygon meshes always run across rows (**N**) and down columns (**M**). (The position of this vertex is **M-0 N-0**.)

```
(
(-1 . <Entity name: 60002a18>)      Entity name (record index).

(0 . "VERTEX")                      Entity type.

(8 . "0")                           Layer name for this entity.

(10 5.0 0.0 0.0)                    X Y Z coordinates.

(40 . 0.0)                          Polyline starting width.

(41 . 0.0)                          Polyline ending width.

(42 . 0.0)                          Polyline bulge factor. Since
                                    this is a 3D polygon mesh,
                                    and adding a bulge factor to
                                    it would be rather strange,
                                    this field isn't used.

(70 . 64)                           Vertex flag. This is a bit-
                                    coded flag. If the first bit (1)
                                    is set, then the next vertex
                                    record was added by
                                    AutoCAD as an extra vertex
                                    to create a smoother curve.
                                    If the second bit (2) is set, a
                                    curve-fitted tangent has
```

been defined, and that tangent information will appear in Group Code **50** below. If the fourth bit (**8**) is set, then this is an extra vertex created by spline fitting. If the fifth bit (**16**) is set, then this vertex is a spline frame control point and is not actually part of the visible polyline. If the sixth bit is set (**32**), then this is a 3D polyline vertex. The seventh bit (**64**) indicates a 3D polygon mesh vertex. Since the value of this flag is 64, then this vertex is part of a 3D polygon mesh.

(50 . 0.0)   Curve-fitted tangent direction. Curve fitting isn't used on 3D polygon meshes, so this field is always 0.

)

The location of this vertex is M-0, N-1.

(

(-1 . <Entity name: 60002a30>)   Entity name (record index).

(0 . "VERTEX")   Entity type.

(8 . "0")   Layer name for this entity.

(10 5.0 2.0 0.75)   **X Y Z** coordinates.

(40 . 0.0)   Polyline starting width.

(41 . 0.0)   Polyline ending width.

(42 . 0.0)   Polyline bulge factor.

(70 . 64)   Vertex flag.

```
(50 . 0.0)                              Curve-fitted tangent direction.
)
```

This vertex is located at M-0, N-2—the upper left corner in Figure 7.

```
(
(-1 . <Entity name: 60002a48>)          Entity name (record index).
(0 . "VERTEX")                          Entity type.
(8 . "0")                               Layer name for this entity.
(10 5.0 4.0 0.0)                        X Y Z coordinates.
(40 . 0.0)                              Polyline starting width.
(41 . 0.0)                              Polyline ending width.
(42 . 0.0)                              Polyline bulge factor.
(70 . 64)                               Vertex flag.
(50 . 0.0)                              Curve-fitted tangent direction.
)
```

This vertex is M-1, N-0.

```
(
(-1 . <Entity name: 60002a60>)          Entity name (record index).
(0 . "VERTEX")                          Entity type.
(8 . "0")                               Layer name for this entity.
(10 3.57938 0.0 1.71268)                X Y Z coordinates.
(40 . 0.0)                              Polyline starting width.
(41 . 0.0)                              Polyline ending width.
(42 . 0.0)                              Polyline bulge factor.
(70 . 64)                               Vertex flag.
(50 . 0.0)                              Curve-fitted tangent direction.
)
```

This VERTEX record is located at M-1, N-1 at the center of the surface.

```
(
(-1 . <Entity name: 60002a78>)        Entity name (record index).
(0 . "VERTEX")                        Entity type.
(8 . "0")                             Layer name for this entity.
(10 3.31078 2.0 1.95153)             X Y Z coordinates.
(40 . 0.0)                            Polyline starting width.
(41 . 0.0)                            Polyline ending width.
(42 . 0.0)                            Polyline bulge factor.
(70 . 64)                             Vertex flag.
(50 . 0.0)                            Curve-fitted tangent direction.
)
```

This is M-1, N-2.

```
(
(-1 .  <Entity name: 60002a90>)       Entity name (record index).
(0 . "VERTEX")                        Entity type.
(8 . "0")                             Layer name for this entity.
(10 3.04218 4.0 0.690391)            X Y Z coordinates.
(40 . 0.0)                            Polyline starting width.
(41 . 0.0)                            Polyline ending width.
(42 . 0.0)                            Polyline bulge factor.
(70 . 64)                             Vertex flag.
(50 . 0.0)                            Curve-fitted tangent direction.
)
```

This vertex is located at the lower right corner in Figure 7 or at M-2, N-0.

```
(
(-1 . <Entity name: 60002aa8>)        Entity name (record index).
(0 . "VERTEX")                        Entity type.
(8 . "0")                             Layer name for this entity.
```

```
(10 1.0 0.0 0.0)                        X Y Z coordinates.
(40 . 0.0)                              Polyline starting width.
(41 . 0.0)                              Polyline ending width.
(42 . 0.0)                              Polyline bulge factor.
(70 . 64)                               Vertex flag.
(50 . 0.0)                              Curve-fitted tangent direction.
)
```

This is vertex M-2, N-1.

```
(
(-1 . <Entity name: 60002ac0>)          Entity name (record index).
(0 . "VERTEX")                          Entity type.
(8 . "0")                               Layer name for this entity.
(10 1.0 2.0 0.75)                       X Y Z coordinates.
(40 . 0.0)                              Polyline starting width.
(41 . 0.0)                              Polyline ending width.
(42 . 0.0)                              Polyline bulge factor.
(70 . 64)                               Vertex flag.
(50 . 0.0)                              Curve-fitted tangent direction.
)
```

This is the ending vertex located at M-2, N-2.

```
(
(-1 . <Entity name: 60002ad8>)          Entity name (record index).
(0 . "VERTEX")                          Entity type.
(8 . "0")                               Layer name for this entity.
(10 1.0 4.0 0.0)                        X Y Z coordinates.
(40 . 0.0)                              Polyline starting width.
(41 . 0.0)                              Polyline ending width.
(42 . 0.0)                              Polyline bulge factor.
```

```
(70 . 64)                               Vertex flag.
(50 . 0.0)                              Curve-fitted tangent direction.
)
```

Finally, the SEQEND record for this POLYLINE structure:

```
(
(-1 . <Entity name: 60002af0>)          Entity name (record index).
(0 . "SEQEND")                          Entity type.
(8 . "0")                               Layer name for this entity.
(-2 .  y name: 60002a00)                Entity name (record index)
                                        of the polyline entity to
                                        which SEQEND is linked.

)
```

TABLE SECTIONS

In AutoCAD Versions 2.6 and later, you can access and read the table sections of the drawing database with AutoLISP. We have found this to be a very valuable tool with many programming applications (see the BLKWRITE program at the end of Chapter 6 for an example).

There are five tables within the drawing database that can be accessed by AutoLISP functions: LAYER, LTYPE, VIEW, STYLE and BLOCK tables.* Since the tables are all accessed initially in exactly the same fashion, we will limit most of our examples to the Block Table.

ACCESSING THE DATA IN THE BLOCK SECTION

This section explains how to access the BLOCK Table of a drawing database, shows you what the association list format looks like, and explains what each record means.

---

*   Release 10 has added UCS, VPORT and DWGMGR tables to the table section.
         These tables will be covered in Appendix C.

Except for the first record of each block definition (the block header record), each block definition looks exactly like the Entity Section in the drawing database. Once you have found a particular block definition, all of the entities that make up that definition can be accessed in the same manner as any entities in the Entities Section of the database.

Two AutoLISP functions can be used to access the Block Section: **tblnext** and **tblsearch**. Both of these functions use a different approach to accessing the table section—which function to use depends on what information you have and what information you want.

tblnext can be used in much the same way as the function **entnext**, but instead of retrieving an entity name, **tblnext** retrieves a record in one of the table sections. The following code retrieves the first entry in the Block Table:

```
(setq blk (tblnext "BLOCK" t))
```

Which would be (from our sample database):

(	
(0 . "BLOCK")	Entity type.
(2 . "ROOMTAG")	The name of this block definition. If the name begins with an asterisk (*), then this is an "anonymous" block definition, such as a hatch pattern.
(70 . 66)	Block type flag. This is a bit-coded flag where the first (1), second (2) or seventh (64) bits are capable of being set. If the second bit (2) is set, this block definition has ATTDEFs or attributes. If the first bit (1) is set, this block is an "anonymous" (or pseudo) block. If the seventh (64) bit is set, then this block is referenced by an INSERT record in the Entities Section

of this drawing. If the seventh bit is set to **0** (false), then the PURGE command will remove this block definition. The possible bit codes for this field are **0, 1, 2, 64, 65** and **66.**

`(10 116.5 88.0 0.0)`

The **X Y Z** coordinate of the base point of this block definition.

`(-2 . <Entity name: 40000018>)`

Entity name (record index) of the first record of the actual block definition—that is, the next record after this one.

`)`

This is the header record of the first block definition in the sample drawing database. Notice that the record index—the **-2** Group Code—is at the end of this list rather than at the beginning, as in the Entities Section. This record index is actually the record index of the first entity record of the block definition—the first record following this header record.

If you wanted to find just the names of all of the defined blocks in the drawing, you could use an AutoLISP function that looks like this:

```
(defun blklist ()
;get the first block
(setq blk (tblnext "BLOCK" t))
;loop while there are blocks in the database
        (while blk
;read the block name
        (setq blkname (cdr (assoc 2 blk)))
;print the block name
        (print blkname)
;get the next block record
        (setq blk (tblnext "BLOCK"))
        )
)
```

As you can see from this example, the function **tblnext** will retrieve only the first record (the header) of each block definition. From this point on, each block definition looks exactly like the Entity Section, and you can then access each record within that definition by using the function **entnext**.

To retrieve the first entity record of this block definition, you could use the following code:

```
;find the first block record
(setq blk (tblnext "BLOCK" t))
;get the record index of the first entity
(setq ent (cdr (assoc -2 blk)))
;print the first entity record
(print (entget ent))
```

The listing would look like this:

```
(
(-1 . <Entity name: 40000018>)     Entity name (record index).
(0 . "LINE")                       Entity type.
(8 . "0")                          Layer name for this entity.
(10 81.0 104.0 0.0)                Starting X Y Z coordinate.
(11 81.0 88.0 0.0)                 Ending X Y Z coordinate.
)
```

This listing is identical to a line listing in the Entities Section of the drawing database, except that the entity name will always start with a 4 instead of a 6.

To get the next record in the block definition, you use the **entnext** function (along with **entget**), like this:

```
(setq ent (entnext ent))
(print (entget ent))
```

which will give you the next entity in the block definition which looks like this:

```
(
(-1 . <Entity name: 40000040>)     Entity name (record index).
(0 . "LINE")                       Entity type.
(8 . "0")                          Layer name for this entity.
```

(10 152.0 104.0 0.0)   Starting **X Y Z** coordinate.

(11 81.0 104.0 0.0)   Ending **X Y Z** coordinate.

)

Here is a very simple AutoLISP function called **blklst** that will read all of the block definitions into a text file. This is same program that we used to generate these listings:

```
(defun c:blklst ()
        (setq outfile (getstring "\nEnter file name for
            Block list: "))
;open a text file to write the block definitions
        (setq outfile (strcat outfile ".txt"))
        (setq a (open outfile "w"))
;get the first block definition header record
        (setq blk (tblnext "BLOCK" t))
;while there are block definitions
        (while blk
;write the block header record to the file
            (print blk a)
;get the first entity record of current block definition
            (setq e (cdr (assoc -2 blk)))
;while there are entities in the current block definition
            (while e
;write the entity record of the current block to the file
                (print (entget e) a)
;get the next entity record of current block definition
                (setq e (entnext e))
            )
;get the next block definition header record
            (setq blk (tblnext "BLOCK"))
        )
;close the output file
        (close a)
)
```

Here is the rest of the commented block definition from our sample database:

(

(-1 . <Entity name: 40000068>)   Entity name (record index).

`(0 . "LINE")`	Entity type.
`(8 . "0")`	Layer name for this entity.
`(10 152.0 88.0 0.0)`	Starting **X Y Z** coordinate.
`(11 152.0 104.0 0.0)`	Ending **X Y Z** coordinate.
`)`	
`(`	
`(-1 . <Entity name: 40000090>)`	Entity name (record index).
`(0 . "LINE")`	Entity type.
`(8 . "0")`	Layer name for this entity.
`(10 81.0 88.0 0.0)`	Starting **X Y Z** coordinate.
`(11 152.0 88.0 0.0)`	Ending **X Y Z** coordinate.
`)`	

ATTRIBUTE DEFINITION (ATTDEF)

The following two records are the attribute definitions (ATTDEF entities), and they are found only inside a block definition. ATTDEF entities are created with the ATTDEF command and they are saved, along with any other entity records, into the Block Section with the BLOCK command. Attribute prompts, default attribute values and constant attribute values are found only in the block definition and they never appear in the Entity Section in the ATTRIB record. If you compare the ATTDEF record with the ATTRIB record in the INSERT section of this appendix, you will find that they are quite similar.

`(`	
`(-1 . <Entity name: 400000B8>)`	Entity name (record index).
`(0 . "ATTDEF")`	Entity type.
`(8 . "0")`	Layer name for this entity.
`(10 84.92857 74.57143 0.0)`	**X Y Z** coordinate starting point for attribute text.
`(40 . 9.0)`	Text height for this attribute definition.

`(1 . "Vacant")`	Default attribute value for this attribute definition.
`(3 . "Employee's Name")`	Prompt for this attribute that appears whenever this block is inserted.
`(2 . "EMPNAME")`	The attribute tag, the key searched for when attributes are extracted using the AT-TEXT command. The attribute tag remains the same for all instances of the attribute, while each instance of the attribute can have different values linked to the attribute tag. Think of the attribute tag as a field name and the attribute value as the value contained in that field in a database record.
`(70 . 0)`	The attribute flag. It is a bit-coded flag with the first (1), second (2), third (4) and fourth (8) bits capable of being set. If no bits are set in this group (0), then this attribute will be visible. If the first (1) bit is set, this attribute will be invisible. If the second (2) bit is set, then the attribute value will be a constant. If the third (4) bit is set, then verification will be required on input of any value for this attribute. If the fourth (8) bit is set, then this will be a preset attribute. See the beginning of Appendix B for more information about bit-coded flags.

(73 . 0)	This is the field length of the attribute value. It isn't currently being used, since there's no way to set it from an AutoCAD command, but it may be used in the future.
(50 . 0.0)	The rotation angle for attribute text in radians.
(41 . 1.0)	Relative width factor of the attribute text.
(51 . 0.0)	The obliquing angle of the attribute text in radians.
(7 . "NORMAL")	Text style for this attribute definition.
(71 . 0)	Text-generation flag for this attribute definition. See the TEXT section in this appendix for more information.
(72 . 1)	Alignment point flag. This is *not* a bit-coded flag. The value of this number determines how the text is justified. **0** means that the text will be left justified and this group code will not appear. Other values: **1** = baseline centered text; **2** = right justified text; **3** = aligned text; **4** = "middle" or fully centered text; and **5** = "fit" text.
(11 116.0 74.57143 0.0)	The actual **centered X Y Z** coordinate base of this attribute text string. This is the point picked for inserting the attribute text after the CENTER option was picked in

the ATTDEF command when
this attribute was defined.

)

The following ATTDEF record is almost identical to the one above; we're
including it so that you can see what a complete block definition looks like.

```
(
(-1 . <Entity name: 4000010D>)
(0 . "ATTDEF")
(8 . "0")
(10 88.78571 90.0 0.0)
(40 . 9.0)
(1 . "")
(3 . "Room Number")
(2 . "ROOMNO")
(70 . 0)
(73 . 0)
(50 . 0.0)
(41 . 1.0)
(51 . 0.0)
(7 . "NORMAL")
(71 . 0)
(72 . 1)
(11 116.0 90.0 0.0)
)
```

TBLSEARCH

If you already know the name of the block (possibly retrieved from an IN-
SERT record in the Entities Section) and you want to get information about
the block definition, you can access the block definition directly with the
function **tblsearch**. **tblsearch** takes as its arguments the table name that

you wish to search and the name of the definition that you are looking for. If you wanted to find the definition of the block ROOMTAG, you would use the following code:

```
(setq blk (tblsearch "BLOCK" "ROOMTAG"))
```

which would return the record header for the block definition of ROOMTAG. You can then retrieve the entity name of the first entity in the block definition from the **-2** group code and then step through the block definition as we did in the previous examples.

ACCESSING OTHER TABLE SECTIONS

The other four table sections (LAYER, LTYPE, VIEW and STYLE) can be accessed using the same techniques that were shown for accessing the Block Section. The only difference is that the other tables do not have subrecords that contain entity information, so that looking at the information in these tables is much simpler. For example, if you wanted to find the parameters for the text style NORMAL, you could use the **tblsearch** function like this:

```
(setq style (tblsearch "STYLE" "NORMAL"))
```

which would return the following association list:

```
(
(0 . "STYLE")
(2 . "NORMAL")



(70 . 64)
```

	Table type.
	The name of this text style definition. NORMAL is the name of the text style that we defined and used in this drawing file.
	Text style group flag. This is a bit-coded flag with the first bit (**1**), the third bit (**4**) and the seventh bit (**64**) capable of being set. If the first flag bit is set (**1**), this definition refers to a shape file rather than a font file. If the third

flag bit is set (4), then a vertically oriented text style has been defined.* If the seventh bit has been set (64), then this text style has been used in either a text string or an attribute in this drawing. If the seventh bit flag is set to 0 (false), then the PURGE command will remove the text style. The possible bit codes for this group are: 0, 1, 4, 64, 65 and 68. See the beginning of this appendix for more information about bit-coded flags.

(40 . 0.0)

Fixed text height. If you had specified a text height in the STYLE command when you were defining a text style, then that height would show up here.

(41 . 1.0)

Width factor for this text style.

(50 . 0.0)

Obliquing angle for this text style.

(71 . 0)

Text generation flag. This is a bit-coded flag with the second (2) and third (4) bits capable of being set. If both bits are 0, then text will appear normal. If the second bit is set (2), then the text will appear mirrored in the X axis (left to right). If the third bit (4) is set, then the text

---

*   if you answered **yes** to Vertical when you defined this style with the STYLE command.

will appear upside down. Only one bit will be set at a time. See the beginning of this appendix for more information about bit-coded flags.

`(3 . "simplex")`

Font file name. The name of the font file that contains the actual vector information that AutoCAD uses to construct the text characters used in this text style definition. This file must be in the same subdirectory as AutoCAD when you load a drawing that uses this font in a text style definition. If you had loaded a SHAPE file into your drawing, the name of that shape file would appear in this group.

`(4 . "")`

If the font used in this style definition was a "bigfont"* then the name of that font would appear in this group. Otherwise, this field remains blank.

`)`

---

*   See Appendix B.5.4 in the *AutoCAD Reference Manual* for information about big fonts.

appendix B DXF DATABASE COMMENTED LISTING

While there's some overlap between Appendix A and this appendix, we feel that it's valuable to present both the association list and the **DXF** formats of the AutoCAD databases. We've chosen to comment on both of these formats because of both their similarity and their differences.

The data formats are similar because for the most part, they carry identical information. The way in which that information is presented, however, is quite different, as you can see by simply comparing the two listings. Deciphering group codes, many of them previously undocumented, is hard enough; but having to deal with two very dissimilar-looking data formats adds another hurdle to the task.

These appendices are meant to be both an overall map of the database structure and a detailed explanation of how every group code works within the AutoCAD database.

We haven't included a listing of the header section of the **DXF** file, because the header variables are explained in Appendix C of the *AutoCAD Reference Manual*.

THE 3D DATABASE IN DXF FORMAT

The database of AutoCAD Release 10 contains complete **X Y Z** coordinate information for all entities, but the **DXF** output file will not list the **Z** coordinates of an entity if **Z** is **0** for that entity or if the system variable FLATLAND is set to **0.**[*]

See the beginning of Appendix A for a discussion of the AutoCAD 3D database.

This appendix is divided into two sections. The first section contains a complete listing of a **DXF** file that was created with Release 10 and is based on the drawing in Figure 1. This **DXF** listing contains all of the 2D entities.

The second section deals with 3D entities and contains a **DXF** listing based on the drawing in Figure 3.

COMPARING DXF AND ASSOCIATION LIST FORMATS

There are more similarities than differences between the **DXF** (Data e**X**change Format) file database and the association list database format. Most group codes are the same in the two data formats; they're just organized differently. Below are some of the differences:

- The **DXF** format has separate group codes for both the **X** and **Y** coordinates of an entity.[**] If you add **10** to the group code for the **X** coordinate, you'll get the group code for the **Y** coordinate. If you add **10** to the group code for the **Y** coordinate, you'll get the group code for the **Z** coordinate (if it's non-zero).

- If a group code for an entity isn't applicable or isn't used for that given entity, then it won't appear in the **DXF** listing for that entity. Two examples: If no attributes are linked to a block insertion, then Group Code **66** (the attributes follow flag) will not appear in the INSERT listing.[***] If a 3D entity is listed but the **Z** coordinate is **0**, then the group codes (**30** and **31**) for the **Z** coordinates won't appear in the database listing.[****]

---

[*]   See Section D.2.1.4 in the *AutoCAD Reference Manual* for more about FLATLAND.
[**]   And for the **Z** coordinate if applicable.
[***]   In the association list format Group Code **66** will appear, but it will be set to **0**.
[****]   It's difficult to comment on fields that don't appear in the database record, so we've added a list of all the group codes that could appear in an entity description at the end of that particular entity listing.

- Entities in a **DXF** file don't have entity names associated with them. Entity names are used within a random-access database framework inside of AutoCAD so that you can access any given entity quickly if you know its entity name. They can, however, have entity handles.

- Group Code **0** appears quite often in the **DXF** file. This group code acts as a flag to indicate that some change will start with the next line. The exact meaning of Group Code **0** varies, depending on what's on the following line; it could mean the start of a new section, the start of a new entity, or the end of a section.

BIT-CODED FLAGS

Any group code between **70** and **78** is usually (but not always) a *bit-coded flag*. In a bit-coded flag, an 8-bit binary code is used. As you may know, a binary number has only two elements: 0 and 1. The number 46 (decimal) would be equal to 00101110 in binary format. The right-most digit of a binary number is the 1 digit, the next digit (moving left) is the 2 digit, followed by the 4 digit, then the 8, then the 16 digit and so on.

The place value of an 8-bit binary number is represented in the following table:

```
128   64   32   16   8   4   2   1
1     1    1    1    1   1   1   1  =255 decimal
0     1    1    1    1   1   1   1  =127 decimal
```

An easy way to convert a binary number to a decimal number is to add the place values of each digit of a binary number that is a 1 (ignoring the digits that are 0). For example:

```
00000111 is, starting from the right digit, 1+2+4=7.
00000101 is 1+4=5
00010101 is 1+4+16=21
01000010 is 2+64=66
01000001 is 1+64=65
01000100 is 4+64=68
```

When an 8-bit binary number is used as a flag, it is sometimes called a *bit field*, and the way certain bits are set (either **0** or **1**) determines what that flag means. One advantage of using a bit-coded field for setting flags is that you can have as many as eight different flags set in one byte (eight bits) of memory—that is, one number can hold as many as eight different pieces of information at one time.

For example, if Group Code **70** has a value of **1**, then the first bit (or flag) is set to **1** (or true) and the other seven flags (or bits) are set to **0** (or false). If the value of the group code is **65**, then the first and the seventh bits are set to true (or **1**). This means that when AutoCAD looks at Group Code **70** in a layer definition, for instance, and sees that the value is **65**, it knows that both the seventh-bit and the first-bit flags have been set to true. Below are some bit fields and their values:

```
00000001 binary=1 decimal  = first bit true.
00000010 binary=2 decimal  = second bit true.
00000100 binary=4 decimal  = third bit true.
01000001 binary=64+1=65 decimal  = first and seventh bit true.
01000010 binary=64+2=66 decimal= second and seventh bit true.
01000100 binary=64+4=68 decimal=  third and seventh bit true.
```

See the listings below for information on how these bit-coded flags are set in specific contexts.

DXF LISTING STRUCTURE

The **DXF** listing for the first section was generated from the same drawing as the database listing in the first section of Appendix A (Figure 3). The format of the **DXF** file is one item per line; the first line carries the group code and the next line carries the value for that group. In most cases we have broken up the **DXF** file into pairs to emphasize this structure. Each group code and group value pair in the following listing will look like this:

10	This is the group code.
10.1	This is the value for the group code above. This is also the line where comments will be found.
20	The next group code.

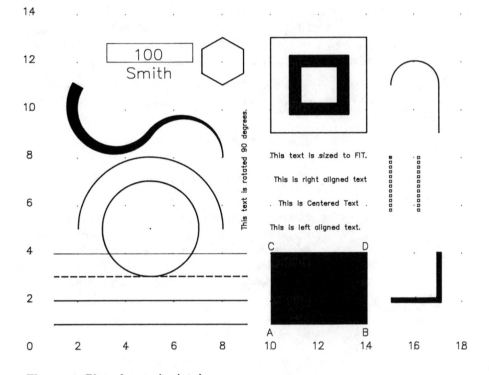

Figure 1: Plot of sample database.

TABLES SECTION

0	
SECTION	The start of the tables section.
2	
TABLES	The name of the table section.

VIEWPORT TABLE

The viewport table is found only in Release 10 or later. This table contains all the definitions for the current viewport (called *ACTIVE) and all of the user-defined viewport configurations saved in this drawing. This section contains the same kind of information that is contained in the header section of the DXF file for the default single viewport.

The following listing presents a configuration of two vertical viewports. The viewpoint in one of these viewports has been rotated.

```
    0
  TABLE                   The start of the VPORT table.

    2
  VPORT                   The name of the VPORT table.

   70
          3             Maximum number of viewports defined.  In this
                        case, there is the default single viewport plus the
                        two active ones that have been defined below.
                        The default viewport isn't defined here, since it's al-
                        ready defined in the header section of this file.
```

The first listing describes the vertical viewport on the right side of the screen.

```
    0
  VPORT                   A viewport definition starts here.

    2
  *ACTIVE               This viewport is active—that is, when this drawing
                        file is loaded, this is one of the viewports that will
                        show up on the screen.

   70
          0             Viewport flag.

   10
  0.5                   This is the lower-left X corner of the viewport.  This
                        number will range from 0.0 to 1.0, and is a ratio
                        relative to the screen.  In this case, 0.5 means that
                        the lower left X of this viewport is 50% of the
                        screen width towards the right.
```

20
0.0

This is the lower-left **Y** corner of the viewport. This number will range from **0.0** to **1.0**, and is a ratio relative to the screen. In this case **0.0** means that the lower left **Y** of this viewport is 0% of the screen height towards the top—at the bottom of the screen.

11
1.0

This is the upper-right **X** corner of the viewport. This number will range from **0.0** to **1.0**, and is a ratio relative to the screen. In this case, **1.0** means that the upper right **X** of this viewport is 100% of the screen width towards the right.

21
1.0

This is the upper-right **Y** corner of the viewport. This number will range from **0.0** to **1.0**, and is a ratio relative to the screen. In this case, **1.0** means that the upper right **Y** of this viewport is 100% of the screen height towards the top—at the top of the screen.

12
10.690296

The view center point **X** coordinate for this viewport. This coordinate is expressed in the **UCS** that was active when this **DXF** file was created.

22
2.3195

The view center point **Y** coordinate for this viewport.

13
0.0

The snap base **X** coordinate for this viewport (in the **UCS**).

23
0.0

The snap base **Y** coordinate for this viewport (in the **UCS**).

14
1.0

The **X** snap spacing for this viewport.

24
1.0

The **Y** snap spacing for this viewport.

```
15
2.0
```
The **X** grid spacing for this viewport.

```
25
2.0
```
The **Y** grid spacing for this viewport.

```
16
0.612372
```
The **X** coordinate of the view direction from the target point. This is the equivalent of the current VPOINT. The viewpoint of this viewport has been rotated from the plan axis as determined by the values found in this and the following two groups. Compare these numbers with those in the next VPORT listing (which defines a plan view).

```
26
-0.353553
```
The **Y** coordinate of the view direction from the target point. This is the equivalent of the current **VPOINT.**

```
36
0.707107
```
The **Z** coordinate of the view direction from the target point. This is the equivalent of the current **VPOINT.**

```
17
0.0
```
The **X** coordinate of the target point. This is always in **WCS** coordinates.

```
27
0.0
```
The **Y** coordinate of the target point. This is always in **WCS** coordinates.

```
37
0.0
```
The **Z** coordinate of the target point. This is always in **WCS** coordinates.

```
40
26.946853
```
View height (the number of drawing units from the bottom to the top of this viewport).

```
41
0.801653
```
Viewport aspect ratio. If you multiply this number by the value in Group **40**, you'll get the width of the viewport in drawing units.

42
50.0   Lens focal length. This is the lens length for an im-
                            aginary camera. This number is set in the **DVIEW**
                            command. This controls the angle of view from
                            the viewpoint to the target point if the projection in
                            this viewport is in perspective. This value is always
                            set to **50** unless it's changed in **DVIEW**.

43
0.0   Front clippng plane, expressed as a distance from
                            the target point on a line between the target point
                            and the viewpoint.

44
0.0   Rear clippng plane, expressed as a distance from
                            the target point on a line between the target point
                            and the viewpoint.

50
0.0   Snap rotation angle, in radians.

51
0.0   View twist angle. This is the angle that the imagi-
                            nary camera is "twisted" or rotated along the line of
                            sight from the viewpoint to the target.

71
    0   View mode. This is a bit-coded flag.[*]

72
    100   Circle zoom percent. This is the VIEWRES setting
                            for this viewport.

73
    1   Fast zoom setting. **1** is on, **0** is off.

74
    1   UCSICON setting. **1** indicates that the **UCS** icon is
                            set to the **WCS**, **0** is that it's set to the **UCS**.

75
    1   Snap toggle — **1** is on, **0** is off.

---

[*]   See the table in Section A.7 in the *AutoCAD Reference Manual* for more about the
      VIEWMODE variable.

76	
1	Grid toggle — **1** is on, **0** is off.
77	
0	Snap style — **0** is standard and **1** is isometric.
78	
0	Snap isometric plane. This is significant only if Group **77** is set to **1**. **0** is left, **1** is top, and **2** is right.

The next listing is for the other active viewport in the two-viewport display. Since most of the parameters in this definition are the same as the last listing, we will comment only on the differences.

0	
VPORT	A viewport definition starts here.
2	
*ACTIVE	This viewport is active.
70	
0	Viewport flag.
10	
0.0	This is the lower-left **X** corner of the viewport. This viewport starts at the lower left corner of the screen.
20	
0.0	The lower-left **Y** corner of the viewport
11	
0.5	This is the upper-right **X** corner of the viewport. In this case, **0.5** means that the upper-right **X** of this viewport is 50% of the screen width towards the right.
21	
1.0	The upper-right **Y** corner of the viewport.
12	
11.263742	The view center point **X** coordinate for this viewport. This coordinate is expressed in the **UCS** that was active when this **DXF** file was created.

22
7.15   The view center point **Y** coordinate for this
                              viewport.

13
0.0   The snap base **X** coordinate.

23
0.0   The snap base **Y** coordinate.

14
1.0   The **X** snap spacing.

24
1.0   The **Y** snap spacing.

15
2.0   The **X** grid spacing.

25
2.0   The **Y** grid spacing.

16
0.0   The **X** coordinate of the view direction from the tar-
                              get point. This is the equivalent of the current
                              VPOINT. The viewpoint of this viewport is a plan
                              view as determined by the values found in this and
                              the following two groups.

26
0.0   The **Y** coordinate of the view direction from the tar-
                              get point. This is the equivalent of the current
                              VPOINT.

36
1.0   The **Z** coordinate of the view direction from the tar-
                              get point. This is the equivalent of the current
                              VPOINT.

17
0.0   The **X** coordinate of the target point.

27
0.0   The **Y** coordinate of the target point.

37
0.0   The **Z** coordinate of the target point.

```
  40
28.653727          View height.

  41
0.801653           Viewport aspect ratio.

  42
50.0               Lens focal length.

  43
0.0                Front clipping plane.

  44
0.0                Rear clipping plane.

  50
0.0                Snap rotation angle, in radians.

  51
0.0                View twist angle.

  71
      0            View mode.

  72
   100             Circle zoom percentage.

  73
      1            Fast zoom setting.

  74
      1            UCSICON setting.

  75
      1            Snap toggle.

  76
      1            Grid toggle.

  77
      0            Snap style.

  78
      0            Snap isometric plane.

   0
ENDTAB             End of VPORT table.
```

LINE-TYPE TABLE

The line-type table contains the definitions of all line types used (or that have been defined by the **LAYER Ltype** command) in a given drawing. Any line type assigned to a layer in the layer table or to an entity in the entity section must first be defined in this table.

The actual line-type definition originally comes from the line-type definition file (either ACAD.LIN or a custom line-type file with a **.LIN** extension) loaded into AutoCAD when you request a new line type in the drawing editor.[*]

0 TABLE	The start of the line-type table.
2 LTYPE	The name of the line-type table.
70 2	Maximum item count. The number of line types that have been defined in this table must appear here. This number may be larger than the number defined, because it represents the count for all line types ever defined in this drawing.[**]
0 LTYPE	A line-type definition starts here.
2 CONTINUOUS	The name of the line type being defined, which is referenced when line types are assigned to layers and entities. CONTINUOUS is the default line type and will appear in the line-type table, even if no line types have been assigned.
70 64	Line-type flag. This is a bit-coded flag and only the seventh bit (**64**) is set. If the seventh bit is set (**64**), that means that this line type is used by an entity or has been assigned to a layer in the layer table.

---

[*]   See Section B.3 in Appendix B of the *AutoCAD Reference Manual* for more information on how line types are defined.

[**]   If a line type definition has been purged from the drawing, that definition won't be written to the DXF file.

If the **PURGE** command sees the seventh bit set to **0**, then it will remove this line type definition from the drawing file unless the line type is continuous.[*] If this line type is not referenced anywhere in the drawing file, then the seventh bit of this flag is set to **0**. See the introduction to this appendix for more information about bit-coded flags.

3
Solid line   This is a "prose description" for this line type.

72
    65   Alignment code. **65** is the ASCII code for the letter **A**. This is the only alignment code AutoCAD supports.[**]

73
0   The number of dash length items. This is the number of dashes (including blanks between dashes) that would be in this line type. Because this is a solid line, there are no dashes.

40
0.0   Total pattern length.

0
LTYPE   A line type definition starts here.

2
HIDDEN   The name of the line type being defined.

70
    64   Line-type flag. This is a bit-coded flag, and only the seventh bit (**64**) is set. If the seventh bit is set (**64**), that means that this line type is used by an entity or has been assigned to a layer in the layer table. If the **PURGE** command sees the seventh bit set to **0**, then it will remove this line type definition from the drawing file.

---

[*]   The **PURGE** command will never remove the continuous line type, since it is the default.

[**]   See Section B.3 in the *AutoCAD Reference Manual* for more information.

3

— —

> This is a "prose description" for this line type. In this particular example, this is just a dash-and-space description of the line type being defined, taken directly from the **.LIN** line type file. This is an optional description in the **.LIN** file, so this group may be blank in certain cases.

72
    65

> Alignment code. **65** is the ASCII code for the letter **A**. This is the only alignment code AutoCAD supports.

73
2

> The number of dash length items. This is the number of dashes (including blanks between dashes) that would be in this line type. Because this is a hidden line with one dash and one space, the number of dash length items is **2**.

40
0.375

> Total pattern length for this line type. This is the total length of the dots and/or dashes and the spaces between them in this pattern. If you added all the values in all of the Group **49**s below, this number would be the result.

49
0.25

> Dash length. This is the length of an individual dash, dot or space (a negative number represents a space) in a line type pattern. Group **49** will appear once in a line type definition for each individual dash, dot or space. The number of times that Group **49** appears in a line type definition must agree with the value of Group **73**.

49
–0.125

> Dash length. Because this number is negative, it indicates that this is the length of the space between the dashes.

0
ENDTAB

> End of the line type table.

LAYER TABLE

The layer table contains the descriptions of all of the layers that have been defined in a particular AutoCAD drawing. Any entity or block assigned to a specific layer must have that layer defined here first. The layers in this layer table have been defined using the **LAYER New** command in AutoCAD.

```
    0
  TABLE
    2
  LAYER                    Start of layer table.

   70
        2                  Layer-table maximum item count. This is the total
                           number of layers that have ever been defined in
                           this table. This number may not agree with the
                           number of layers in the table. See Group 70 in the
                           line type table for more information.

    0
  LAYER                    A layer definition starts here.

    2
0                          Name of the layer to be defined. Layer 0 is the
                           default layer, and will appear in the layer table
                           even if no layers have been assigned to the draw-
                           ing.

   70
       64                  Layer flag. This is a bit-coded flag where both the
                           first and seventh bits can be set. If the first bit is
                           set (1), this layer is currently frozen. If the seventh
                           bit is set (64), this layer is used by an entity in
                           either the entity section or in the block section. If
                           the PURGE command sees the seventh bit set to
                           0, then it will remove this layer definition from the
                           drawing file unless it is layer 0.* If this layer is not
                           referenced anywhere in the drawing file, then the
                           seventh bit is set to 0. The possible bit combina-
                           tions for this flag are 0 (layer not referenced and
                           not frozen), 1 (layer not referenced and frozen), 64
```

---

*   The PURGE command will never remove layer "0," since it is the default layer.

(layer referenced and not frozen) and **65** (layer referenced and frozen). See the beginning of this appendix for more information on bit-coded flags.

```
  62
7
```

Color number assigned to this layer (**7** is white). If this is a negative number, then this layer is turned **OFF**.

```
  6
CONTINUOUS
```

The line type assigned to this layer. The CONTINUOUS line type is automatically assigned to any new layer when it is defined by the **LAYER** command.

```
  0
LAYER
```

A layer definition starts here.

```
  2
1
```

Name of the layer to be defined. The name of this layer is **1**; a text string, not a number.

```
  70
        0
```

Layer flag. This is a bit-coded flag where both the first and seventh bits can be set. If the first bit is set (**1**), this layer is currently frozen. If the seventh bit is set (**64**), this layer is used by an entity in either the entity section or in the block section. If the **PURGE** command sees the seventh bit set to **0**, then it will remove this layer definition from the drawing file. This layer is not referenced by an entity since none of the bit flags have been set.

```
  62
7
```

Color number assigned to this layer (**7** is white). If this is a negative number, then this layer is turned **OFF**.

```
  6
HIDDEN
```

The line type assigned to this layer.

```
  0
ENDTAB
```

End of the layer table.

TEXT STYLE TABLE

The text style table contains the definitions of all the text styles that have been defined with the **STYLE** command. If any shapes are used in the drawing, the SHAPE file is also defined in this table.

0 TABLE 2 STYLE	Start of the text style table.
70 3	Text style table maximum item count. The total number of text styles that have been defined in this table. See Group **70** in the line type table section for more information.
0 STYLE	A text style definition starts here.
2 STANDARD	The name of this text style definition. STANDARD is the default text style that is assigned to all text in the drawing unless another text style is defined as current with the **TEXT S** command.
70 0	Text style group flag. This is a bit-coded flag with the first bit (**1**), the third bit (**4**) and the seventh bit (**64**) capable of being set. If the first flag bit is set (**1**), this definition refers to a shape file rather than a font file. If the third flag bit is set (**4**), then a vertically oriented text style has been defined.[*] If the seventh bit has been set (**64**) then this text style has been used in either a text string or as an attribute in this drawing. If the seventh bit flag is set to **0** (false), then the **PURGE** command will remove the text style. The possible bit codes for this group are **0, 1, 4, 64, 65** and **68**. See the beginning of this appendix for more on bit-coded flags.

---

[*]   If you answered **yes** to Vertical when you defined this style with the **STYLE** command.

40		
0.0		Fixed text height. If you had specified a text height in the **STYLE** command when you were defining a text style, then that height would show up here.
41		
1.0		**X** scale factor for this text style.
50		
0.0		Obliquing angle for this text style.
71		
	0	Text generation flag. This is a bit-coded flag with the second (**2**) and third (**4**) bits capable of being set. If both bits are **0**, text will appear normal. If the second bit is set (**2**), text will appear mirrored in the **X** axis (left to right). If the third bit (**4**) is set, text will appear upside down. Only one bit will be set at a time. See the beginning of this appendix for more about bit-coded flags.
42		
0.2		The last text height used for this style in this drawing. Unlike Group **40** (fixed height), this just sets a default height for this style.
3		
txt		Font file name; the name of the font file containing the actual vector information with which AutoCAD constructs the text characters used in this text style definition. This file must be in the same subdirectory as AutoCAD when you load a drawing that uses this font in a text style definition. If you had loaded a shape file into your drawing, the name of that shape file would appear in this group.
4		
		If the font used in this style definition was a "big-font"[*] then its name would appear in this group. Otherwise, this field remains blank.
0		
STYLE		A text style definition starts here.

---

[*]   See Appendix B.5.4 in the *AutoCAD Reference Manual*.

```
   2
NORMAL                    The name of this text style definition.  NORMAL is
                          the name of the text style that we defined and used
                          in this drawing file.

  70
      64                  Text style group flag.  This is a bit-coded flag.  See
                          the previous style listing for more information.

  40
0.0                       Fixed text height size.

  41
1.0                       X scale factor for this text style.

  50
0.0                       Obliquing angle for this text style.

  71
       0                  Text generation flag.  See the previous listing for
                          more information.

  42
0.2                       The last text height used for this style in this draw-
                          ing.

   3
simplex                   Font file name used in this text style.

   4
                          "Bigfont" file name, if any.
```

SHAPE FILE LOAD REQUEST

If a shape file is loaded into the drawing, that fact will show up in the style table as a style definition. This is not a true style definition, however, and only three groups in this definition are meaningful for shapes. All of the other groups are output by AutoCAD, but they seem to carry values from other style definitions. You can ignore these other groups, but they must be present in the definition.

```
   0
STYLE                     A style definition starts here  (IMPORTANT).

   2
                          The name of this style definition.  Because this is a
                          shape load, this field is blank (IGNORE).
```

70

    65   Text style group flag. This is a bit-coded flag and it is set to **65**, which indicates that this is a shape load request. It is referenced by a shape insertion in this drawing file; the seventh bit (**64**) and the first bit (**1**) are set to **1** (IMPORTANT).

40
0.0   Fixed-text height size (IGNORE).

41
1.0   **X** scale factor for this text style (IGNORE).

50
0.0   Obliquing angle for this text style (IGNORE).

71
    0   Text generation flag (IGNORE).

42
9.0   The last text height used (IGNORE).

3
PC   The name of the shape file loaded (IMPORTANT).

4

0
ENDTAB   End of the text style table.

VIEW TABLE

The view table holds the coordinates of all the views that were saved with the **VIEW SAVE** or **VIEW WINDOW** commands. This table contains one view window of the room tag on the sample drawing.

0
TABLE
2
VIEW   The view table starts here.

70
    1   Maximum number of views in this table. See Group **70** in the line type table for more information.

0
VIEW   A view definition starts here.

2
ROOM   The name of the view.

70
        0   View flag — not used. This is a bit-coded flag.

40
2.609776   View height.

10
4.973454   **X** coordinate of the view center point.

20
11.713717   **Y** coordinate of the view center point.

41
4.109143   View width.

11
0.0   **X** coordinate of the view direction from the target
                        point. This value is the default for the Plan view.

21
0.0   **Y** coordinate of the view direction from the target
                        point. This value is the default for the Plan view.

31
1.0   **Z** coordinate of the view direction from the target
                        point. This value is the default for the Plan view.

12
0.0   The **X** coordinate of the target point. This is al-
                        ways in **WCS** coordinates.

22
0.0   The **Y** coordinate of the target point. This is al-
                        ways in **WCS** coordinates.

32
0.0   The **Z** coordinate of the target point. This is al-
                        ways in **WCS** coordinates.

42
0.0   Lens focal length. This is the lens length for an im-
                        aginary camera. This number is set in the **DVIEW**
                        command. This controls the angle of view from
                        the viewpoint to the target point if the projection in
                        this viewport is in perspective.

```
43
0.0                      Front clippng plane, expressed as a distance from
                         the target point on a line between the target point
                         and the viewpoint.

44
0.0                      Rear clippng plane, expressed as a distance from
                         the target point on a line between the target point
                         and the viewpoint.

50
0.0                      View twist angle. This is the angle that the imagi-
                         nary camera is "twisted" or rotated along the line of
                         sight from the viewpoint to the target.

71
0.0                      View mode. This is a bit-coded flag.*

0
ENDTAB                   End of the view table.
```

THE UCS TABLE

The **UCS** table stores coordinate information about User Coordinate Systems that you have saved in the drawing with the **UCS S(ave)** command. The following listing contains all of the information necessary to restore a **UCS** called "3D." All coordinates in this table are world coordinates.

```
0
TABLE
2
UCS                      The UCS table starts here.

70
     1                   Maximum number of saved UCSs in this table.
                         See Group 70 in the line type table for more infor-
                         mation.

0
UCS                      A UCS definition starts here.

2
3D                       Name of saved UCS.
```

---

*   See the table in Section A.7 in the *AutoCAD Reference Manual* for more on the
      VIEWMODE variable.

```
70
      0                 UCS flag — not used.  This is a bit-coded flag.
10
0.0                     X coordinate of UCS origin.
20
0.0                     Y coordinate of UCS origin.
30
0.0                     Z coordinate of UCS origin.
11
0.500000                X coordinate of X axis direction, relative to 1.
21
0.866025                Y coordinate of X axis direction, relative to 0.
31
0.0                     Z coordinate of X axis direction, relative to 0.
12
-0.612372               X coordinate of Y axis direction, relative to 0.
22
0.353553                Y coordinate of Y axis direction, relative to 1.
32
0.707107                Z coordinate of Y axis direction, relative to 0.
  0
ENDTAB
  0
TABLE
  2
```

The DWGMGR table is reserved for future use, and none of the groups has been defined.

```
DWGMGR
70
      0
  0
ENDTAB
  0
ENDSEC                  End of the tables section.
```

BLOCKS SECTION

The blocks section contains all entity information about every block in the drawing. Each block definition in this section is structured exactly like the entity section in this file.[*] When you create a block with AutoCAD, the records of all the drawing entities you've included in the block are copied from the entities section to the blocks section, and are then deleted from the entities section.

When you write a block out to disk as a separate drawing with the **WBLOCK** command, the entity information for the desired block is written to a new file. Other information written to this new file includes the header section and any line type, layer or text definitions referenced by entities in the block definition.

BLOCK DEFINITION

```
      0
SECTION
      2
BLOCKS
```
The beginning of the blocks section.

```
      0
BLOCK
```
A block listing starts here. This block definition consists of four LINE entities and one ATTDEF entity.^{**} You'll see the block definition for the block INSERT entity later in this file. The header section for this block contains information about the overall properties of the block.

```
      8
0
```
Layer name for this block.

```
      2
ROOMTAG
```
The name of the block definition that **INSERT** uses to reference this block description.

---

[*]   Except that entities in the block section do not have entity handles associated with them.

[**]   There should be two ATTDEFs, but we took one out for brevity.

70		
	66	Block type flag. This is a bit-coded flag where the first (1), second (2) and seventh (64) bits are capable of being set. If the second bit (2) is set, this block definition has ATTDEFs or attributes. If the first bit (1) is set, this block is an "anonymous" (or pseudo) block. If the seventh (64) bit is set, then this block is referenced by an INSERT record in the entities section of this drawing. If the seventh bit is set to 0 (false), then the PURGE command will remove this block definition. The possible bit codes for this field are 0, 1, 2, 64, 65 and 66.

10	
116.5	**X** coordinate of the base point for this block.
20	
88.0	**Y** coordinate of the base point for this block.

Now the entities list begins for this block.

0	
LINE	A line definition starts here.
8	
0	Layer name for this entity.
10	
81.0	Start **X** coordinate.
20	
104.0	Start **Y** coordinate.
11	
81.0	End **X** coordinate.
21	
88.0	End **Y** coordinate.
0	
LINE	A line definition starts here.
8	
0	Layer name for this entity.

```
   10
  152.0                    Start X coordinate.

   20
  104.0                    Start Y coordinate.

   11
   81.0                    End X coordinate.

   21
  104.0                    End Y coordinate.

    0
  LINE                     A line definition starts here.

    8
  0                        Layer name for this entity.

   10
  152.0                    Start X coordinate.

   20
   88.0                    Start Y coordinate.

   11
  152.0                    End X coordinate.

   21
  104.0                    End Y coordinate.

    0
  LINE                     A line definition starts here.

    8
  0                        Layer name for this entity.

   10
   81.0                    Start X coordinate.

   20
   88.0                    Start Y coordinate.

   11
  152.0                    End X coordinate.

   21
   88.0                    End Y coordinate.
```

ATTRIBUTE DEFINITION (ATTDEF)

The attribute definition (ATTDEF) entity is always found inside a block definition. You create this with the **ATTDEF** command in AutoCAD and then save it (along with other entities) with the **BLOCK** command to make up the block-with-attributes structure.

0 ATTDEF	Start of the ATTDEF entity.
8 0	Layer name for this entity.
10 84.928571	**X**-coordinate starting point for attribute text.
20 74.571429	**Y**-coordinate starting point for attribute text.
40 9.0	Text height for this attribute definition.
1 Vacant	Default attribute value for this attribute definition.
3 Employee's Name	Prompt for attribute value that appears whenever this block is inserted.
2 EMPNAME	The attribute tag, the key searched for when attributes are extracted with the **ATTEXT** command. The attribute tag remains the same for all instances of this attribute, while each instance can have different values linked to the tag. Think of the attribute tag as a field name and the attribute value as the value contained in that field in a database record.
70 0	The attribute flag. It is a bit-coded flag with the first (**1**), second (**2**) third (**4**) and fourth (**8**) bits capable of being set. If no bits are set in this group (**0**), then this attribute will be visible. If the first (**1**) bit is set, this attribute will be invisible. If the second (**2**) bit is set, then the attribute value will be a constant. If the third (**4**) bit is set, then

verification will be required on input of any value for this attribute. If the fourth bit (8) is set, then this is a preset attribute. See the beginning of this appendix for more information about bit-coded flags.

7
NORMAL   Text style for this attribute entity.

72
        1   Alignment point flag. This is *not* a bit-coded flag. The value of this number determines how the text is justified. **0** means that the text will be left justified and this Group Code will not appear. Other values: **1** = baseline centered text; **2** = right-justified text; **3** = aligned text; **4** = "middle" or fully centered text; and **5** = "fit" text.

11
116.0   The actual **centered X** coordinate base of this attribute text string. This, along with Group **21** below, is the point picked for inserting the attribute text after the CENTER option was picked in the **ATTDEF** command. These two groups are optional, and will appear only in an entity listing if Group **72** is present and non-zero.

21
74.571429   The actual **centered Y** coordinate base of this attribute text string.

0
ENDBLK   End of this block definition.

8
0   Layer name for the preceding block definition.

0
ENDSEC   End of the blocks section.

ENTITIES SECTION

The entities section is the main part of the **DXF** file. All entities in your drawing are described here—either as complete entity descriptions or as instances of block insertions.

START OF THE ENTITIES SECTION

```
  0
SECTION
  2
ENTITIES
```
The name of the entities section. Any line following Group Code **2** is the name of something.

LINE

This first line listing is for a simple line entity.

```
  0
LINE
```
Entity type.

```
  8
0
```
Layer name for this entity.

```
  10
1.0
```
Start **X** coordinate.

```
  20
1.0
```
Start **Y** coordinate.

```
  11
9.0
```
End **X** coordinate.

```
  21
1.0
```
End **Y** coordinate.

```
210
0.0
```
Offset **Z** extrusion **X** coordinate from the **WCS**. This line was constructed on a plane rotated 90 degrees counterclockwise around the **X** axis of the **WCS**. This group and the next two groups will show up in a **DXF** record only if the entity was constructed on a **UCS** plane that was different from the **WCS**. See Appendix A for more on the **UCS**.

```
220
1.0
```
Offset **Z** extrusion **Y** coordinate from the **WCS**.

```
230
0.0
```
Offset **Z** extrusion **Z** coordinate from the **WCS**.

EXTRUDED LINE

This line listing is for a line that has a **Z** coordinate thickness and elevation assigned to it — Groups **38** and **39**, respectively. These groups will be in the entity record *only* if their value is non-zero. Otherwise, this listing is the same as for a line entity.

```
    0
  LINE                    Entity type.

    8
  0                       Layer name for this entity.

   38
  2.0                     If the 38 Group exists in the DXF file, then this en-
                          tity has a Z elevation that is not zero, and the next
                          line is the elevation.

   39
  4.0                     If Group 39 appears in the DXF file, then this entity
                          has a Z thickness that is greater than zero. The
                          next line is the thickness.

   10
  1.0                     Start X coordinate.

   20
  2.0                     Start Y coordinate.

   11
  9.0                     End X coordinate.

   21
  2.0                     End Y coordinate.
```

LINE BY LINETYPE

This next line listing is for a line that has a different linetype than the one set for the layer on which this entity resides.

```
    0
  LINE                    Entity type.

    8
  0                       Layer name for this entity.
```

6 HIDDEN	If Group Code **6** appears, then the linetype for this entity is not the same linetype (HIDDEN) set for the layer for this entity.
10 1.0	Start **X** coordinate.
20 3.0	Start **Y** coordinate.
11 9.0	End **X** coordinate.
21 3.0	End **Y** coordinate.

LINE "BYCOLOR" WITH AN ENTITY HANDLE

This last line listing has a different color than the one assigned to that entity's layer.

0 LINE	Entity type.
8 0	Layer name for this entity.
62 1	If Group Code **62** appears, then the color for this entity is different than the entity's layer color. Color number 1 is RED.
10 1.0	Start **X** coordinate.
20 4.0	Start **Y** coordinate.
11 9.0	End **X** coordinate.
21 4.0	End **Y** coordinate.
1F	This is the entity handle. Entity handles are automatically assigned to each entity in a drawing after the **HANDLES ON** command is invoked. The entity handle is a sequentially assigned, 4-byte

long integer, expressed as a string with any leading zeros removed. This ID number is permanently assigned to this entity and it is very useful for linking individual entities to database records outside of AutoCAD. This example is just a simulation, because once you turn entity handles on you won't be able to turn it off again and all subsequent records will contain the entity handles field.

POINT

POINT is a simple entity; it has only one coordinate. The different point modes available are set with the variable $PMODE in the header section of the data file.[*]

```
   0
POINT                  Entity type.

   8
0                      Layer name for this entity.

  10
5.0                    X coordinate.

  20
5.0                    Y coordinate.
```

CIRCLE

CIRCLE has only two defining measurements: the **X Y** coordinates for the center and the **radius**.

```
   0
CIRCLE                 Entity type.

   8
0                      Layer name for this entity.

  10
5.0                    X coordinate for the center of the circle.

  20
5.0                    Y coordinate for the center of the circle.
```

---

[*]   See Section 4.2 in the *AutoCAD Reference Manual* for more on points.

```
    40
   2.0                   Radius of circle.
```

ARC

ARC is described with a center, a radius, a starting angle and an ending angle. An arc is always drawn counterclockwise from the starting angle to the ending angle.

```
     0
   ARC                   Entity type.

     8
   0                     Layer name for this entity.

    10
   5.0                   X coordinate for the center of the arc.

    20
   5.0                   Y coordinate for the center of the arc.

    40
   3.0                   Arc radius.

    50
   0.0                   Starting angle in degrees.

    51
  180.0                  Ending angle in degrees.
```

SOLID

A SOLID is a three- or four-sided figure that is usually filled. A solid is uniquely described by two opposing pairs of points rather than by four points around the perimeter, as a normal rectilinear shape would be described.

In Figure 1, the solid is properly defined by the first pair of points, **A** and **B** (the base) and then by the second pair of points, **C** and **D** (the top). If this were a square figure rather than a solid, it would be correctly described by the following sequence of points: **A, C, D, B** and **A**. If a solid were triangular, it would be described with the first two points as the base (**10** and **11**), and the third point as the apex (**12**).

```
    0
  SOLID                    Entity type.

    8
  0                        Layer name for this entity.

   10
  10.0                     First X coordinate for the base.

   20
  1.0                      First Y coordinate for the base.

   11
  14.0                     Second X coordinate for the base.

   21
  1.0                      Second Y coordinate for the base.

   12
  10.0                     First X coordinate for the top.

   22
  4.0                      First Y coordinate for the top.

   13
  14.0                     Second X coordinate for the top.

   23
  4.0                      Second Y coordinate for the top.
```

TEXT AND SHAPE

The next several listings describe various types of TEXT and SHAPE entities.

There's only one TEXT entity, but it can vary, based on how the text has been formatted in the drawing editor. Those variations can be very confusing, so we'll illustrate most of them explicitly by example listings.

In all TEXT entity listings below, the text is the same height and the same style; only the way that the text has been formatted is different (i.e., CENTER, RIGHT, FIT, etc.).

For more information on TEXT and SHAPE entities, see the text section in Appendix A.

LEFT TEXT

This first listing is for standard left-justified text, or the kind of text that you get when you just pick a starting point in response to the **TEXT** command.

```
     0
TEXT
```
Entity type.

```
     8
0
```
Layer name for this entity.

```
    10
10.0
```
Insertion point **X** coordinate for this line of text. This coordinate, and the **Y** coordinate that follows, is the actual starting point of the line of text. This point is always at the *beginning* of the text string.

```
    20
5.0
```
Insertion point **X** coordinate for this line of text.

```
    40
0.2
```
The body height of the uppercase letters for this line of text. This group will not appear in the **DXF** listing if the text style has been defined with a height in the tables section.

```
     1
This is left-
aligned text.
```
The actual text string for this entity. These are the characters that will appear on your screen. This text string can have a maximum length of 255 characters. Because everything stored in disk files is stored as strings, this text string doesn't have to be explicitly quoted as it does in the association list format.

```
     7
NORMAL
```
The name assigned to the style definition for this text style. In this example, the text style is named NORMAL. This is *not* the name of the font file, which appears in the style table in the tables section of the drawing database, where the complete definition for NORMAL text style is found (the font file for NORMAL is SIMPLEX).

CENTERED TEXT

The only difference between this TEXT entity listing and the preceding one is that this text is **centered** on an **alignment point** (Groups **11** and **21**). Text always has a base point at the *beginning* of the TEXT entity (in this example, just before the "T" in "This"). If you specify **center** alignment when you insert your line of text into the drawing, AutoCAD will calculate a point to the left of the center point, half the length of your text string. This is the actual insertion point for the TEXT entity.

```
  0
TEXT                    Entity type.

  8
0                       Layer name for this entity.

 10
10.357143               Insertion point X coordinate for this line of text.
                        This, combined with Group 20 below, is the actual
                        starting point of the line of text.

 20
6.0                     Insertion point Y coordinate for this line of text.

 40
0.2                     The body height of the uppercase letters for this
                        line of text.

  1
This is
Centered Text           The actual text string for this entity.

  7
NORMAL                  Text style for this entity.

 72
      1                 Text-justification type flag. The value of this num-
                        ber determines how the text is justified. In this ex-
                        ample, 1 means that the text will be centered. This
                        is an optional group.

 11
12.0                    The centered insertion X coordinate of this text
                        string. This group, and Group 21 that follows, is
                        the point picked for inserting the text after you
                        picked the CENTER option in the TEXT command.
```

	This is an optional group, and will appear only if Group **72** is in the data description and is non-zero.
21 6.0	The actual **centered** insertion **Y** coordinate of this text string. This is an optional group.

RIGHT-ALIGNED TEXT

If you chose **right-aligned** text, then the actual TEXT entity insertion point will be a point to the left of the alignment point, equal in distance to the total width of the TEXT entity.

0 TEXT	Entity type.
8 0	Layer name for this entity.
10 10.161905	Insertion point **X** coordinate for this line of text. This, combined with Group **20** below, is the actual starting point of the line of text.
20 7.0	Insertion point **Y** coordinate for this line of text.
40 0.2	The body height of the uppercase letters for this line of text.
1 This is right aligned text	The actual text string for this entity.
7 NORMAL	The name of the text style for this text.
72 2	Text-justification type flag. The value of this number determines how the text is justified. In this example, **2** means that the text will be right aligned.

```
 11
14.0
```
The actual **right-aligned** insertion **X** coordinate of this text string. This group, and Group **21** that follows, is the point picked for inserting the text after you picked the RIGHT option in the **TEXT** command. This is an optional group, and will appear only if Group **72** is in the data description and is non-zero.

```
 21
7.0
```
The actual **right-aligned** insertion **Y** coordinate of this text string. This is an optional group.

TEXT TO FIT

The difference between this TEXT entity listing and a standard TEXT entity is that this text is fitted between a starting and ending point. After you pick these points, AutoCAD will adjust the **relative X-scale factor** (Group **41**) for this TEXT entity so that it will fit. An **alignment point** (Groups **11** and **21**), halfway between the starting and ending points, is also calculated. Again, text always has a base point at the *beginning* of the TEXT entity (in this example, just before the "T" in "This"), or at the starting point for fitted text. This is the actual insertion point for the TEXT entity.

```
  0
TEXT
```
Entity type.

```
  8
0
```
Layer name for this entity.

```
 10
10.0
```
Insertion point **X** coordinate for this line of text. This, combined with Group **20** below, is the actual starting point of the line of text.

```
 20
8.0
```
Insertion point **Y** coordinate for this line of text.

```
 40
0.2
```
The body height of the uppercase letters for this line of text.

```
  1
This text is
sized to FIT.
```
The actual text string for this entity.

```
  41
1.042184
```
Relative **X** scale, or width factor. This is the factor that changes when a TEXT entity is "stretched" or "squeezed" to fit between two points. In this example, the text had to be stretched slightly to fit, because the factor is slightly greater than **1**.

```
   7
NORMAL
```
Text style for this entity.

```
  72
     5
```
Text-justification type flag. The value of this number determines how the text is justified. In this example, **5** means the text will be sized to fit.

```
  11
14.0
```
The actual **centered** insertion **X** coordinate of this text string. This group, and Group **21** that follows, is the point calculated by AutoCAD to be halfway between the starting and ending points picked for inserting the text after you picked the FIT option in the **TEXT** command. This is an optional group, and will appear only if Group **72** is in the data description and is non-zero.

```
  21
 8.0
```
The actual **centered** Insertion **Y** coordinate of this text string. This is an optional group.

ROTATED TEXT

This example is simply left-justified text, rotated **90** degrees counterclockwise. It illustrates Group **50**.

```
   0
TEXT
```
Entity type.

```
   8
0
```
Layer name for this entity.

```
  10
9.0
```
Insertion point **X** coordinate for this line of text. This, combined with Group **20** below, is the actual starting point of the line of text.

```
  20
 5.0
```
Insertion point **Y** coordinate for this line of text.

```
  40
 0.2
```
The body height of the uppercase letters for this line of text.

```
   1
This text is
rotated 90
degrees.
```
The actual text string for this entity.

```
  50
90.0
```
The rotation angle for this line of text in degrees.

```
   7
NORMAL
```
Text style for this entity.

SHAPES

A shape file is identical in structure to a text file, and almost all information presented about text files and TEXT entities is also true for shapes. The following is the listing for a shape insertion. Notice how close it is in structure to a text insertion.

```
   0
SHAPE
```
Entity type.

```
   8
0
```
Layer name for this entity.

```
  10
15.0
```
Insertion point **X** coordinate for this shape. This, combined with Group **20** below, is the insertion point for this shape.

```
  20
 8.0
```
Insertion point **Y** coordinate for this shape.

```
  40
 2.0
```
The size, or relative scale factor for this shape. This shape was inserted at 2x scale. This is an optional group.

2 DIP24	The name of this shape (the name is contained in the shape file referenced in the style table in the table section of this **DXF** file).

OPTIONAL GROUP CODES FOR TEXT AND SHAPES

The following group codes will appear only in a **DXF** file TEXT entity listing if the value for the group code in question is non-zero.[*] The order in which these "optional" group codes may appear is not fixed, and may vary.

30	Insertion point **Z** coordinate. This will show up only if it is non-zero.
50	The rotation angle for the line of text, in degrees. The pivot point for this angle is always at the insertion point (Group Codes **10** and **20**), which may be different from the starting point of the text (depending on the type of text formatting).
41	Relative **X** scale, or width factor. If, when you defined your text style with the **STYLE** command,[**] you used a width factor other than **1**, then this group code will show up in the **DXF** file with the width factor (other than **1**) that was specified for the text style.
51	The obliquing angle of the text, in degrees. If you had defined a text style to have slanting letters, the angle of that slant would be in this group code and it would appear in the **DXF** file entry for TEXT.
71	Text-generation flag. This is a bit-coded flag with the second (**2**) and third (**4**) bits capable of being set. If both bits are 0, text will appear normal. If the second bit is set (**2**), the text will appear mirrored in the **X** axis (left to right). If the third bit (**4**)

---

[*]   In the association list format all group codes, with a few exceptions, will appear in the entity record regardless of their value.

[**]   See Section 4.10.1 of the *AutoCAD Reference Manual*.

is set, the text will appear upside down. Only one bit will be set at a time. See the beginning of this appendix for more on bit-coded flags.

72   Text-justification type flag. This is *not* a bit-coded flag. The value of this number determines how the text is justified. **0** means that the text will be left justified and this group code will not appear. Other values: **1** = baseline-centered text; **2** = right-justified text; **3** = aligned text; **4** = "middle" or fully centered text; and **5** = "fit" text.

11
21
31   Alignment point. These three group codes represent the **X Y Z** coordinate point where the text was inserted. These groups will appear in a record description only if Group **72** appears. See the comments on the different types of TEXT entities for examples of how to use these two groups.

OTHER TEXT ENTITY TYPES

Two remaining text-justification types that we haven't illustrated are ALIGNED and MIDDLE.

ALIGNED is similar to FIT except the text height (Group **40**) is adjusted to fit instead of the relative **X** scale factor (Group **41**). The text-justification type (Group **72**) for ALIGNED is **3**.

MIDDLE is similar to CENTER, but the text is centered with the alignment point (Groups **11** and **21**) in both the **X** and the **Y** axis. The text-justification type (Group **72**) for MIDDLE is **4**.

BLOCK INSERTION, ATTRIBUTE AND SEQEND

The following four **DXF** entity listings represent an insertion of a block that contains two attributes. The only difference between this block insertion record and that of a block that doesn't contain attributes is that in the latter, Group **66** doesn't appear.

The actual list of entities that makes up any given block or attribute is in the block section of this **DXF** file.

Many "optional" groups for block insertions and attributes don't appear in the following **DXF** listings. These groups are listed and commented on at the end of this section.

BLOCK INSERTION

```
     0
INSERT
```
Entity type.

```
     8
0
```
Layer name for this entity.

```
    66
        1
```
"Attributes Follow" flag. If this group appears in the **DXF** listing for a block insertion, then all records that follow this record will be attributes attached to this block until a SEQEND entity type is reached. This is an optional group and will appear only if attribute entities are linked with the block.

```
     2
ROOMTAG
```
The name of this block. If an INSERT record is found with a block name starting with an asterisk (*), then that block is "anonymous," created by an internal AutoCAD operation. Hatch patterns and arrowheads are examples of anonymous blocks.

```
    10
5.0
```
The **X** coordinate of the insertion point for this instance of the block.

```
    20
12.0
```
The **Y** coordinate of the insertion point for this instance of the block.

```
    41
0.05
```
The **X** scale for this insertion of the block. This is an optional group—if the **X** scale of this block insertion were **1**, this group would not appear in this record.

```
 42
0.05
```
The **Y** scale for this insertion of this block. This is an optional group—if the **Y** scale of this block insertion were **1**, this group would not appear in this record.

```
 43
0.05
```
The **Z** scale for this insertion of this block. This is an optional group—if the **Z** scale of this block insertion were **1**, this group would not appear in this record.

ATTRIBUTES

The next two listings are for the two attributes linked to the block insertion above. Notice the similarity to the TEXT entity listings. Because the attribute entity carries mainly textual data, it could be considered a specialized type of TEXT entity. All text formatting features available with the **TEXT** command are available with attributes. The attribute prompts that appear when this block is inserted are stored in the block section of this **DXF** file, in an entity called ATTDEF.

A number of optional groups for the ATTRIBUTE entity will not appear in this example. These groups carry text-formatting information and are identical to the optional groups for the TEXT entity.[*]

```
  0
ATTRIB
```
Entity type.

```
  8
0
```
Layer name for this entity.

```
 10
4.085714
```
Insertion point **X** coordinate for this attribute. This, combined with Group **20** below, is the actual starting point of the text of this attribute.

```
 20
11.328571
```
Insertion point **Y** coordinate for this attribute.

---

[*]   See the TEXT section of this appendix for more information on these groups.

```
40
0.45
```

The body height of the uppercase letters for this attribute. The original height of this text when this attribute was defined was 9". When we inserted the block that this attribute was attached to into the drawing, we scaled the block to .05x scale. AutoCAD automatically recalculated all sizes of the attributes associated with that block to be the same relative size.

```
1
Smith
```

The attribute value we gave to this particular insertion of the attribute, linked to the attribute tag EMPNAME.

```
2
EMPNAME
```

The attribute tag, the key searched for when attributes are extracted using the **ATTEXT** command. The attribute tag remains the same for all instances of this attribute, while each instance of this attribute can have different values linked to this attribute tag. Think of the attribute tag as a field name and the attribute value as the value contained in that field in a database record.

```
70
  0
```

The attribute flag. It is a bit-coded flag with the first (**1**), second (**2**), third (**4**) and fourth (**8**) bits capable of being set. If no bits are set in this group (**0**), then this attribute will be visible. If the first (**1**) bit is set, this attribute will be invisible. If the second (**2**) bit is set, then the attribute value will be a constant. If the third (**4**) bit is set, then verification will be required on input of any value for this attribute. If the fourth bit (**8**) is set, then this is a preset attribute. See the beginning of this appendix for more on bit-coded flags.

```
7
NORMAL
```

Text style for this attribute entity.

```
 72
     1
```
Text-justification type flag. The attribute text in this example is centered. This group has the same values as the TEXT entity Group **72**. This is an optional group.

```
 11
 4.975
```
The actual **centered** insertion **X** coordinate of this attribute text string. This, along with Group **21** below, is the point picked for inserting the attribute text after the CENTER option was picked in the **ATTDEF** command when this attribute was defined. These two groups are optional and will appear in an entity listing only if Group **72** is present and non-zero.

```
 21
 11.328571
```
The actual **centered** insertion **Y** coordinate of this attribute text string.

The following ATTRIB listing is almost identical to the one above. We wanted to show you how two (or more) attributes can be linked with the same Block INSERT record. We'll comment only on those fields that are different from the preceding ATTRIB record.

```
  0
ATTRIB
  8
0
 10
 4.439286
     20
 12.1
 40
 0.45
  1
100
```
The attribute value for the attribute tag ROOMNO.

```
  2
ROOMNO
```
The attribute tag to which the value 100 is linked.

```
 70
  0
  7
STANDARD
```

```
    72
     1
    11
 4.975
    21
 12.1
```

The next entity, SEQEND, appears only at the end of a series of attribute records (or, as we'll see later, at the end of a series of polyline vertices). SEQEND marks the end of a series of attributes that are linked to a block insertion.

```
     0
SEQEND                      Entity type.

     8
0                           Layer name for this entity.
```

OPTIONAL GROUP CODES FOR BLOCKS AND ATTRIBS

Several optional group codes did not appear in these sample listings and will appear in a **DXF** record only if their value is other than the standard default value (usually **0**) for that group code. They are as follows:

30	Insertion point **Z** coordinate. This will show up only if it is non-zero.
50	The rotation angle of the block insertion in degrees. This will appear only if the angle is *not* **0** degrees.
70	Column count for MINSERT. If this or any of the next three groups have a value other than **0**, then these group codes will appear in the INSERT record of the **DXF** file. They indicate that the insertion was done with the **MINSERT** command, and the record represents multiple occurrences of the referenced block in the drawing file.[*]
71	Row count for **MINSERT**.
44	Column spacing for **MINSERT**.
45	Row spacing for **MINSERT**.

---

[*]   See Section 9.1.6 in the *AUTOCAD Reference Manual* for more on **MINSERT**.

210	
220	
230	Offset **X Y Z** extrusion coordinate from the **WCS**. These groups will show up in a **DXF** record only if the entity was constructed on a **UCS** plane that was different from the **WCS**. See Appendix A for more on the **UCS**.

The following optional group codes are found in ATTRIB records and are identical in meaning to the same codes found in text entities. See the end of the text entities section in this appendix for a complete explanation of these group codes:

50	Rotation angle for the attribute text in degrees. Will appear only if the angle is not **0**.
41	Relative **X** scale, or width factor of the attribute text. This group code will show up in an attribute record only if this value is *not* **1**.
51	The obliquing angle of the attribute text in degrees. This is used only if this value is *not* **0**.
71	Text generation flag. See Group Code **71** in the text section of this appendix for explanation of the codes.
210	
220	
230	Offset **X Y Z** extrusion coordinate from the **WCS**. These groups will show up in a **DXF** record only if the entity was constructed on a **UCS** plane that was different from the **WCS**. See Appendix A for more on the **UCS**.

TWO-DIMENSIONAL (2D) POLYLINES

The **POLYLINE** entity in Release 10 can now be either a 2D polyline or a 3D polyline, depending on the value of certain groups within the POLYLINE and the VERTEX records. 3D polylines are described in detail in the 3D entity section of this appendix. Here we will touch on the differences between a 2D polyline and a 3D polyline.

There are two types of 3D polylines. The first type is generated by the **3DPOLY** command and will construct a 0-width, non-extruded polyline in 3D space. The second type is called a 3D polygon mesh, and although it's described by the polyline entity record in the drawing database, it's generated internally by the AutoCAD commands **3DMESH, RULESURF, TABSURF, REVSURF** and **EDGESURF**. The most important thing to know at this point is that if the value of Group **70** in the polyline entity record is greater than 7, then that polyline, and the vertex records that follow, describe a 3D polyline.

POLYLINE DATA FORMAT

The polyline data format has three parts. The first part is the header record entity, called POLYLINE. The POLYLINE record signals the start of the polyline data structure and contains some general information about the polyline. The structure of this record is quite similar to the INSERT record followed by ATTRIB. The second part of the polyline data structure is a series of entity records, called VERTEX. A vertex record contains the coordinates and other information about each vertex or point in the polyline. Finally, the SEQEND entity appears as the last record in the polyline data structure; it signals the end of that structure.[*]

There are several optional group codes for polyline and vertex records that will appear in the **DXF** file for those records only if their value is not zero. These are listed at the end of the first polyline listing.

POLYLINE HEADER

0	
POLYLINE	Entity type.
8	
0	Layer name for this entity.
66	
1	Vertex follows flag. Because the polyline header record cannot exist unless there are at least two VERTEX entities following it, this flag would seem to be redundant. It does, however, follow a consistent data structure.

---

[*]   See the section on polylines in Appendix A for more information.

70

1   Polyline flag. This is a bit-coded flag. If the bit is not set (**0**), then this is an open polyline; if the bit is set (**1**) (as in this example), it's a closed polyline. When a polyline is **closed**, it appears on the screen with a line connecting its last vertex with its first vertex. You close a polyline by using the C option in the **PLINE** command. If this flag were set to **0**, then this polyline would be U-shaped instead of square. The following applies to Release 9 or later: If bit 2 (**2**) is set, then this polyline has been curve fitted and if bit 3 (**4**) has been set then this polyline has been spline fitted. The following bit flags are used in Release 10 and later to indicate whether this is a 3D polyline or a 3D polygon mesh: If the fourth (**8**) bit is set, then this is a 3D polyline. If the fifth bit (**16**) is set, then this is a 3D polygon mesh. These bit flags are described in more detail in the 3D section of this appendix.

VERTEXES

The following four VERTEX records describe a polyline square with the polylines having zero width.

0
VERTEX   Entity type.

8
0   Layer name for this entity.

10
10.0   **X** coordinate for this vertex.

20
13.0   **Y** coordinate for this vertex.

0
VERTEX   Entity type.

8
0   Layer name for this entity. Theoretically, you could place each vertex of a polyline on a separate layer, but this doesn't seem to have any practical use.

10	
14.0	**X** coordinate for this vertex.
20	
13.0	**Y** coordinate for this vertex.
0	
VERTEX	Entity type.
8	
0	Layer name for this entity.
10	
14.0	**X** coordinate for this vertex.
20	
9.0	**Y** coordinate for this vertex.
0	
VERTEX	Entity type.
8	
0	Layer name for this entity.
10	
10.0	**X** coordinate for this vertex.
20	
9.0	**Y** coordinate for this vertex.

POLYLINE SEQEND

This SEQEND record is the same record found at the end of a list of AT-TRIB records. It marks the end of the list of vertex records that define a polyline.

0	
SEQEND	Entity type.
8	
0	Layer name for this entity.

OPTIONAL GROUP CODES FOR POLYLINE AND VERTEX RECORDS

The following optional group codes will appear in polyline and/or vertex records if the value of the group code is *not* zero.

30	Z coordinate for the vertex. This group shows up in a DXF record only if the value is non-zero.
40	Starting width. The only time Group **40** is not **0** and will appear either in the polyline record or at the specific vertex record is when the starting width is changed. The starting polyline width is assumed to always be the same until it's changed.
41	Ending width. The only time Group **41** is not **0** and will appear either in the polyline record or at the specific vertex record is when the ending width is changed. The ending polyline width is assumed to be always the same until it is changed. The ending width of the current vertex becomes the starting width of the next vertex.
42	Polyline bulge factor. If this group code appears in a vertex record, it means that the polyline segment between the vertex this group appears in and the following vertex record will be a polyarc. This group code will appear only in a vertex record. See the section on bulge factor calculations in Appendix A.
70	Polyline flag. This is a bit-coded flag. If the bit is not set (**0**), then this is an open polyline, and if the bit is set (**1**) (as in this example), it's a closed polyline. When a polyline is **closed**, it appears on the screen with a line connecting its last vertex with its first vertex. You close a polyline by using the C option in the **PLINE** command. If this flag were set to **0**, then this polyline would be U-shaped instead of square. The following applies to Release 9 or later: If bit 2 (**2**) is set, then this polyline has been curve fitted and if bit 3 (**4**) has been set, then this polyline has been spline fitted. The following bit flags are used in Release 10 and later: If the fourth (**8**) bit is set, then this is a 3D polyline. If the fifth bit (**16**) is set, then this is a 3D polygon mesh. These bit flags are described in more detail in the 3D section of this appendix.

70	Vertex flag. This is a bit-coded flag where only the first (**1**) and second (**2**) bits are set. If the first bit (**1**) is set, then AutoCAD added the next vertex record as an extra vertex to create a smoother curve. If the second bit (**2**) is set, a curve-fitted tangent has been defined, and that information will appear in Group Code **50** below. The following applies to Release 9 or later: If the fourth bit (**8**) is set, then this is an extra vertex created by spline fitting. If the fifth bit (**16**) is set, then this vertex is a spline-frame control point and is not actually part of the visible polyline. 3D polyline vertex flags are discussed in the 3D section (bits **6** and **7**).
50	Curve-fitted tangent direction, in degrees. This group code will appear in a vertex record only if "Fit Curve" has been used on this polyline and the second bit (**2**) flag in Group Code **70** above has been set.*
210	
220	
230	Offset **X Y Z** extrusion coordinate from the **WCS**. These groups will show up in a 2D POLYLINE DXF record only if the 2D polyline was constructed on a **UCS** plane that was different from the **WCS**. See Appendix A for more on the **UCS**.

There are several other optional group codes for polylines that apply only to 3D polygon meshes. They're covered in the section on 3D polylines.

WIDE POLYLINE

This next polyline record describes a closed polyline box in which the polyline is .5 inch wide. Note that the starting and ending widths of .5" (Groups **40** and **41**) appear only in the polyline record and not in any of the subsequent vertex records. The only time these fields are *not* **0** in a polyline or a vertex record is when the starting or ending widths are changed *in that record*. These values are kept until changed in another record.

---

*   See Section 5.4.1.1 in the *AutoCAD Reference Manual* for more on curve fitting.

```
   0
POLYLINE                Entity type.

   8
0                       Layer name for this entity.

  66
      1                 Vertex follows flag.


  70
      1                 Polyline flag.

  40
0.5                     Default starting polyline width.  This is where the
                        polyline starting width is defined; it's an optional
                        group code.

  41
0.5                     Default ending polyline width.  This is where the
                        polyline ending width is defined; it's an optional
                        group code.

   0
VERTEX                  Entity type.

   8
0                       Layer name for this entity.

  10
11.0                    X coordinate for this vertex.

  20
10.0                    Y coordinate for this vertex.

   0
VERTEX                  Entity type.

   8
0                       Layer name for this entity.

  10
11.0                    X coordinate for this vertex.

  20
12.0                    Y coordinate for this vertex.

   0
VERTEX                  Entity type.
```

```
   8
0                      Layer name for this entity.

  10
13.0                   X coordinate for this vertex.

  20
12.0                   Y coordinate for this vertex.

   0
VERTEX                 Entity type.

   8
0                      Layer name for this entity.

  10
13.0                   X coordinate for this vertex.

  20
10.0                   Y coordinate for this vertex.

   0
SEQEND                 Entity type.

   8
0                      Layer name for this entity.
```

SIMPLE POLYLINE WITH POLYARC

This polyline structure is one straight line followed by a semicircle (a 180-degree half circle, the largest arc that can be created with a single polyarc). The only difference between the first and the second vertex records (other then the coordinates) is that the second vertex contains a **polyline bulge factor** of **1**. The bulge factor is 1/4 of the tangent of the included angle of the arc. If the bulge factor is **0**, then the polyline segment that extends from that vertex will be straight. If the bulge factor is **1**, as in this case, then the polyline segment will appear as a semicircle. See "Bulge Factor Calculations" in Appendix A to learn how to derive the arc information from the bulge factor.

```
   0
POLYLINE               Entity type.

   8
0                      Layer name for this entity.

  66
      1                Vertex follows flag.
```

```
  0
VERTEX              Entity type.

  8
0                   Layer name for this entity.

 10
17.0                X coordinate for this vertex.

 20
9.0                 Y coordinate for this vertex.

  0
VERTEX              Entity type.

  8
0                   Layer name for this entity.

 10
17.0                X coordinate for this vertex.

 20
11.0                Y coordinate for this vertex.

 42
1.0                 Polyline bulge factor.  A bulge factor of 1 means
                    that this polyline segment will be a semicircle.

  0
VERTEX              Entity type.

  8
0                   Layer name for this entity.

 10
15.0                X coordinate for this vertex.

 20
11.0                Y coordinate for this vertex.

 42
1.0                 Polyline bulge factor.  This is the bulge factor if the
                    preceding polyarc were continued back to the
                    starting point of of the polyarc (a full circle).

  0
SEQEND              Entity type.

  8
0                   Layer name for this entity.
```

TAPERED POLYARCS

This entry describes two different types of polyline structures: tapered polylines and polyarcs. Figure 2 is a detailed illustration of this polyline structure. The first thing to notice about this polyline is that, although the illustration shows only two arcs and three vertexes, there are actually four vertex sub-records in this polyline record—the coordinates for the first two vertex records are identical. Because there are actually three polyarcs, the first polyarc was forced to have the same starting and ending point.[*] "Bulge Factor Calculations" in Appendix A describes how to extract the arc description information from the bulge factor.

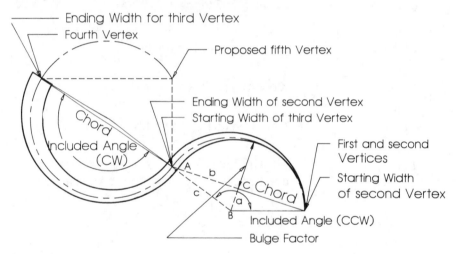

Figure 2

0		
POLYLINE		Entity type.
8		
0		Layer name for this entity.
66		
	1	Vertex follows flag.
0		
VERTEX		Entity type.

---

[*]   You have to use this technique if you're starting a polyline with a polyarc and want that arc to be less than 180 degrees.

8	Layer name for this entity.
0	
10	
8.0	**X** coordinate for this vertex.
20	
8.0	**Y** coordinate for this vertex.
42	
1.0	Polyline bulge factor. This is the first polyarc, forced to the same starting and ending point—in this circumstance, the bulge factor is always **1**.
0	
VERTEX	Entity type.
8	
0	Layer name for this entity.
10	
8.0	**X** coordinate for this vertex.
20	
8.0	**Y** coordinate for this vertex.
41	
0.25	Ending polyline width. The first visible polyarc of this structure starts at **0** width, and ends with a width of **.25**.
42	
0.720759	Polyline bulge factor.
0	
VERTEX	Entity type.
8	
0	Layer name for this entity.
10	
5.0	**X** coordinate for this vertex.
20	
9.0	**Y** coordinate for this vertex.

```
40
0.25
```
Starting polyline width. This is the same width as the ending polyline width of the previous vertex, but since it's different than the starting width of the previous vertex, then the starting width has changed, which must show up here.[*]

```
41
0.5
```
Ending polyline width.

```
42
-0.945986
```
Polyline bulge factor. If the bulge factor is a negative number, it means that the polyarc was generated clockwise from its starting point.

```
0
VERTEX
```
Entity type.

```
8
0
```
Layer name for this entity.

```
10
2.0
```
X coordinate for this vertex.

```
20
11.0
```
Y coordinate for this vertex.

```
40
0.5
```
Starting polyline width. This width is, of course, different than the starting width of the last vertex — the starting width of the *next* polyline segment (if there were one).

```
41
0.5
```
Ending polyline width.

```
42
-0.571429
```
Polyline bulge factor. This is the bulge factor of a proposed polyarc of the same radius as the last polyarc. This assumes that it was continued until it intersected with the right angle of a right triangle

---

[*]   The starting and ending width fields *always* remain *at 0 unless* there is a change in width from the previous vertex record.

	constructed so that the hypotenuse was congruent with the chord of the last polyarc (see Figure 2).

```
    0
SEQEND                  Entity type.

    8
0                       Layer name for this entity.
```

POLYGONS

Polygons are not separate entity types, but are simply closed polylines generated by AutoCAD according to your specifications when you use the **POLYGON** command. Below is the DXF data record for a hexagon generated with the **POLYGON** command:

```
    0
POLYLINE                Entity type.

    8
0                       Layer name for this entity.

   66
        1               Vertex follows flag.

   70
        1               Polyline flag. A polyline generated with the
                        POLYGON command is always properly closed.

    0
VERTEX                  Entity type.

    8
0                       Layer name for this entity.

   10
8.0                     X coordinate for this vertex.

   20
11.0                    Y coordinate for this vertex.

    0
VERTEX                  Entity type.

    8
0                       Layer name for this entity.
```

```
    10
8.866025              X coordinate for this vertex.

    20
11.5                  Y coordinate for this vertex.

     0
VERTEX                Entity type.

     8
0                     Layer name for this entity.

    10
8.866025              X coordinate for this vertex.

    20
12.5                  Y coordinate for this vertex.

     0
VERTEX                Entity type.

     8
0                     Layer name for this entity.

    10
8.0                   X coordinate for this vertex.

    20
13.0                  Y coordinate for this vertex.

     0
VERTEX                Entity type.

     8
0                     Layer name for this entity.

    10
7.133975              X coordinate for this vertex.

    20
12.5                  Y coordinate for this vertex.

     0
VERTEX                Entity type.

     8
0                     Layer name for this entity.

    10
7.133975              X coordinate for this vertex.
```

```
  20
11.5
```
Y coordinate for this vertex.

```
   0
SEQEND
```
Entity type.

```
   8
   0
```
Layer name for this entity.

TRACE

A trace looks something like a polyline, but if you examine the data structure, you'll find that it's more like a solid. Generally, traces have been superseded by polylines.

TRACE records can also contain the optional group codes **30, 31, 32, 33** (**Z** coordinates), **210, 220** and **230**.

```
   0
TRACE
```
Entity type.

```
   8
   0
```
Layer name for this entity.

```
  10
15.0
```
X coordinate of the first corner of the starting side.

```
  20
 2.1
```
Y coordinate of the first corner of the starting side.

```
  11
15.0
```
X coordinate of the second corner of the starting side.

```
  21
 1.9
```
Y coordinate of the second corner of the starting side.

```
  12
16.9
```
X coordinate of the first corner of the ending side. This, along with Group Code **22** below, is a mitered corner that shares this coordinate with the first corner of the starting side in the next TRACE.

```
  22
 2.1
```
Y coordinate of the first corner of the ending side.

13 17.1	**X** coordinate of the second corner of the ending side. This, along with the Group Code **23** below, is a mitered corner that shares this coordinate with the second corner of the starting side in the next TRACE.
23 1.9	**Y** coordinate of the second corner of the ending side.
0 TRACE	Entity type.
8 0	Layer name for this entity.
10 16.9	**X** coordinate of the first corner of the starting side. This, along with Group Code **20** below, is a mitered corner that shares this coordinate with the first corner of the ending side in the previous TRACE.
20 2.1	**Y** coordinate of the first corner of the starting side.
11 17.1	**X** coordinate of the second corner of the starting side. This, along with Group Code **21** below, is a mitered corner that shares this coordinate with the second corner of the ending side in the previous TRACE.
21 1.9	**Y** coordinate of the second corner of the starting side.
12 16.9	**X** coordinate of the first corner of the ending side.
22 4.0	**Y** coordinate of the first corner of the ending side.
13 17.1	**X** coordinate of the second corner of the ending side.

23
4.0   **Y** coordinate of the second corner of the ending
                          side.

ASSOCIATIVE DIMENSION BLOCK

Ordinarily, when you dimension a drawing with the DIM commands, the parts of the dimension structure such as extension lines, dimension lines and text are made up of LINE and TEXT entities and are not obvious as dimensions in the drawing database.[*]

An associative dimension entity is a unique type of entity. On the one hand, it has many of the properties of a BLOCK entity in that its data description is in the blocks section; and the whole dimension structure of text, extension lines, dimension lines and arrowheads is treated as a single entity in the drawing. On the other hand, when you operate on this entity with the **STRETCH**, **SCALE** or **ROTATE** commands, AutoCAD updates the dimension text to reflect its new size or orientation. When you stretch or move the associative dimensioning DIMENSION entity, not only do all defining point coordinates in the entity record change to reflect the new position of the entity; the block definition in the blocks section also changes to reflect the new coordinates of all points in the drawing. Whenever you add a dimension, AutoCAD creates an unique block definition for that dimension in the blocks section, then references that block with a DIMENSION record in the entities section.[**]

We suggest that you use this associative dimension sparingly—it seems to take up much more space in the drawing database than an ordinary dimension and tends to create larger drawing files than necessary.[***]

The associative dimension entity is created any time that you add a dimension to a drawing with the system variable **DIMASO** set to **ON**. When a associative dimension entity is created, a number of special points are inserted into your drawing at strategic locations. These points are called

---

[*]   The only unique entity that shows up in this type of dimension is the arrowhead, which strictly speaking is an "anonymous" block.

[**]   If you delete a DIMENSION entity in your drawing, the block reference for that entity will remain in the blocks section.

[***] The associative dimension in this example uses 13 records. If this dimension were created using the regular dimensioning command, it would take only seven records to describe it. Also, if this associative dimension were erased from the drawing, the twelve records in the blocks section would still exist.

definition points, and their coordinates are found in Group Codes **10** through **16** and **20** through **26**. Definition points are always inserted on a special layer that AutoCAD creates, named DEFPOINTS. For example, if you were to dimension a line, then definition points would be placed at the beginning and end of the line, at the end point of the dimension line and at the center of the dimension text. If you later lengthened this line with the **STRETCH** command, the **defining point** for the endpoint of the line would have a new coordinate location and AutoCAD would recalculate the dimension[*] and display it as the dimension text.

Below is a block section and an entities section listing for a simple horizontal dimension. Compare the coordinates for the different entities (such as LINE, POINT and SOLID) in the block section with the defining points in the DIMENSION entity in the entities section.

ASSOCIATIVE DIMENSION BLOCK DEFINITION

The first information below is the block definition for the associative DIMENSION entity. It's described in the entities section which follows. Rather than give group by group comments on each entity, which would get redundant, we identify and comment only on how each entity record refers to the DIMENSION entity in the entities section.

0 SECTION	Start of section.
2 BLOCKS	Start of blocks section.
0 BLOCK	Start of block definition.
8 0	Layer name for this block.
2 *D3	The name of this block. The leading asterisk indicates that this is a "pseudo" block created by AutoCAD, and the **D** indicates it's a DIMENSION block.

---

[*]   And possibly the dimension text location, to keep the dimension text centered.

```
70
  1
```
Block type flag. This is a bit-coded flag where the first (**1**), second (**2**) or seventh (**64**) bits are capable of being set. If the second bit (**2**) is set, this block definition has ATTDEFs or attributes. If the first bit (**1**) is set, this block is an "anonymous" (or pseudo) block. If the seventh (**64**) bit is set, this block is referenced by an INSERT record in the entities section of this drawing. If the seventh bit is set to **0** (false), then the **PURGE** command will remove this block definition. The possible bit codes for this field are **0, 1, 2, 64, 65** and **66**.

```
10
0.0
```
X coordinate of the base point for this block. Since this is a "pseudo" block, there is no base point.

```
20
0.0
```
Y coordinate of the base point for this block.

This line is the left extension line of the DIMENSION entity.

```
 0
LINE
```
Entity type.

```
8
0
```
Layer name for this entity.

```
6
BYBLOCK
```
This indicates a floating linetype.

```
62
  0
```
Color number **0** is a floating color.

```
10
-8.163841
```
Start **X** coordinate.

```
20
5.997929
```
Start **Y** coordinate.

```
11
-8.163841
```
End **X** coordinate.

```
21
6.386479
```
End **Y** coordinate.

This line is the right extension line of the DIMENSION entity.

```
    0
   LINE                    Entity type.

    8
   0                       Layer name for this entity.


    6
   BYBLOCK                 This indicates a floating linetype.
   62
          0               Color number 0 is a floating color.
   10
   -6.663841              Start X coordinate.

   20
   5.997929               Start Y coordinate.

   11
   -6.663841              End X coordinate.

   21
   6.386479               End Y coordinate.
```

This line is the left dimension line of the DIMENSION entity.

```
    0
   LINE                    Entity type.

    8
   0                       Layer name for this entity.

    6
   BYBLOCK                 This indicates a floating linetype.

   62
          0               Color number 0 is a floating color.

   10
   -7.983841              Start X coordinate.

   20
   6.206479               Start Y coordinate.

   11
   -7.968841              End X coordinate.

   21
   6.206479               End Y coordinate.
```

This line is the right dimension line of the DIMENSION entity.

```
   0
   LINE                 Entity type.

   8
   0                    Layer name for this entity.

   6
   BYBLOCK              This indicates a floating linetype.

   62
        0               Color number 0 is a floating color.

   10
   -6.843841            Start X coordinate.

   20
   6.206479             Start Y coordinate.

   11
   -6.858841            End X coordinate.

   21
   6.206479             End Y coordinate.
```

This solid is the left arrowhead in the DIMENSION entity.

```
   0
   SOLID                Entity type.

   8
   0                    Layer name for this entity.

   6
   BYBLOCK              This indicates a floating linetype.

   62
        0               Color number 0 is a floating color.

   10
   -7.983841            First corner X coordinate.

   20
   6.176479             First corner Y coordinate.

   11
   -7.983841            Second corner X coordinate.

   21
   6.236479             Second corner Y coordinate.
```

```
  12
-8.163841              Third corner X coordinate.

  22
6.206479               Third corner Y coordinate.

  13
-8.163841              Fourth corner X coordinate.

  23
6.206479               Fourth corner Y coordinate.
```

This solid is the right arrowhead in the DIMENSION entity.

```
   0
  SOLID                 Entity type.

   8
  0                     Layer name for this entity.

   6
  BYBLOCK               This indicates a floating linetype.

  62
         0             Color number 0 is a floating color.

  10
-6.843841              First corner X coordinate.

  20
6.176479               First corner Y coordinate.

  11
-6.843841              Second corner X coordinate.

  21
6.236479               Second corner Y coordinate.

  12
-6.663841              Third corner X coordinate.

  22
6.206479               Third corner Y coordinate.

  13
-6.663841              Fourth corner X coordinate.

  23
6.206479               Fourth corner Y coordinate.
```

This is the current dimension text for the DIMENSION entity—the actual dimension between the two extension defining points formatted in the current UNITS format. This dimension text *will not* appear in the dimension if an explicit dimension has been typed in when you were prompted for dimension text when this dimension was created.

```
   0
TEXT                    Entity type.

   8
0                       Layer name for this entity.

   6
BYBLOCK                 This indicates a floating linetype.

  62
       0                Color number 0 is a floating color.

  10
-7.788841               Text insertion point X coordinate.

  20
6.116479                Text insertion point Y coordinate.

  40
0.18                    Dimension text height.

   1
1.5000                  The dimension text string.
```

This point is the extension defining point for the starting point of the DIMENSION entity. This corresponds to Group Codes **13** and **23**.

```
   0
POINT                   Entity type.

   8
DEFPOINTS               Layer name for this entity.

   0
BYBLOCK                 This indicates a floating linetype.

  62
       0                Color number 0 is a floating color.

  10
-8.163841               X coordinate.

  20
5.935429                Y coordinate.
```

This POINT is the extension defining point for the ending point of the DIMENSION entity. This corresponds to Group Codes **14** and **24**.

```
   0
POINT                   Entity type.

   8
DEFPOINTS               Layer name for this entity.

   6
BYBLOCK
   62                   Color number 0 is a floating color.

        0
  10
-6.663841               X coordinate.

  20
 5.935429               Y coordinate.
```

This point is the dimension line defining point for the DIMENSION entity. This corresponds to Group Codes **10** and **20**.

```
   0
POINT                   Entity type.

   8
DEFPOINTS               Layer name for this entity.

   6
BYBLOCK                 This indicates a floating linetype.

  62
        0               Color number 0 is a floating color.

  10
-6.663841               X coordinate.

  20
 6.206479               Y coordinate.

   0
ENDBLK                  End of associative dimension block definition.

   8
0                       Layer name for this block.

   0
ENDSEC                  End of the blocks section.
```

```
   0
SECTION
   2
ENTITIES
```
Start of the entities section.

ASSOCIATIVE DIMENSION INSERT

This is the INSERT entity for the associative dimension block listed above.

```
   0
DIMENSION
```
Entity type.

```
   8
0
```
Layer name for this entity.

```
   2
*D3
```
Block name. The asterisk at the beginning of the block name indicates that it's an "anonymous" block created by AutoCAD. **D** indicates that this is an associative dimension block and **3** is the unique block number for this dimension entity.

```
  10
-6.663841
```
The **X** coordinate of the dimension line *defining point*. This, along with Group Code **20** below, is the actual end point of the dimension line. The distance between this defining point and the Group Codes **13** and **23** defining point below determines the distance between the dimensioned object and the dimension line (and also the length of the extension line).

```
  20
6.206479
```
The **Y** coordinate of the dimension line defining point.

```
  11
-7.413841
```
The **X** coordinate of the middle-of-text defining point. This, along with Group **21** below, is usually a point midway along the dimension line. This point is recalculated to remain at the midpoint of the dimension line if any of the other defining points are moved. There is no point for this defining point listed in the block definition.

```
21
6.206479
```
Y coordinate of the middle-of-text defining point.

```
13
-8.163841
```
X coordinate of the extension defining point for the starting point of the dimension entity. This point also corresponds to the starting point of the line being dimensioned in this example.

```
23
5.935429
```
Y coordinate of the extension defining point for the starting point of the dimension entity.

```
14
-6.663841
```
X coordinate of the extension defining point for the ending point of the dimension entity. This point also corresponds to the ending point of the line being dimensioned in this example.

```
24
5.935429
```
Y coordinate of the extension defining point for the ending point of the dimension entity.

OPTIONAL GROUP CODES FOR THE DIMENSION ENTITY

Several optional group codes may appear in the DIMENSION entity if their value is *not* zero:

```
12
24
```
Insertion points for CLONES of a dimension. This would be the insertion point (Group Codes **10** and **20**) of the *next* associative dimension entity if you used the BASELINE or CONTINUE options to do a string of dimensions in one direction.

```
70
```
Dimension type flag. This is a bit-coded flag with the first (**1**), second (**2**) and third (**4**) bit capable of being set. If no bits are set (**0**), then this is a horizontal, vertical or rotated dimension. Other flag codes: **1** = aligned, **2** = angular, **3** = diameter and **4** = radius.

1	Explicit dimension text string. When you create a dimension, you're prompted for the dimension text. You can press < RETURN > to accept the actual measured dimension, or you can type in your own text. If you type in your own text, then it will show up here, and it *will not* be updated if you stretch this dimension later. The null string (two quotation marks) means that the dimension text will be updated. The dimension is calculated from the distance between the coordinates in Group Codes **13** and **23** and **14** and **24**.
15 25	Extension defining point for diameter, radius and angular dimensions. If this dimension is not a diameter, radius or angular dimension, then this group code will not appear in the **DXF** file record.
16 26	Extension defining point for the dimension arc in angular dimensions. This would be analogous to Group Codes **10** and **20** for other dimension types.
40	Leader length for radius and diameter dimensions.
50	Angle of rotation for linear dimensions; specifically, horizontal, vertical or rotated dimensions.

3D ENTITIES

This section describes the association list data structure of 3D entities. There are five types of 3D entities: LINE, POINT, 3DFACE, 3D POLYLINE and 3D POLYGON MESH. 3D POLYLINE and 3D POLYGON MESH are actually variations of the standard polyline structure; they differ from 2D polylines only in the way the Group **70** polyline flags are set.

We have extracted the 3D entity data from Figure 3 to use as examples of the data record listings.

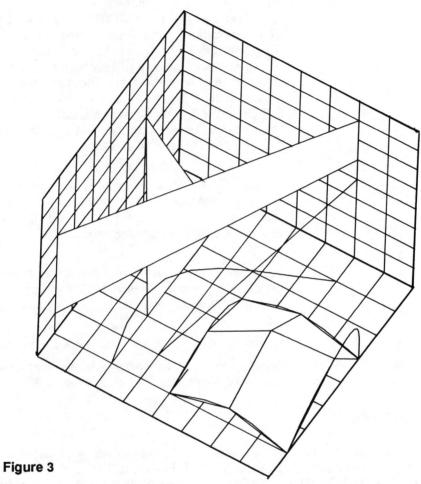

Figure 3

LINE

This is a listing for a LINE entity that was drawn in 3D space. The only major difference between this listing and the LINE listing in the 2D section is that the **Z** coordinate of the end point is not **0**.

One other interesting thing about LINE is that you can extrude a line into the **Z** axis — even if it's drawn in 3D space. The line is extruded into the **Z** axis of the current **UCS** plane and the end points are perpendicular to the current **Z** axis. If the line has been extruded into a **UCS** that differs from the **WCS**, then the entity record will contain a Group **210** field.

```
    0
    LINE                Entity type.

    8
    0                   Layer name for this entity.

    10
    2.0                 Start X coordinate.

    20
    5.0                 Start Y coordinate.

    30
    -0.0                Start Z coordinate.

    11
    8.0                 End X coordinate.

    21
    2.0                 End Y coordinate.

    31
    -4.0                End Z coordinate.
```

3DFACE

The 3DFACE entity is similar in structure to the SOLID entity. Unlike SOLID, however, 3DFACE is constructed by picking the corners in a circular fashion, rather than by describing two points for the base and either one or two points for the top of the surface. 3DFACE always has three coordinates given for each corner and can have either three or four vertexes or corners. When you use the **HIDE** command, the 3DFACE will appear opaque when the view has its hidden lines removed.

One new feature has been added to 3DFACES in Release 10 — you can now make one or more edges of a 3DFACE invisible. This is particularly useful for constructing an irregularly shaped seamless surface with 3DFACES.

This first 3DFACE is triangular, so the first and the fourth corners are the same.

```
    0
    3DFACE              Entity type.

    8
    0                   Layer name for this entity.
```

10 3.0	**X** coordinate of the starting corner.
20 6.0	**Y** coordinate of the starting corner.
30 0.0	**Z** coordinate of the starting corner.
11 7.0	**X** coordinate of the second corner.
21 6.0	**Y** coordinate of the second corner.
31 0.0	**Z** coordinate of the second corner.
12 6.0	**X** coordinate of the third corner.
22 8.0	**Y** coordinate of the third corner.
32 5.0	**Z** coordinate of the third corner.
13 3.0	**X** coordinate of the last corner. Since this face is triangular, this coordinate will be the same as the first corner.
23 6.0	**Y** coordinate of the last corner.
33 0.0	**Z** coordinate of the last corner.

This is a four-sided 3DFACE.

0 3DFACE	Entity type.
8 0	Layer name for this entity.
10 1.0	**X** coordinate of the starting corner.

```
20
8.0                    Y coordinate of the starting corner.

30
1.0                    Z coordinate of the starting corner.

11
1.0                    X coordinate of the second corner.

21
8.0                    Y coordinate of the second corner.

31
5.0                    Z coordinate of the second corner.

12
8.0                    X coordinate of the third corner.

22
2.0                    Y coordinate of the third corner.

32
7.0                    Z coordinate of the third corner.

13
8.0                    X coordinate of the last corner.

23
2.0                    Y coordinate of the last corner.

33
5.0                    Z coordinate of the last corner.
```

OPTIONAL GROUP CODE FOR 3DFACE

70   Invisible edge, bit-coded flag. If bit one (**1**) is set, then the first edge will be invisible. If bit two (**2**) is set, then the second edge will be invisible. Bits three (**4**) and four (**8**) control the visibility of the third and fourth edges, respectively. All four bits can be set to make all of the edges of a 3DFACE invisible.

3D POINT

The point is defined by its **X Y Z** coordinates in 3D space. A point can also be extruded into the **Z** axis from the current **UCS** plane.

```
       0
  POINT                Entity type.

       8                Layer name for this entity.

       0
      10
     5.0                X coordinate.

      20
     3.0                Y coordinate.


      30
     7.0                Z coordinate.
```

A 3D POINT also has an optional group code:

    50   The angle of the **X** axis of the **UCS**, relative to the **WCS**, that was current when this point was created. This information is used by point display mode (PDMODE) to display the alternate point graphic symbols (see Section 4.2 of the *AutoCAD Reference Manual* for information on PDMODE).

3D POLYLINE

This **DXF** data listing describes a 3D polyline that was created by constructing four vertexes in space and then smoothing it with **PEDIT** into a 3D spline curve. This 3D polyline is shown in Figure 3.

In the following polyline listing there are 13 vertexes, but only four of them (the first and the last three) actually control the shape of the curve — they are called the control points. AutoCAD adds the other nine vertexes to the polyline to smooth the curve.

```
       0
  POLYLINE             Entity type.

       8
  0                    Layer name for this entity.

      66
          1            Vertex follows flag.
```

70
    12   Polyline flag. This is a bit-coded flag. If the bit is not set (0), this is an open polyline; if the bit is set (1), it's a closed polyline. If bit 2 (2) is set, then this polyline has been curve fitted and if bit 3 (4) has been set, then this polyline has been spline fitted. If the fourth (8) bit is set, this is a 3D polyline. If the fifth bit (16) is set, it's a 3D polygon mesh. The sixth bit (32) is set only to indicate that this structure is a polygon mesh, closed in the N direction. Since the value of this group is 12, the third and the fourth bits have been set (4 + 8 = 12); that means that this is a 3D polyline that has been spline fitted.

75
    6   Smooth curve type flag. This is not a bit-coded flag. Since this is a 3D polyline and not a 3D polygon mesh, this field indicates the type of curve fitting applied: The type depends on the value set in the system variable SPLINESEGS, specifying either a quadratic B-spline (5) or a cubic B-spline curve (6). Don't confuse the SPLINESEGS variable with the SURFTYPE variable, which controls the surface fitting of 3D meshes—they're independent of one another. A 0 value means that this polyline has not been curve fitted. A 5 means that this is a quadratic B-spline curve. A 6 defines the polyline as a cubic B-spline curve. These are the only valid values for a polyline that's not a polygon mesh. This is an optional group.

This first vertex is the starting point for this polyline, and it's also a control point. This is one of only four vertexes (out of 13) that was used to define this 3D polyline before it was curve fitted. Usually the only spline frame control points that actually lie on the fitted curve are the first and last vertexes of a polyline.

    0
VERTEX   Entity type.

    8
0   Layer name for this entity.

10		
1.0		X coordinate for this vertex.
20		
6.0		Y coordinate for this vertex.
30		
0.0		Z coordinate for this vertex.
70		
	48	Vertex flag. This is a bit-coded flag. If the first bit (**1**) is set, then AutoCAD added the next vertex record as an extra vertex to create a smoother curve. If the second bit (**2**) is set, a curve-fitted tangent has been defined, and that information will appear in the optional Group Code 50. If the fourth bit (**8**) is set, then this is an extra vertex created by spline fitting. If the fifth bit (**16**) is set, then this vertex is a spline-frame control point and is not actually part of the visible polyline. If the sixth bit is set (**32**), then this is a 3D polyline vertex. The seventh bit (**64**) indicates a 3D polygon mesh vertex. Since the value of this flag is 48 (16 + 32 = 48), then this vertex is a spline-frame control point of a 3D polyline.

OPTIONAL GROUP CODES FOR 3D POLYLINE VERTEX

The following optional group code may appear in a 3D polyline vertex record if its value is non-zero:

50	Curve-fitted tangent direction, in radians. This is always **0**, unless "fit curve" has been used on this polyline, the system variable SPLINESEGS has been set to 5 (quadratic B-spline), and the second bit (**2**) flag in Group Code **70** above has been set.[*]

The next nine vertex records were generated internally by AutoCAD with the spline curve option of the **PEDIT** command to generate a smooth curve based on the location of the original four vertexes (now control points). If you want to modify the shape of this curve, move only the control point vertexes and then use **PEDIT** to resmooth the curve.

---

[*]   See Section 5.4.1.1 in the *AutoCAD Reference Manual* for more on curve fitting.

```
   0
VERTEX                    Entity type.

   8
0                         Layer name for this entity.


  10
1.0                       X coordinate for this vertex.

  20
6.0                       Y coordinate for this vertex.

  30
0.0                       Z coordinate for this vertex.

  70
     40                   Vertex flag.  This is a bit-coded flag.  Since the
                          value of this flag is 40 (32 + 8 = 40),  this is a spline
                          vertex created by spline fitting (8); also, this is a 3D
                          polyline vertex (32).
```

The next eight vertex records are identical in function to the previous record, so we comment on them only briefly.

```
   0
VERTEX                    Entity type.

   8
0                         Layer name for this entity.

  10
1.667969                  X coordinate for this vertex.

  20
5.910156                  Y coordinate for this vertex.

  30
1.3125                    Z coordinate for this vertex.

  70
      40                  Vertex flag.

   0
VERTEX                    Entity type.

   8
0                         Layer name for this entity.
```

```
    10
2.21875              X coordinate for this vertex.

    20
5.65625              Y coordinate for this vertex.

    30
2.25                 Z coordinate for this vertex.

    70
        40           Vertex flag.

     0
VERTEX               Entity type.

     8
0                    Layer name for this entity.

    10
2.722656             X coordinate for this vertex.

    20
5.261719             Y coordinate for this vertex.

    30
2.8125               Z coordinate for this vertex.

    70
        40           Vertex flag.

     0
VERTEX               Entity type.

     8
0                    Layer name for this entity.

    10
3.25                 X coordinate for this vertex.

    20
4.75                 Y coordinate for this vertex.

    30
3.0                  Z coordinate for this vertex.

    70
        40           Vertex flag.

     0
VERTEX               Entity type.
```

```
   8
0                          Layer name for this entity.

  10
3.871094                   X coordinate for this vertex.

  20
4.144531                   Y coordinate for this vertex.

  30
2.8125                     Z coordinate for this vertex.

  70
     40                    Vertex flag.

   0
VERTEX                     Entity type.

   8
0                          Layer name for this entity.

  10
4.65625                    X coordinate for this vertex.

  20
3.46875                    Y coordinate for this vertex.

  30
2.25                       Z coordinate for this vertex.

  70
     40                    Vertex flag.

   0
VERTEX                     Entity type.

   8
0                          Layer name for this entity.

  10
5.675781                   X coordinate for this vertex.

  20
2.746094                   Y coordinate for this vertex.

  30
1.3125                     Z coordinate for this vertex.

  70
     40                    Vertex flag.
```

```
     0
  VERTEX                    Entity type.

     8
  0                         Layer name for this entity.

    10
  7.0                       X coordinate for this vertex.

    20
  2.0                       Y coordinate for this vertex.

    30
  0.0                       Z coordinate for this vertex.

    70
      40                    Vertex flag.
```

The last three vertex records are spline frame control points. None of the control points are actually part of the curve, but they control how the curve should look. You can tell that these are control points because the third bit **(8)** is set in Group **70**.

```
     0
  VERTEX                    Entity type.

     8
  0                         Layer name for this entity.

    10
  3.0                       X coordinate for this vertex.

    20
  6.0                       Y coordinate for this vertex.

    30
  4.0                       Z coordinate for this vertex.

    70
      48                    Vertex flag.

     0
  VERTEX                    Entity type.

     8
  0                         Layer name for this entity.

    10
  3.0                       X coordinate for this vertex.
```

```
    20
    4.0                         Y coordinate for this vertex.

    30
    4.0                         Z coordinate for this vertex.

    70
    48                          Vertex flag.

    0
    VERTEX                      Entity type.

    8
    0                           Layer name for this entity.

    10
    7.0                         X coordinate for this vertex.

    20
    2.0                         Y coordinate for this vertex.

    30
    0.0                         Z coordinate for this vertex.

    70
        48                      Vertex flag.
```

The SEQEND record always comes at the end of a series of polyline vertexes.

```
    0
    SEQEND                      Entity type.

    8
    0                           Layer name for this entity.
```

3D POLYGON MESH

3D polygon meshes are used to describe complex curved surfaces in 3D space. They are generated by the **3DMESH, RULESURF, TABSURF, REVSURF** and **EDGESURF** commands in AutoCAD Release 10. These commands will generate a polyline record in the drawing database with one VERTEX record for each vertex that shows up in the drawn 3D surface.

See the 3D section in Appendix A for more on 3D surfaces.

3D POLYGON MESH DATA STRUCTURE

The following 3D polygon mesh data structure represents the simplest 3D surface that can be generated by the **EDGESURF** command. This 3D surface is the one with four sides in Figure 3. If you look closely at Figure 3 you can see the four curved polylines that were used to define the edges of this surface. The curved polyline on the right side is particularly evident. As you can imagine, the greater the number of surfaces defined, the smoother the curved surface will be and the more closely its edges will follow the defining polyline edges.

0	
POLYLINE	Entity type.
8	
0	Layer name for this entity.
66	
1	Vertex follows flag.
70	
16	Polyline flag. This is a bit-coded flag. If the bit is not set (**0**), then this is an open polyline, and if the bit is set (**1**), it's a closed polyline. If bit 2 (**2**) is set, then this polyline has been curve fitted and if bit 3 (**4**) has been set, then this polyline has been spline fitted. If the fourth (**8**) bit is set, this is a 3D polyline. If the fifth bit (**16**) is set, it's a 3D polygon mesh. The sixth bit (**32**) is set only to indicate that this structure is a polygon mesh, closed in the **N** direction. Since the value of this group is 16, the fourth bit has been set; that tells us that this is a 3D polygon mesh.
71	
3	Polygon mesh **M** vertex count. This is the number of vertexes in the **M** direction of this surface as defined by the value of SURFTAB1 +1.[*]

---

[*]   See Section 4.9 in the *AutoCAD Reference Manual* for more on **M** and **N** directions.

72

    3   Polygon mesh **N** vertex count. This is the number of vertexes in the **N** direction of this surface as defined by SURFTAB2 + 1.

One way of determining the number of VERTEX records that follow the POLYLINE record is to multiply the values found in Groups **71** and **72** and then add that value to the product of multiplying the values of optional Groups **73** and **74**. In this example, it's $(3 \times 3) + (0 \times 0) = 9$.

OPTIONAL GROUP CODES FOR 3D POLYGON MESHES

The following optional group codes may appear in a 3D POLYLINE record for a 3D polygon mesh if their value is non-zero:

73   Polygon mesh smooth surface **M** density. If **PEDIT** was used to smooth this surface, the value in the system variable SURFU would be found here.

74   Polygon mesh smooth surface **N** density. If **PEDIT** was used to smooth this surface, the value in the system variable SURFV would be found here.

75   Smooth surface type flag. This is *not* a bit-coded flag. In the case of a 3D polygon mesh, this field indicates the type of surface fitting applied: The type depends on the value set in the system variable SURFTYPE, specifiying a quadratic B-spline surface (**5**), a cubic B-spline surface (**6**) or a Bezier surface (**8**). Don't confuse SURFTYPE with the SPLINESEGS variable, which controls the curve fitting of polylines—they're independent of one another.

3D POLYGON MESH VERTEX

The following listing is the first vertex record of this 3D polygon mesh. 3D polygon meshes always run across rows (**N**) and down columns (**M**). The position of this vertex is **M-0, N-0**.

    0

VERTEX   Entity type.

```
  8
0                              Layer name for this entity.

 10
5.0                            X coordinate for this vertex.

 20
0.0                            Y coordinate for this vertex.

 30
0.0                            Z coordinate for this vertex.

 70
      64
```
Vertex flag. This is a bit-coded flag. If the first bit (1) is set, then AutoCAD added the next vertex record as an extra vertex to create a smoother curve. If the second bit (2) is set, a curve-fitted tangent has been defined, and that information will appear in Group Code 50 below. If the fourth bit (8) is set, then this is an extra vertex created by spline fitting. If the fifth bit (16) is set, then this vertex is a spline-frame control point and is not actually part of the visible polyline. If the sixth bit is set (32), then this is a 3D polyline vertex. The seventh bit (64) indicates a 3D polygon mesh vertex. Since the value of this flag is 64, then this vertex is part of a 3D polygon mesh. The location of this vertex is M-0, N-1.

```
  0
VERTEX                         Entity type.

  8
0                              Layer name for this entity.

 10
5.0                            X coordinate for this vertex.

 20
2.0                            Y coordinate for this vertex.

 30
0.75                           Z coordinate for this vertex.

 70
      64                       Vertex flag.
```

This vertex is located at M-0, N-2 or the upper left corner in Figure 3.

```
   0
VERTEX                    Entity type.

   8
0                         Layer name for this entity.

  10
5.0                       X coordinate for this vertex.

  20
4.0                       Y coordinate for this vertex.

  30
0.0                       Z coordinate for this vertex.

  70
      64                  Vertex flag.
```

This vertex is **M-1, N-0**.

```
   0
VERTEX                    Entity type.

   8
0                         Layer name for this entity.

  10
3.579379                  X coordinate for this vertex.

  20
0.0                       Y coordinate for this vertex.

  30
1.712678                  Z coordinate for this vertex.

  70
      64                  Vertex flag.
```

This vertex record is located at **M-1, N-1** at the center of the surface.

```
   0
VERTEX                    Entity type.

   8
0                         Layer name for this entity.

  10
3.310781                  X coordinate for this vertex.

  20
2.0                       Y coordinate for this vertex.
```

```
30
1.951535
```
Z coordinate for this vertex.

```
70
   64
```
Vertex flag.

This is **M-1, N-2**.

```
0
VERTEX
```
Entity type.

```
8
0
```
Layer name for this entity.

```
10
3.042182
```
X coordinate for this vertex.

```
20
4.0
```
Y coordinate for this vertex.

```
30
0.690391
```
Z coordinate for this vertex.

```
70
   64
```
Vertex flag.

This vertex is located at the lower right corner in Figure 3 or at **M-2, N-0**.

```
0
VERTEX
```
Entity type.

```
8
0
```
Layer name for this entity.

```
10
1.0
```
X coordinate for this vertex.

```
20
0.0
```
Y coordinate for this vertex.

```
30
0.0
```
Z coordinate for this vertex.

```
70
   64
```
Vertex flag.

This is vertex **M-2, N-1**.

```
0
VERTEX
```
Entity type.

```
    8
0                         Layer name for this entity.

   10
1.0                       X coordinate for this vertex.

   20
2.0                       Y coordinate for this vertex.

   30
0.75                      Z coordinate for this vertex.

   70
        64                Vertex flag.
```

This is the ending vertex located at **M-2**, **N-2**.

```
    0
VERTEX                    Entity type.

    8
0                         Layer name for this entity.

   10
1.0                       X coordinate for this vertex.

   20
4.0                       Y coordinate for this vertex.

   30
0.0                       Z coordinate for this vertex.

   70
        64                Vertex flag.

    0
SEQEND                    Entity type.

    8
0                         Layer name for this entity.
```

appendix C

THE DXB FILE FORMAT

The **DXF** format described in the previous appendix is the most commonly used method of exchanging drawing data from one format to another. There is, however, another drawing exchange format that AutoCAD can use that has several advantages over the **DXF** format in certain circumstances — the **DXB** format. The **DXB** (for **D**rawing e**X**change **B**inary) format was designed for transferring pure graphics data into AutoCAD from a medium that may or may not be a CAD system. **DXB** files were first used for translating data from digital scanners into an AutoCAD drawing format.

The **DXB** format stores the graphic information in a very compact binary format, similar to the way graphic information is stored in the **DWG** drawing file. The main advantage of a **DXB** file is that it's compact, allowing AutoCAD to read the file much faster than it can a **DXF** file. For example, a simple line entity description in **DXF** format takes up approximately 82 bytes of file space. The **DXB** file only uses 9 bytes (or 17 bytes depending on the number mode) to describe that same line.

The **DXB** format is not a true drawing exchange format, because it does not carry a complete representation of the drawing database and because AutoCAD does not have a **DXBOUT** function. AutoCAD can produce a **DXB** file through the ADI plotter driver interface, but all the drawing entities are translated into lines and line segments (plotter pen moves) to drive a plotter.

The **DXB** format is currently capable of storing only graphic data. There's no way of storing the drawing header information (the drawing defaults), text, block definitions, block attributes, linetypes or views.

About the only information that a digital scanner can derive by scanning a paper drawing are entities such as lines, arcs and points. So the original **DXB** format was limited to storing very simple entity types. In the last few years, we've noticed that Autodesk has been expanding the **DXB** format so that it will now carry more complex entities such as polylines, 3dfaces, layer names and entity colors. There's some speculation that one day the **DXB** format may be capable of storing as much information as the **DXF** format — and much more efficiently.

WHY USE DXB FILES?

If you want to translate a pure vector graphics file into an AutoCAD drawing file, consider using the **DXB** format because the files are much more compact than **DXF** files and are much faster to read and write.

Here is an example of some of the advantages of using the **DXB** file format. We recently wrote a program in C to translate map graphic data from a graphics format used by the U. S. Geological Survey (Digital Line Graph) into **DXB** files to generate AutoCAD drawings of those maps. The resulting **DXB** file generated from a typical **DLG** file was less than 5 percent the size of the original **DLG** file and less than 10 percent the size of the same data in **DXF** format. The size of the original map data file was 439k. From that file, we produced a **DXB** file of 22k and a **DXF** file of 242k. The size of the resulting drawing file was 107k. It took less than two minutes to generate a **DXB** file from the original map data file.

WRITING DXB FILES

You can't "write" a **DXB** file by hand, since it's a pure binary format. But once you understand the structure of the **DXB** file (and if you have a little programming experience in C), you'll find it very simple to write a program to write a **DXB** file based on another graphic data file format.

We're going to assume, at this point, that you have some experience with the C programming language, since we'll be explaining the **DXB** entities by using the C structure format.

THE DXB FILE FORMAT

The **DXB** file format consists of three parts:

The file header simply declares that the file is indeed a **DXB** file, and what follows is a list of graphic entities in binary format.

The body is a list of graphic entity records of variable length in binary format. The first byte in each record declares what entity will be found in the record, and by definition, the length of that record.

The terminator is a nul byte that lets AutoCAD know that it has come to the end of the file.

The length of an entity record is determined by two factors: the number of coordinates needed to describe that entity and whether the coordinates are expressed as integer numbers or real numbers. Let's look at a line entity record and see how this works:

Line record in integer format

```
1               byte 1                    entity type
1               byte 2-3                  from x
1               byte 4-5                  from y
9               byte 6-7                  to x
1               byte 8-9                  to y
```

If the number mode record had been set to 1, which declares that the records following will have the coordinates as floating point numbers, then AutoCAD will expect the line record to be 33 bytes long rather than 9 bytes as in the preceding example.

Line record in real format

```
1                       byte 1       entity type
1.000000   byte 2-9                  from x
1.000000   byte 10-17   from y
9.000000   byte 18-25   to x
1.000000   byte 26-33   to y
```

If you store all the coordinates in the **DXB** file as floating point numbers, rather than as integers, you can see that the file will be almost four times as long. There's a way to effectively store floating point coordinates from another file as integers in the **DXB** file (to keep the file size small) by using a scale factor.

The scale factor is a number by which all succeeding coordinate values in the **DXB** file are multiplied by to arrive at an actual AutoCAD drawing coordinate number.

If the graphic data that you're converting is taken from a paper drawing, and the accuracy of that data is not expected to be greater than .001 inches, chances are that if you multiplied all the coordinate values by 1000, the range of coordinate values wouldn't exceed integer values (-32767 to 32767). If that's the case, you could multiply each coordinate value from the input file by 1000 (creating an integer value) and place a SCALE FACTOR record at the beginning of your **DXB** file with the value of .001.

THE DXB FILE STRUCTURE

Because the **DXB** file is a binary file, you'll never be able to read it; so we can't really show you a commented file listing as we did with the Association List and the **DXF** formats. What we can show you are the C structure formats for all the current **DXB** record types and a few examples of how to fill these structures with data.

```
/*the following structure will write the DXB file header*/
struct
        {
        char head_string[15];
        char cr;
        char lf;
        char control_z;
        char nul;
        } dxb_file_head = {"AutoCAD DXB 1.0", 13, 10,
        26, '\0'};
/*LINE structure.  To use this, and any other structure*/
/*for floating point numbers, change the data type */
/*declarations from int to double and change the variable */
/*initialization from 0 to 0.0 */
struct
        {
        char entity_type;
        int from_x;
        int from_y;
        int to_x;
        int to_y;
        }line = {1,0,0,0,0};
/*POINT structure */
```

```c
        struct
                {
                char entity_type;
                int x;
                int y;
                }point = {2,0};
/*CIRCLE Structure */
        struct
                {
                char entity_type;
                int center_x;
                int center_y;
                int radius;
                }circle = {3,0,0,0};
/*ARC structure.  Notice that the starting and ending */
/*angles are declared as long ints.  If those are long ints,*/
/*then the number will represent the angle in millionths */
/*of a degree.  If the angles are declared as doubles, the */
/*angle is in decimal degrees */
        struct
                {
                char entity_type;
                int center_x;
                int center-y;
                int radius;
                long int start_angle;
                long int end_angle;
                }arc = {8,0,0,0,0,0};
/*TRACE structure */
        struct
                {
                char entity_type;
                int x1;
                int y1;
                int x2;
                int y2;
                int x3;
                int y3;
                int x4;
                int y4;
                }trace = {9,0,0,0,0,0,0,0,0};
/*SOLID structure */
```

```
struct
        {
        char entity_type;
        int x1;
        int y1;
        int x2;
        int y2;
        int x3;
        int y3;
        int x4;
        int y4;
        }solid = {11,0,0,0,0,0,0,0,0};
/*SEQEND is not a structure, but a char type constant */
char seqend = 17;
/*Polyline structure.  This flag is always an int.*/
struct
        {
        char entity_type;
        int closure_flag;
        }polyline = {19,0};
/*VERTEX structure.  Always follows a polyline record */
struct
        {
        char entity_type;
        int to_x;
        int to_y;
        }vertex = {20,0,0};
/*3DLINE structure. */
struct
        {
        char entity_type;
        int from_x;
        int from_y;
        int from_z;
        int to_x;
        int to_y;
        int to_z;
        }3dline = {21,0,0,0,0,0,0};
/*3DFACE structure */
```

```
struct
            {
            char entity_type;
            int x1;
            int y1;
            int z1;
            int x2;
            int y2;
            int z2;
            int x3;
            int y3;
            int z3;
            int x4;
            int y4;
            int z4;
            }solid = {22,0,0,0,0,0,0,0,0,0,0,0,0};
/*SCALE FACTOR structure.  This record must be placed */
/*before any of the other records that you want to have */
/*scaled.  The scale factor can also be reset to 1 at */
/*any point in the file.  The default scale factor */
/*is 1, so if you don't want to scale any of the */
/*coordinates, then you don't have to use this record */
struct
            {
            unsigned char entity type;
/*since these numbers will be greater than 127*/
            double scale_factor;
/*this number is always declared a double*/
            }scalefac = {128,1};
/*NEW LAYER structure.  Any entity that follows this */
/*record will be placed on the layer named in this record */
/*until the next NEW LAYER record is encountered in the file */
struct
            {
            unsigned char entity_type;
            char layer_name[32];
/*maximum length of layer name in Acad*/
            int nul;
            }new_layer = {129," ",'\0'};
/*LINE EXTENSION structure.  This record must always */
/*follow a LINE record.  This record can be used when you have */
/*a series of connected lines.  It's used in the way */
```

```
/*that polyline vertex records are used in polyline */
/*structures. */
struct
        {
        unsigned char entity_type;
        int to_x;
        int to_y;
        }line_extension = {130,0,0};
/*TRACE EXTENSION.  This record must always follow a TRACE */
/*record.  It's used with traces the same way LINE EXTENSION */
/*is used with lines. */
struct
        {
        unsigned char entity_type;
        int x3;
        int y3;
        int x4;
        int y4;
        }trace_extension = {131,0,0,0,0};
/*BLOCK BASE structure.  If the DXB file will be converted */
/*into a drawing file ultimately to be used as a block, then */
/*this record needs to be used to define the block base */
/*coordinates used for inserting that block into another */
/*drawing */
struct
        {
        unsigned char entity_type;
        int base_x;
        int base_y;
        }block_base = {132,0,0};
/*BULGE structure.  This is the bulge factor for a polyline */
/*vertex.  See page 382 of the AutoCAD Reference Manual for */
/*more information. */
struct
        {
        unsigned char entity_type;
        long int factor;
/*if number mode is 1 then this is a double */
        }bulge = {133,0};
/*WIDTH structure.  This structure declares the width of any */
/*polyline vertexes that follow this record until another */
/*record of this type is encountered. */
```

```
struct
        {
        unsigned char entity_type;
        int start;
/*these widths type must be doubles if number mode is 1*/
        int end;
        }width = {134,0,0};
/*NUMBER MODE structure.  Number mode can either be 0 or 1. */
/*If number mode is set to one, all subsequent records must */
/*have their coordinate values stored as doubles (8 bytes)*/
/*until the number mode is reset to 0.  The default value of */
/*the number mode is 0, so if all coordinates are to be */
/*expressed as integer numbers, then this record does */
/*not have to appear in the DXB file. */
struct
        {
        unsigned char entity_type;
        int mode;     /*always an int*/
        }number = {135,0};
/*NEW COLOR structure.  All entities following this record */
/*will be assigned the color number in this record.  The */
/*standard AutoCAD color numbers of 0-256 are used. */
struct
        {
        unsigned char entity_type;
        int number;
        }new_color = {136,0};
/*3DLINE EXTENSION structure.  This record is to 3DLINES */
/*what the LINE EXTENSION record is to lines. */
struct
        {
        unsigned char entity_type;
        int to_x;
        int to_y;
        int to_z;
        }3dline_extension = {137,0,0,0};
/*We must also define a null character to add to the end */
/*of the DXB file */
char null_char = '\0';
```

USING THE DXB DATA STRUCTURES IN C

We don't know how your input data might be formatted, so we'll end this appendix by including several short **C** functions for writing data to a **DXB** file. The data structure is quite straightforward. You should find it easy to adapt these functions to write any of the other record types. The only difficulty you may have is remembering that if you're writing a **DXB** file using floating point coordinates, then you must declare all the coordinate variables to be type double instead of type int.

For sake of argument, we'll assume you've opened an input file and an output file, and you'll be translating line and circle data. The file pointer for the **DXB** file will be defined as *fpout*. The first function will write the **DXB** file header:

```
int write_header ()
        {
/*just writes the declared structure to a file since */
/*it is a constant */
        fwrite (&dxb_file_head, sizeof(dxb_file_head), 1,
        fpout);
        }
```

The next function will write the LINE record using the starting and ending X-Y coordinates as arguments:

```
int write_line_record (int start_x, int start_y, int end_x,
        int end_y)
        {
/*loads the different variables of the structure with the */
/*coordinates    */
        line.from_x=start_x;
        line.from_y=start_y;
        line.to_x=end_x;
        line.to_y=end+y;
/*writes the loaded structure to the file including the */
/*entity type char */
        fwrite(&line,sizeof(line), 1, fpout);
        }
```

Assuming the next line has the same starting coordinate as the ending coordinate of the previous line, you can use this next function to write the line extension:

```
int write_line_extension_record (int end_x, int end_y)
        {
```

```
line_extension.to_x=end_x;
line_extension.to_y=end+y;
fwrite(&line_extension, sizeof(line_extension),
1, fpout);
}
```

Here's a function to write a CIRCLE DXB record:

```
int write_circle_record (int center_x, int center_y,
        int radius)
        {
        circle.center_x=center_x;
        circle.center_y=center_y;
        circle.radius=radius;
        fwrite(&circle, sizeof(circle), 1, fpout);
        }
```

Finally, when your program has written all the entity records to the DXB file, it must add the NULL character and close the file:

```
fwrite(&null_char, 1, 1, fpout);
close(fpout);
```

HOW TO CREATE YOUR OWN SWD FILES

appendix D

An **.SWD** file is simply a list of the character widths of each character in the font file along with their ASCII codes. The BASIC text formatting program at the end of Chapter 9 uses this file to determine how many characters should be placed in each line of text. An **.SWD** file *must* have the same name as the font file it's used for with an **.SWD** file extension attached to it. See the **SIMPLEX.SWD** listing in the next section as an example of what the file should look like.

SWD FILE STRUCTURE

There are two numbers on each line separated by a comma. The first number is the ASCII code for the character and the second number is the *total width for that character, in vectors,* including any space before and/or after that character. The first line of the .SWD file is **0**, followed by the total height in vectors of an upper case character (the first number on the second line of the **.SHP** file).

The second line is **10**, followed by the line feed (ASCII code **10**) length in vectors (the number after the minus on the fifth line of the **.SHP** file). *

---

*   See Appendix B in the *AutoCAD Reference Manual* for more information on how fonts are constructed.

If your .SHP file starts out looking like this:

```
*0,4,[Name of a font]
35,9,0,0
*1,2,sot
5,0
*10,5,1f
2,8,(0,-50),0
```

then your .SWD file should start out like this:

```
0,35
10,50
32,(width of space in vectors)
33,(etc,etc)
. . . .
228,50  (last entry in file-vector width the same as the second entry.)
```

If there are some ASCII numbers that haven't been coded in your .SHP file, simply skip those numbers in the .SWD file.

HOW TO DETERMINE THE VECTOR WIDTH OF YOUR FONT

Using the above .SHP file fragment as an example, go into your drawing editor. Set the style of your font and in the text command set the text height for 3.5 inches (35 vectors high). Set snap to .1 inch and type in several letters. Every time you hit the right cursor key, you will be moving the screen crosshair one vector width across the character. Be sure to include any leading or trailing space as part of that character's width.

THE SIMPLEX.SWD FILE

Below is the complete listing of the **SIMPLEX.SWD** file that is used with the text formatting program that appears at the end of Chapter 9. This file contains all of the ASCII character codes, followed by the vector width of each character in the **SIMPLEX.SHX** font file that comes with AutoCAD. To use this file, type in each pair of numbers (including the comma) in the listing below into your text editor and save it under the file name **SIMPLEX.SWD**. The listing below has been formatted into three columns to save space.

0,21	64,24	98,19
10,36	65,22	99,18
32,19	66,21	100,19
33,13	67,21	101,18
34,15	68,21	102,12
35,19	69,19	103,19
36,20	70,18	104,19
37,30	71,21	105,8
38,23	72,22	106,10
39,9	73,8	107,17
40,14	74,16	108,8
41,14	75,21	109,30
42,16	76,17	110,19
43,26	77,24	111,19
44,10	78,22	112,19
45,26	79,22	113,19
46,10	80,21	114,13
47,22	81,22	115,17
48,20	82,21	116,14
49,16	83,20	117,19
50,20	84,18	118,16
51,20	85,22	119,22
52,20	86,20	120,17
53,20	87,24	121,16
54,20	88,20	122,17
55,20	89,20	123,12
56,20	90,20	124,7
57,20	91,15	125,11
58,15	92,22	126,26
59,14	93,12	127,8
60,20	94,20	128,26
61,26	95,24	129,19
62,20	96,9	228,36
63,18	97,19	

appendix E   USING A TEXT EDITOR INSIDE AUTOCAD

First, find a small text editor or word processor that you would like to use. We've been using PC-WRITE Version 1.05[*] and find it to be quite adequate. PC-WRITE is a SHAREWARE product and can be obtained from numerous sources for $10 or less. When you've decided on a suitable text editor, find out how large it is by listing the file in DOS with **DIR**. Take the file size for your text editor and add 17,000 to it for necessary DOS functions and then add 30,000 or 40,000 to that number for file buffer. The example below could be the memory requirements for a typical text editor:

	SIZE
TEXT EDITOR	50,000
DOS	17,000
TEXT FILE AREA	40,000
TOTAL MEMORY REQUIRED	107,000

---

[*]   The later versions with more features are too large.

Using your text editor, load the **ACAD.PGP** file that came with your copy of AutoCAD. Add the following line to the end of this file using the file name of the text editor that you've chosen and the total memory required number based on the size of the text editor chosen:

```
EDIT,[your text editor command], [memory required],,0
```

For example, the entry on our **ACAD.PGP** file is:

```
EDIT, ED, 107000
```

Save the modified **ACAD.PGP** file and copy the chosen text editor program to your AutoCAD subdirectory on your hard disk.

Now, whenever you want to create a text file from inside the AutoCAD drawing editor, simply type **EDIT** at the **Command** line and you'll enter your text editor. When you exit your text editor, you'll be back in the AutoCAD drawing editor exactly where you left. You may find some "garbage" on your drawing screen when you leave the text editor, but issuing a **REDRAW** command should eliminate the problem.

FOR FURTHER READING:

- Bradlee, R. C., *Programming AutoCAD Volume I,* ADSI, Naperville IL.

- Head, George O., Charles Pietra, Kenneth J. Segal, *The AutoCAD 3D Book*, Ventana Press, Chapel Hill, NC.
  ISBN 0-940087-18-9

- Head, George O., *AutoLISP in Plain English, Second Edition*, Ventana Press, Chapel Hill, NC.
  ISBN 0-940087-29-4

- Jones, Frederic H., *Computer Aided Architecture and Design*, William Kauffman, Los Altos CA.
  ISBN 0-86576-102-7.

- Schaefer, A. Ted and Brittain, James L., *The AutoCAD Productivity Book, Third Edition*, Ventana Press, Chapel Hill, NC.
  ISBN 0-940087-27-8.

- Schilling, Terrence G. and Particia M., *Intelligent Drawings*, McGraw-Hill, New York NY.
  ISBN 0-07-055317-3.

Index

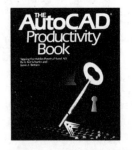

HATE TO TYPE?

The AutoCAD Database Diskette runs on any 360K IBM-standard format computer and can save hours of tedious, error-prone typing. All programs, functions and routines listed in the book appear on the diskette, including:

- The bill of materials program from Chapter Four (provided in dBASE or compiled so it can be run without dBASE).

- An AutoLISP program that allows you to update any chosen attribute in an AutoCAD drawing from an outside database.

- A program that automatically writes all blocks in a drawing to a disk file.

- The text program from Chapter Nine that allows you to format text within a drawing, including text size, type size, line length, proportional spacing and multiple columns. A compiled version is also included that will run five times as fast.

Bonus! *The AutoCAD Database Diskette* includes a text editor designed specifically for AutoLISP; includes an automatic indent feature; also "error-checks" for pairs of parentheses.

____Yes, please send____ copies of *The AutoCAD Database Diskette* at $49.95 per diskette. Add $2.20/diskette for normal UPS shipping. Add $5.00/diskette for UPS "two-day air." NC residents add 5% sales tax. Immediate shipment guaranteed.

Name_____ Firm _____

Address (no P.O. Box)_____ _____

City_____ State _____ Zip _____

Telephone_____

____ Payment enclosed (check or money order; no cash please)

VISA Acc't # _____ Exp. Date_____

MC Acc't # _____ Exp. Date_____

Signature _____

MAIL TO: Ventana Press, P.O. Box 2468, Chapel Hill, NC 27515. Or, if you'd like it even sooner, call 919/942-0220.

TEAR HERE

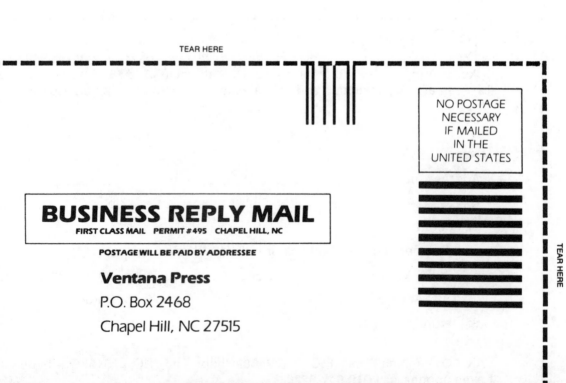

NO POSTAGE
NECESSARY
IF MAILED
IN THE
UNITED STATES

BUSINESS REPLY MAIL
FIRST CLASS MAIL   PERMIT #495   CHAPEL HILL, NC

POSTAGE WILL BE PAID BY ADDRESSEE

Ventana Press

P.O. Box 2468

Chapel Hill, NC 27515

TEAR HERE

HATE TO TYPE?

The AutoCAD Database Diskette runs on any 360K IBM-standard format computer and can save hours of tedious, error-prone typing. All programs, functions and routines listed in the book appear on the diskette, including:

- The bill of materials program from Chapter Four (provided in dBASE or compiled so it can be run without dBASE).

- An AutoLISP program that allows you to update any chosen attribute in an AutoCAD drawing from an outside database.

- A program that automatically writes all blocks in a drawing to a disk file.

- The text program from Chapter Nine that allows you to format text within a drawing, including text size, type size, line length, proportional spacing and multiple columns. A compiled version is also included that will run five times as fast.

Bonus! *The AutoCAD Database Diskette* includes a text editor designed specifically for AutoLISP; includes an automatic indent feature; also "error-checks" for pairs of parentheses.

TEAR HERE

BUSINESS REPLY MAIL
FIRST CLASS MAIL   PERMIT #495   CHAPEL HILL, NC

POSTAGE WILL BE PAID BY ADDRESSEE

Ventana Press

P.O. Box 2468

Chapel Hill, NC 27515

9331

TEAR HERE